THE
ROCK GARDEN
month-by-month

THE
ROCK GARDEN

month-by-month

MICHAEL JEFFERSON-BROWN

Consultant editor

MICHAEL UPWARD

Secretary, The Alpine Garden Society

David & Charles

PAGE 1: The forget-me-not blue flowers of Eritrichium nanum

PAGE 3: The pretty spring flowers of Chionodoxa frame the single nodding head of a fritillary

A DAVID & CHARLES BOOK

Book design by Diana Knapp

Most of the photographs were supplied by the Alpine Garden Society Slide Library –
photographers include: A. M. Edwards pp. 14, 42 (right), 60, 61 (top), 75; Mike Ireland pp. 23 (top
& bottom), 31 (top & middle), 39 (top), 42 (left), 43 (bottom), 50 (bottom), 51, 65 (top & bottom),
71 (top & middle), 74 (top & middle), 83, 113, 117; D. Joyce p. 103 (top); Phil Phillips p. 103.
Other photographs were supplied by: Neil Campbell-Sharp pp. 2, 57; Clive Nichols pp. 6, 9, 11,
27, 47, 67, 89; Garden Picture Library – photographers are Lamontagne p. 19, John Glover pp.
86, 99, Neil Holmes p. 109; S & O Mathews p.3; Harry Smith Collection p. 79.

Colour and black and white artwork by Eva Melhuish

First published in the UK in 1996

Copyright © Michael Jefferson-Brown 1996
Artwork and Layout Copyright © David & Charles 1996

A catalogue record for this book is available from the British Library.

ISBN 0 7153 0232 9

Typeset by ABM Typographics Ltd, Hull
and printed in Italy by New Interlitho SpA
for David & Charles
Brunel House   Newton Abbot   Devon

CONTENTS

Introduction 6

JANUARY 10
Practical project: Building raised beds 16

FEBRUARY 18
Practical project: Building an outcrop 24

MARCH 26
Practical project: Renovating a rock garden 32

APRIL 34
Practical projects: Making a grassy alpine lawn 40
Making a grassless alpine lawn 44

MAY 46
Practical projects: The scree garden 52
Making an 'antique' trough 54

JUNE 56
Practical project: Creating a peat bed 62

JULY 66
Practical projects: Ponds and waterfalls 72
Making a bog garden 76

AUGUST 78
Practical projects: The alpine house 1 84
The alpine house 2 86

SEPTEMBER 88
Practical projects: Making a bulb and propagating frame 94
Planting the bulb frame 96

OCTOBER 98
Practical projects: Paved and gravelled areas 1 104
Paved and gravelled areas 2 106

NOVEMBER 108
Practical project: Planning an expedition 114

DECEMBER 116
Practical projects: Creating special collections 1 122
Creating special collections 2 124

Appendix 1: *Plants for alpine lawns* 126

Appendix 2: *Checklist of alpines* 128

Useful Addresses 141

Further Reading 142

Index 143

INTRODUCTION

Rock gardens and the cultivation of small plants whose homes are high in the hills or elsewhere has been one of the major innovations in recent horticulture. Interest in this area of gardening shows no sign of slackening, indeed it appears to be increasing every season, and it is not really surprising. Gardens are shrinking and we want to get more plants into our given space – quarts into pint pots. And, of course, the range of small plants is huge: they can be most beautiful, they are full of interest, and there is something for all tastes. Very lovely easy plants abound for those with less time or inclination to take up the challenge offered by some of the more tricky kinds. There are also surprises. The experts are expert – but even they are often confounded. A difficult plant may flourish in the garden of a newcomer to the cult, growing and blooming with little special care – a most satisfactory state of affairs. However, this is not always the case and it does help to know not to do the obvious wrong thing, and here we hope to help.

PRACTICAL POLITICS

This is a practical book. Purple prose is kept to the minimum. Suggestions are put forward simply and without any aura of inviolable dogma. Readers are expected to adapt what is written to their circumstances – and prevailing weather conditions. If a job suggested for early spring is impossible to perform because the ground is frozen as hard as concrete, it does not have to be postponed for a year, do what suits you when it suits you. We have an apt metaphor,

Linum arboreum *and* Erinus alpinus *in an alpine bed at Copton Ash, Kent*

'nothing is cast in stone'; flexibility is the name of the game. One of the joys of gardening is evolving one's own methods for tackling the various jobs.

There are two main aspects to the book: the rock garden, its various adjuncts and modern adaptations; and the plants. A balance is needed between both these aspects. Certainly, one does not need a rock garden to grow alpine plants, but the converse is less true: a rock garden permanently without alpines is a very unhappy construction.

Fashions change in rock gardens as in all else. Grottoes are very Victorian and can still be found, probably surrounded by prodigious tons of rock. Today we preach economy in its use. There are two very good reasons for this: rock is very expensive; and we hope to thwart the activities of those who denude the landscape of our natural heritage. Some keen alpine gardeners can argue persuasively for growing alpines without a rock garden, indeed some of the greatest practitioners have never had 'rock' gardens.

ALPINES AND ROCK GARDEN PLANTS

Some definition of terms peculiar to rock or alpine gardening may be helpful for those new to it. The term 'alpine' relates to the early days of interest in mountain plants when most of the small plants being introduced in rock gardens actually came from the Alps; plants from these mountainous habitats became known as alpines. Nowadays no one is so purist as to restrict the name to plants from this one mountain range. The terms rock-garden plant and alpine are virtually interchangeable, although there is sometimes a residual nuance that suggests an alpine is a plant from high in the hills while a rock-garden plant is merely a plant that by its stature and habit looks right in a rock garden.

SEASONS AND MONTHS

Under average conditions, the seasons used throughout this book correspond to the following months:

SPRING
Early: March
Mid: April
Late: May

SUMMER
Early: June
Mid: July
Late: August

AUTUMN
Early: September
Mid: October
Late: November

WINTER
Early: December
Mid: January
Late: February

TYPES OF HABITATS

Open rock garden
Shaded pocket in rock garden
Crevice
Niche in wall
Scree
Paved area
Gravelled area
Peat bed
Bog
In pond
Pond margin
Raised bed
Container
Trough
Alpine house
Bulb frame
Light woodland

In this book the term alpine and rock-garden plant are used without discrimination. Our 'alpines' may have been originally found growing by the seashore or even in a desert. If they grow and give pleasure they are welcome, it is the plants not the terms that are important.

After the influx of plants from the Alps, others followed from further European ranges. Then the treasure store of the East was opened and plants from the Himalayas and the highlands around north Burma, Tibet and China came flooding in. Many were surprisingly hardy and quickly became established in gardens. Further explorations of China and Japan gave even more choice. The flora of South Africa is also included although it is often too tender to grow outside in cooler climes. There is also a large number of plants from New Zealand that are suitable and recently attention is being directed to plants dwelling high up in the mountains of South America, not forgetting the species from North American mountains and woodlands. The whole world is providing us with a choice of plants. It could be bewildering if it was not so fascinating.

PLANT AVAILABILITY

Nowadays most good garden centres have well established plants in one-, two- or even three-litre pots. The larger ones may seem expensive but they can be good value for those wanting to establish a display quickly. Garden centres vary in the choice of plants offered. One has to face the fact that they depend on a relatively quick turnover and most only stock plants that do not require very expert attention so the range is likely to be of reliable, relatively easy plants. If you are searching for some rarer plants you need to look to one of the many more specialist nurseries. They often have 'choice' kinds; 'choice' often meaning difficult or slow to grow. If your patience is really limited you could find the garden centre stock the most rewarding.

Societies, such as the prestigious Alpine Garden Society in Britain, publish literature carrying the advertisements of specialist growers. Catalogues are also very educational. In Britain, the source of plants in commerce can be found in a current edition of The Plant Finder. Plants not in commerce may often be raised from the seed offered by specialist societies in their seed exchange schemes.

CHOOSING PLANTS

Patience is one of the prime virtues of the good gardener. A visit to a flower show or a garden exhibition may have stimulated your interest so that you want to rush out and accomplish something equally fine. Punch's advice to those about to get married, 'Don't', is too severe; what is needed is to 'Hasten slowly'. You are reading this book which is a good indication that you have chosen the prudent path. There are also lots of less practical, but very helpful reference books. Names you have noted at shows or elsewhere can be looked up and something learned of them. It could be that the plant you covet is one that will die in your soil conditions or needs to be carefully cultivated under glass when you want a robust outsider; it could be a rarity of which the only other known example in captivity is grown by a dedicated enthusiast who lives on the side of a hill on an island in the middle of the Pacific.

Choosing plants is fun. Almost everyone enjoys making lists of plants they feel they need to get. The difficult thing is to ensure that the list includes a range of plants to give interest and beauty all the year round. This book helps you make your choice.

This book also helps you to avoid the pitfalls of planting a miniature landscape. For example, caution is needed when choosing trees and shrubs. These are very useful for giving scale and shape, especially when many perennials have sensibly put up the shutters for winter, but beware of 'dwarf' conifers; the adjective is one that deals in relative measures. How dwarf is dwarf? We were once shown into a wilderness of conifers, the owner of which had purchased a collection of 'dwarf' conifers. There was not one under 3m (10ft)!

SITES AND SOILS

These points will be covered in detail through the book. The point to make here is to emphasise that to have a successful rock garden one must be willing to give it the site and conditions that will promote this success, not to handicap oneself hopelessly from the start.

There was a tendency in the past to put rock gardens in corners where 'nothing else will grow'. This is a short recipe for disaster. As one authority said, the word 'else' should be omitted. Another mistake, still frequently made, is to use a space under trees. There are several reasons why this is completely wrong. The trees are likely to make the site dark and dry and any rain that does get through may drip persistently into the centre of precious plants causing them to rot. Fallen leaves may instigate rotting.

An ill-drained site is death to the vast majority of plants, especially to those alpines that have mountain homes with instant drainage. Roots also need oxygen in the soil.

The chemical balance of the soil is important in the selection of plants, but generally the most important features are good drainage, some moisture-retentive properties and a healthy structure. Well-worked garden soil is a good start. A very heavy sticky clay is not ideal but even this can be tamed. Acid sandy soil can be very hungry and may need feeding with rotted compost, leaf-mould and peat. The low pH level, under the 7.5 neutral mark, indicating its acidity, can be carefully adjusted by applications of lime or chalk.

OTHER EQUIPMENT

There are certain adjuncts that help us grow rock plants and alpines. One such is the alpine house, which can be expensive to purchase but is well within the scope of the DIY enthusiast. What it provides is a control of overhead water for particularly sensitive plants; as much air movement as possible is needed inside it. A useful back-up feature for the rock garden is a frame, helpful for propagating plants and for growing special bulbs. These items are covered as well as such features as the bog garden, screes and trough gardens.

You are allowed to leave your garden sometimes to go on holiday. There is great pleasure to be had in travelling abroad to places where alpines grow naturally. We give you hints about arranging an expedition.

USING THIS BOOK

This book looks at rock gardening month-by-month. This discipline has emphasised certain verities that might have been overlooked, and has underlined points that ought to be made to anyone new to rock gardening.

Each month is introduced with some words about its 'flavour' and importance in the garden. Next, the jobs that might be tackled at this time are listed and described. 'Plants of the Month' feature a selection of leading plants that are attention grabbing in that particular month. Space allows only a taste of the 'star performers' but we augment this with mention of important relatives and elsewhere there are copious margin lists of other plants of various types that are worthwhile investigating. The appendix checklist may also help. Everyone has their own favourites, so apologies if some of yours have been missed out – there are so many good things to choose from.

'Practical Projects' contain some heavyweight input. 'You heave, we'll grunt.' No one need follow every project in every month, and certainly not in one year – at least if anyone does, please would they write and let us know; we could do with a little extra help in the garden. The main principles behind each project are outlined and there are suggestions on how to carry them out with the minimum of expenditure and effort by you and/or your ever-willing partner. The projects have been shared around the year; some are best tackled in the month they are featured, others may be deferred until it is convenient. Once you have your rock garden or rock beds organised, it would be surprising if you did not wish to add some new element, perhaps a scree, a pool or a bog garden. This could enrich the whole concept.

At the end of the book, appendices give extra tabulated information, which may save a lot of research.

Apart from the chapter headings all times of the year have been given by season and not by the month – southern- and northern-hemisphere enthusiasts should be able to make equal sense of the text. You will find a definition of the seasons in the margin at the beginning of this chapter.

Enjoy your gardening; enjoy your plants.

ERIGERON KARVINSKIANUS

PLANT TYPES

There are many plant forms among rock-garden plants. Those listed in this book may be all safely assumed to be hardy unless otherwise stated.

Dwarf trees, eg *Salix × boydii*
Dwarf conifers, eg *Juniperus communis* 'Compressa'
Dwarf shrubs, eg *Coprosma* 'Indigo Lustre'
Herbaceous perennials, eg *Primula clarkei*
Carpeting perennials, eg *Raoulia australis*
Evergreen perennials, eg *Gentiana acaulis*
Bulbs, eg *Tulipa humilis*
Corms, eg *Crocus goulimyi*
Tubers, eg *Erythronium tuolumnense*
Rhizomatous perennials, eg *Anemone nemorosa*
Grasses, eg *Festuca orina glauca*
Sedges, eg *Carex buchananii*

JANUARY

This is the middle of the winter and little changes from last month.
However the days are getting longer and in mild seasons there is some
activity among the plants that are up and about early. Smaller bulbs,
the snowdrops, bulbous irises, winter aconites and crocus species often
risk a really cold snap and bravely show colour this month. They also
have relatives under the protection of greenhouse, alpine house glass or
in frames. It is rare that the weather is so poor that at least some of
these small plants do not suggest that winter will end. Even in the
coldest weather we can find plants in bud or bloom among our potted
treasures; perhaps they may be brought into the conservatory to be
admired for a day or two without softening them up too much.

If prevented from much active work outside, there is normally plenty
to be done under glass, checking pots and perhaps sowing seeds. In the
comfort of an armchair there can be some pleasant planning to do,
perhaps a feature to be designed for the garden, lists of plants to be
checked.

The winter allows us to appreciate the need for care in the positioning
of the permanent features in the rock garden. Now rocks and dwarf
trees and shrubs stand out and we need to be able to appreciate their
form from a warm room. Rocks should be placed to please the eye.
Imagine a traditional Japanese garden with a few rocks surrounded
by raked sand and gravel. Perhaps our eyes are greedy for more
details; these can be provided with the evergreen shrubs and trees, and
later in the year with other flowering plants.

Television and radio programmes on holidays abroad may stimulate
thoughts about a break with a decidedly horticultural bias, an
expedition to see some of the small plants in their high mountain
homes.

tasks

FOR THE

month

'HEALTHY LOAM'
This is a rare commodity
defined as a well-balanced,
natural top soil somewhat
greasy to the touch and without
a preponderance of either clay
or sand particles, with plenty of
humus and full of fibre. In the
past it was often sold as
'Kettering loam'.
In the absence of this ideal it
is necessary to make do with
what is available and a worthy
alternative may be obtained
from stripping turf perhaps
when preparing an area for the
rock garden. Stack it neatly
upside down and allow the
grass to rot, water the pile and
cover it with black polythene to
ensure all green life is killed off.

◀ *PAGES 10–11*
The stunning, clear blue
flowers of Iris 'Harmony' will
brighten any rock garden

12

CHECKLIST

- ☑ Outside tidying
- ☑ Alpine house hygiene
- ☑ Mixing composts
- ☑ Repotting
- ☑ Pest eradication

OUTSIDE TIDYING

This task appears regularly in the checklist. There is no need to be obsessive about keeping everything tidy, but for want of a few seconds to pick up loose leaves or debris on the rock garden, one may find that rotting has started in a precious plant. Save a few ferns that enjoy the splashing water from waterfalls, alpines hate excessive water around their neck and foliage. What happens is that a leaf or two gets wedged in a cushion-like plant and then tends to funnel rainfall into it. For a start this is not helpful and then the dead leaves begin to rot naturally and the rot spreads to the living plant. It is much easier to prevent rotting by timely leaf clearing, than to effect a cure. Cutting away the affected part will leave the plant with a hole in it, making it vulnerable to further wet and rot.

ALPINE HOUSE HYGIENE

Rain, wind and cold may make the garden a little uninviting, so get fresh air and enjoyment in the alpine house. Just as with a greenhouse, the alpine house should be kept as clean as possible to discourage pests and diseases. There must be no accumulation of bits and bobs, no half-used seed packets, used cartons, loose labels and no litter of dirty trays and pots. As far as possible when a pot is

emptied it should be washed and put away.

Keep the ground as clear as possible. Probably the most sensible arrangement is to have a central path of paving slabs, with dug soil under the benches on the two sides. The soil can be raked and topped off with a couple of inches of gravel on top of a layer of black polythene to discourage weeds. This ensures a buoyant and healthy atmosphere and helps the temperature balance. The door and all the ventilators are best hung on rustproof hinges or if of steel then these must be well greased or oiled.

Check that there are no drips due to condensation or leaks. Repeated drips on to plants, especially through the winter months, is an unpleasant death.

MIXING COMPOSTS

These winter months can be just the time for a little energetic work. It makes sense to get quantities of compost mixed up now for immediate use and more especially, for the busier months soon arriving when there will be plants to be repotted, seed to be sown, and seedlings and cuttings to pot up.

Basic compost by bulk is:

- 2 parts healthy loam/good top-soil
- 1 part humus as leaf-mould or/and peat

- 1 part grit or washed sharp-sand

These are the basic proportions of the John Innes seed compost and this or JI No 2 potting compost can be used with most alpines. The John Innes-type composts are made from sterilised components so that one should be starting with a standard product. There is variation in quality of loam-based composts and some are better than others, though much is being done by trade organisations to ensure high standards; the difficult ingredient is 'healthy loam'.

John Innes-type **potting composts** are made by bulk of:

- 7 parts healthy loam
- 3 parts peat
- 2 parts sand

JI Base fertiliser and ground chalk is added to the potting composts.

JI Base fertiliser is made by weight of:

- 2 parts hoof and horn
- 2 parts superphosphate of lime
- 1 part sulphate of potash

JI No 1 has one dose of fertiliser: 112g (4oz) and 28g (1oz) ground chalk per 51kg (1cwt), No 2 has a double dose and No 3 a treble one.

For lime-hating plants use an ericaceous compost or your own mix with no chalk or lime added. A suitable mix for such plants is:

- 2 parts leaf-mould and/or peat
- 1 part healthy loam/good top-soil
- 1 part grit or washed sharp-sand

Leaf-mould can be made simply by collecting the fallen autumn leaves. Leave them in a compact pile for six months, then turn them or put them through a shredder and leave for a further six months when the leaves will have decomposed and the leaf-mould is ready for use. A mixture of leaves normally gives best results, oak and beech leaves are particularly good.

For plants demanding particularly sharp drainage and gritty conditions the compost mix might be:

- 2 parts grit or washed sharp-sand
- 1 part healthy loam/good top-soil
- 1 part leaf-mould and/or peat

Mixed composts or the separate ingredients can be kept in bunkers or dustbins ready for use. It is difficult to have too much; it is surprising what quantities are used when the busy times come.

REPOTTING

It is expedient to make an early start on any repotting that may seem necessary. Check the primulas first. They are becoming active and some of the Vernales section of Primulas will be in bloom. *P. allionii* is at the top of the queue; the plants should be even mounds of clean healthy foliage, but the odd dead leaf needs teasing out before it starts any disastrous rotting. You need patience and a pair of tweezers.
- Having cleaned the plants up, turn them gently out of the pot and if there is a mass of root decide on repotting
- Gently work away some of the soil so that the outer roots hang free
- Repot in a similar-sized or just slightly larger pot introducing fresh compost between the roots and leaving all as little disturbed as possible

Other primulas may also be ready for a spring clean. *P. marginata* and *P. auricula* types can have old dead leaves removed and, by turning the pots out on a clean bench, possibly on to newspaper most of the soil can be worked at. Keep a look out for two particularly nasty enemies, the vine weevil and the root aphid. Such nasties may be suspected if the plants look limp, have a lot of dead leaves, and seem ready to leave the soil with the slightest tug.

PEST ERADICATION

Vine weevils, aphids and slugs can cause havoc in alpine house or bulb frame. Prevention being better than cure it is best to work cleanly and quickly, and tackle an attack early, before it has a chance to become widespread. The sooner in the year preparations are made, the less chance of survival the pests will have. (See February tasks p20, and March tasks p28, for 'seek and destroy' plans.)

PLANTS FOR REPOTTING

Primula allionii
P. marginata
P. pubescens
Dwarf, deciduous shrubs/trees

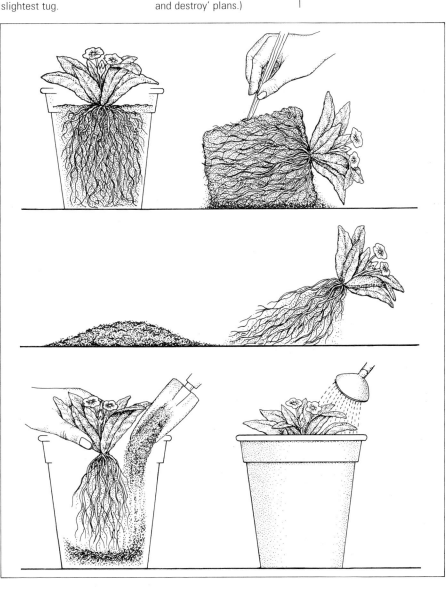

plants
OF THE
month

FALSE BOX

FALSE BOX
(Polygala chamaebuxus)

False box belongs to a varied genus of annuals and perennial plants, hardy and tender, deciduous and evergreen. The perennial alpine species are neat little plants, making slow steady growth, requiring little attention and perfectly hardy. They are usually blue- or pink-flowered; this is the exception.

type	Low, woody, evergreen perennial shrublet
foliage	Very tough, oval dark leaves, close to the ground. Included here for its winter foliage
flowers	Most commercial forms have pea-like blooms of bright yellow, with contrasting magenta-mahogany centres, in early summer
height	5cm (2in)
spread	20cm (8in)
planting	Spring or late summer
site	Base of a shaded rock, in a peat-bed or in a shady trough
soil	Peat- or humus-rich, best moist but well-drained
propagation	Detach rooted pieces in spring
relatives	*P. vayrediae*, similar-sized, low shrub

with narrow leaves, purple-red and yellow flowers. *P. calcarea* (Milkwort), usually prostrate perennial with dark, oval leaves and blue flowers, late spring or early summer. *P.c.* 'Bulley's Variety' good, deep blue form

SWEET BOX
(Sarcococca hookeriana humilis)

Sweet box belongs to a small genus of evergreen shrubs useful for their pleasing foliage and the fragrance in winter – the flowers are so tiny they are almost invisible but the perfume that they provide is nothing short of generous. These neat, easy plants are good for the lower reaches of rock gardens or light woodlands.

type	Neat, evergreen shrub with new stems arising directly from ground
foliage	Small, pointed, oval, dark green, glossy leaves
flowers	Small tight racemes of very highly fragrant, tiny, white petal-less, flowers, with pink anthers, borne in the leaf-axils in late winter and followed by round black fruits
height	30–60cm (1–2ft)
spread	90cm (3ft)

planting Firmly, possibly best early spring
site Moist, semi-shade
soil Not fussy
propagation Summer cuttings
relatives *S. hookeriana*, narrower, pointed
leaves, more upright shrub.
S. ruscifolia (Butchers Broom),
upright, arching shrub, oval leaves,
dark red fruits

SNOWDROP

(Galanthus nivalis 'Viridapicis'*)*

Galanthus are related to daffodils and have such a wide range of species that we need not be without snowdrops in bloom from autumn until spring.

type Bulb
foliage Grey-green, like miniature daffodil
flowers Typical snowdrop flowers but with
green tips to the three outer petals as
well as the three inner ones in mid to
late winter
height 20–30cm (8–12in)
spread Makes clumps of increasing size, a
few bulbs making a spread of some
40cm (16in) wide in about 4 years
planting Dry bulbs 5–8cm (2–3in) deep in
early autumn. 'In the green' bulbs just
after flowering, having split clumps
into smaller groups. Very best time is
as foliage dies down in late spring
site Between heathers, in woodland, at
bottom of rock garden
soil Open, well-drained, with plenty of
humus for maximum increase
care Avoid heavy overgrowth of
neighbouring shrubs and plants
propagation Split clumps when leaves are still
green and replant immediately
relatives There are many other forms of the
common snowdrop, all worth
growing. Some of the larger, taller
ones like the graceful 'Atkinsii' may
be a bit big for the rock garden.
Species such as *G. ikariae* are
distinct with polished, bright green
leaves. *G. plicatus* has broader
leaves and plump, shining white
flowers. *G. reginae-olgae* is
autumn-flowering

CROCUS

(Crocus minimus)

All the crocus species and hybrids are welcome. Selections of this species bloom at the end of the winter – especially in the alpine house – up till the more usual late spring outside. They are par-

ticularly attractive in pots and need a dry period in summer.

type Corm, frost hardy
foliage Narrow, nearly erect, dark, with a
central white stripe
flowers Buff-mauve in bud but stained or
feathered dark violet, inside purple-
mauve, orange stigmas. Dainty, bright
and tiny
height 6–8cm (2¹/₂–3in)
spread 3–8cm (1¹/₄–3in)
planting Early autumn
site Sunny, warm spot, or a pot in bulb
frame/alpine house
soil Gritty
propagation Lift plants when foliage dies down
and split off new corms
relatives *C. corsicus*, another small late mid-
spring species, slightly larger than *C.
minimus*, pale lilac, violet inside

'VIRIDAPICIS' SNOWDROP

practical project

BUILDING RAISED BEDS

Outcrops and natural rock gardens can look incongruous in some sites, especially those surrounded by walls, fences and buildings. In those cases raised beds may provide the answer. They can use space economically and, if well sited, they can be very attractive. A complete range of plants can be grown in them and their walls can also be planted thus providing a new dimension.

Raised beds have several advantages. As long as they are surrounded by safe paths they are easy to look after. All plants are within reach without clambering and, being raised off the ground, they are more easily examined and appreciated. They need not involve too much expense, indeed they can be cheaper than a rock garden which may have large pieces of rock almost valuable enough to insure. Soil mixes can be made to suit the plants. Drainage – essential for most alpines – can easily be provided. Many leading alpine enthusiasts confine their gardening to beds and containers.

MATERIALS

Choice of materials for building the walls will depend on aesthetics and finance, as well as the practical points of ease of construction, maintenance and safety.

▪ *Stone* This the natural first choice. If you have a source of local stone that can be obtained in pieces neither too large nor too small this may be the ideal answer. While thin flat pieces is not my first choice (because problems can arise with the huge number of crannies and spaces between the rocks which might draw conventions of slugs and snails), I admit to having seen some effective beds made with such stone

▪ *Old, used bricks* could look right near a brick house, so long as they are of similar colouring

▪ *Reconstituted stone* Although rather uniform and raw in colour when first built this soon loses this appearance, acquiring a patina of moss and algae. Any gauntness is quickly broken by plants falling over the tops and draping the sides from vertical planting sites and holes left during construction

▪ *Railway sleepers* Sleepers and alpines may not seem a natural twosome but provided the beds are not over-high, sleepers can provide a safe and not unattractive background for small plants. The walls are quickly secured in position and, having been intended for heavy-duty railway work, are persistent

SITES

The majority of alpines crave light, therefore an open site not under trees or any over-hanging building is ideal. If the finished bed is going to be an all-round-the-year attraction, the site is perhaps best fairly close to the house, so that the beds can be seen from one or more of the windows. Although alpines are better in an open site, a bed in a shady area might be sensible if you are particularly interested in small woodland plants, not strictly alpines but with the same miniature appeal.

Practical considerations include ease of access for yourself and a wheelbarrow or tools, and being within a reasonable distance of a water supply. There should be adequate drainage away from the site so that the surrounding paths are not constantly wet.

DESIGN

Your bed or beds can be tailor-made to suit your chosen site but there are some general factors:

▪ The higher the bed, the more care is needed to ensure the stability of the walls. Too high a structure can look like a prehistoric burial site and will require huge quantities of material for filling. Wall heights from 12–45cm (5–18in) are within the normal recommended range

▪ The width of the beds should be such that nowhere is out of easy reach from one side or the other. In effect this means a width of 2–2.2m (6–7ft) if the bed can be approached from two sides and 1–1.2m (3–4ft) if one can work from only one side

▪ The most obvious shape is an oblong outline – squares seem less aesthetically pleasing – but beds beyond 3m (9ft) will look

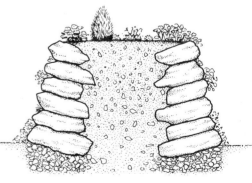

Cross-section of a raised bed

formidable. If a considerable planting area is desired it is advisable to have more than one bed. This also allows dedicated beds – for example, one solely for the use of lime-hating plants

▪ Stone – and to a lesser extent brick – allows a deviation from straight sides and right angle corners, railway sleepers do not.

▪ Finally, consider whether your site might be attractive with beds formed in an L-shape, with one arm longer than the other

BUILDING

Stone and brick walls should have firm foundations going into the ground and will be safer if they slope inwards slightly. No stone should project to create a major overhang.

Ensure that the site has free drainage. Allow for drainage holes through the walls every metre/yard and put a layer of rough drainage material perhaps 10–15cm (4–6in) deep on the bottom of the bed before covering it with turves or humus material to prevent the compost filling every drainage cavity. Use composts as suggested p12.

PLANTING

It could be wise to incorporate plants in the sides of the walls as you build. See margin for suitable wall plants. When you have finished, allow the compost to settle before planting the top of the bed. A number of rocks could be placed on the level surface of the bed to relieve the flatness. It will also provide growing niches for some plants.

PLANTS FOR GROWING IN WALLS

Arabis caucasica	*H. ferdinandi-coburgii*	*O. tauricum*
Asarina alpina	*Helianthemum*	*Persicaria affinis*
A. procumbens	*Hieraceum villosum*	*Ramonda myconi*
Asperula suberosa	*H. waldsteinii*	*Saponaria ocymoides*
Aubrieta	*Iberis sempervirens*	*Saxifraga encrusted kinds*
Campanula cochlearifolia	*Leucanthemum hosmariense*	*Scutellaria alpina*
C. portenschlagiana*	*Lewisia*	*S.scordiifolia*
C. poscharskyana*	*Linaria alpina*	*Sedum*
Cymbalaria aequitriloba	*L. maroccana*	*Sempervivum*
C. hepaticifolia	*Lithodora diffusa*	*Tanacetum densum amanum*
C. muralis 'Nana Alba'	*Lychnis alpina*	*Both campanulas can be
Erigeron karvinskianus	*L. flos-jovis 'Nana'*	invasive and need to be kept
Haberlea rhodopensis	*Onosma albo-roseum*	under control.

▪ *The colour illustration shows a suggested planting arrangement for a raised bed*

1 *Aubrieta*	10 *Dianthus*	20 *Juniperus*
2 *Crocus*	11 *Tulipa humilis*	21 *Juniperus*
3 *Saxifraga*	12 *Saxifraga*	22 *Dianthus alpinus*
4 *Lewisia*	13 *Saxifraga*	23 *Primula*
5 *Gentiana verna*	14 *Lewisia*	24 *Dionysia aretoides*
6 *Dianthus*	15 *Maidenhair spleenwort*	25 *Asperula suberosa*
7 *Dryopteris affinis* 'Congesta'	16 *Primula marginata*	26 *Aubrieta 'Carnival'*
8 *Snowdrop*	17 *Primula marginata*	27 *Areniaria balearica*
9 *Juniperus*	18 *Saxifraga*	28 *Saxifraga*
	19 *Dianthus*	29 *Primula*

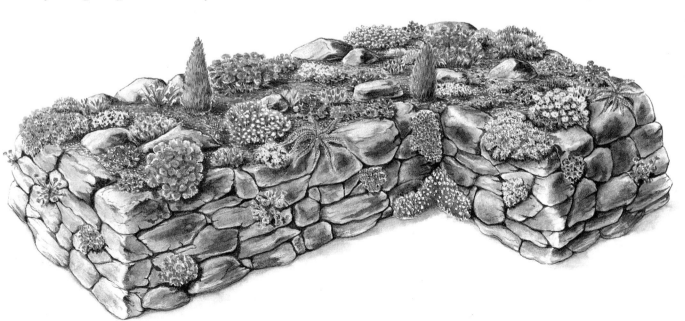

FEBRUARY

This spells the end of winter: in a short while there will be plenty of signs of growth among outside plants while under cover there may already be lots of colour. Some of the smaller Narcissus and Leucojum forms, together with irises and Romulea species, even if perfectly hardy, can be better enjoyed under cover where they will not get battered by the weather. These, together with early primulas, saxifrages and the enthusiast's dionysias may all be performing now for your benefit.

At this time of year wet can be the main danger to many alpines. It is important to ensure that preparations are made in good time so that no plant drowns in too much rain. On a bright day a little top-dressing can be done in the rock garden, perhaps using spent compost, and it is certainly worth trying to clear any small threatening weed growth and giving the whole area a face-lift by raking the gritty top-dressing or adding a fresh layer of chippings or pea-gravel.

There may be serious work to be done. In the tasks for the month there are suggestions of what may be timely. This might include giving the entire landscape a light dressing of fertiliser, starting serious warfare on slugs if they are a problem (it is at the beginning of the spring that these pests do their greatest damage), some propagation work may be attempted, and if any rocks have got dislodged, loosened or simply seem ill-placed this is the best time to realign them so that they do not continue to cause visual offence.

By the end of the month the most exciting period of the year is beginning.

tasks

FOR THE

month

PAGES 18–19
Posies of double primulas which
come in a wide variety of
colours, thus providing subjects
to suit any colour scheme

CHECKLIST

- Slug limitation outside
- Fertilisers
- Watering under glass
- Seed sowing
- Old foliage

PEST ERADICATION UNDER GLASS

The worst pests of plants under glass and in pots are likely to be vine weevil, root aphids, white fly and red spider mites. If you start checking pot plants this month you need to look out for weevils and aphids. For treatment see March tasks, p29.

SLUG LIMITATION OUTSIDE

Now until mid to late spring is the most vital time to limit the damage by slugs and snails. If they are controlled now they will have a much lesser chance of doing real damage. It is the beginning of their busiest period and, with the plants starting into growth, it is the time when they can cause greatest harm; a short snack can ruin an important plant and their most dangerous attacks can be made on tissue just below the soil's surface.

Fortunately a well-maintained rock garden is not their first choice of homes; gritty surfaces and well-drained, gritty soils do not appeal. On the other hand, wet smooth rocks with crannies are welcome bases. Make sure there is no slug- and snail-friendly rotting vegetable matter in the garden and the plants themselves should not be very wet and certainly not soft, easy, lettuce-like fodder. A generous layer of grit below and around plants will help keep them from getting sodden.

Slug populations can be reduced by distributing slug pellets; there are now types that are harmless to pets and birds. Pellets are most effective in moist conditions as in periods of drought the pests are likely to keep under the soil or in damper, sheltered spots. Traps are well-worth using – saucers of stale beer collect surprising numbers and orange peel, old apples, damp newspapers or similar material placed at intervals and collected regularly each morning will reveal a number of sheltering slugs and snails. Unless checked daily *and* early these traps are a waste of time; 5am is a good time, before the slimy fellows have moved away!

FERTILISERS

Although in their native habitat they can be considerable drinkers of the water from melting snow and ice flowing past their roots alpine plants are not gross feeders. In the rock garden many find conditions fairly soft after the rigour of the hills. The aim is to keep all plants healthy and moving towards their optimum performance without promoting any threatening personality changes.

Some growers are antipathetic to the use of any fertiliser on rock gardens. They might be right, but on the other hand their puritan approach may be bolstered by the fact that they have a rock garden built over a healthy soil that their deep-rooting alpines delve into. The truth is that the gritty composts recommended for rock garden plants can be leached of much of their mineral nutrition over the year and a light dusting of a slow-acting, balanced fertiliser can keep soil and plants healthy. A good mix by weight would be:

- 1 part sulphate of potash
- 6 parts bone meal

This should be distributed so that garden looks as if it has had a light dusting all over, but avoiding the plants as

SLUGS

Our main foes are the **field slug**, *Deroceras reticulatum;* **garden slug**, *Arion hortensis;* **garden snail**, *Helix aspera and the* **strawberry snail**, *Trichia striolata*

The large black slug, Arioin ater, looks horrendous and greedy but is less of a threat than the smaller ones listed above.
Field slugs *are usually grey, sometimes light brown and occasionally white. They will never be longer than 4cm (1¹/₂in). When touched or attacked they exude a white slime.*
Garden slugs *are about the same size in greys and browns with a characteristic bright golden orange underside. This underside is called a foot.*

much as possible. It will soon wash away and the clean appearance will be restored, especially if it is spread before forecast rain. Fertilising can be done now in late winter/early spring or late summer/early autumn. It will certainly help to prolong the healthy life of the plants.

After a few seasons, the rock garden may benefit from a top dressing, especially if the basic soil is hungry sand. Collect the surface grit, tickle the soil surface with a hand fork and add an inch or two of fresh compost before replacing the surface grit/chippings/gravel. The compost will contain fertiliser so there is no need for separate feeding that year.

WATERING UNDER GLASS

With plants beginning to come out of winter rest, extra water is needed. It is sensible to provide this in discreet quantities. In beds or plunged pots, the soil will not have been allowed to dry out completely in the winter; a flush of water now will stimulate growth and any surplus should drain away. Introduce the water around plants not on them; this discourages disease. If the month is open and relatively warm watering can start early; if there is still some very frosty weather it is best delayed.

SEED SOWING

Usually seed is best sown as soon as ripe and with alpines this is likely to be in the summer or autumn. In natural habitats some seed germinates almost immediately and the young plants get themselves established before the rigours of winter. However, a considerable proportion of seed, having fallen to the ground, is programmed to await at least one frost before germinating. For the alpine gardener now is a sensible time to sow seeds of these plants and leave them to the weather outside; there should be a frost or two to trigger germination and then the pots can be covered in a frame or alpine house, where seedlings will grow on strongly as the weather improves.

There are other more pragmatic reasons for sowing now: specialist societies send out their seeds in the winter so there are exciting seed packets awaiting attention and this is a month when jobs under cover may be welcomed.

A word of caution: if you know the seed is likely to be highly fertile, do not use too much. Raising vast excesses of plants is a pointless exercise and either means having the heartbreak of throwing away the surplus after potting up the number you want, or, and this is a temptation too easy to fall into, potting up too many so that for the rest of the year you have to care for a population you are hawking around at all suitable functions.

OLD FOLIAGE

In autumn some clump-making or tufted plants were left with dead leaves clustered around their crowns as protection from frost, and to mark their stations. As new growth starts the old foliage should be removed. Pulling is not always effective and living pieces can be detached by mistake: it is better to use scissors or pruning shears. Ferns come into new growth at varying times, some very late. The developing new fronds are beautiful; it makes sense to remove dead, damaged and worn-out old fronds that detract from the developing picture. The same applies to other plants.

Removing old foliage

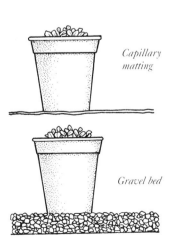

Capillary matting

Gravel bed

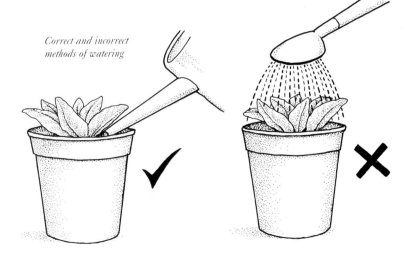

Correct and incorrect methods of watering

plants
OF THE
month

PASQUE FLOWER

 ### PASQUE FLOWER
(Pulsatilla vulgaris)

Pulsatillas were for many years included with the anemones, and are closely related. The genus has some very attractive members, none easier or more worth having than this robust plant, quickly getting into action in the early spring and always looking well through the growing months. It needs no special attention and can last a gardener's lifetime provided it is left undisturbed.

type	Herbaceous, tufted perennial, with fibrous, woody rootstocks
foliage	Much-divided, ferny, light green leaves
flowers	Silvery hairy buds arise early to mid-spring and open as large, nodding, velvety bells complete with large bosses of golden stamens. Usually rich purple-mauve, but there are whites, silver-greys, lilacs, purples and reds. After blooming the stems elongate, the tops straightening, and showy seedheads develop with glistening long, hairy wind-beckoning tails
height	15–24cm (6–10in)

spread	15–24cm (6–10in)
planting	Plant end of winter or when potted plants available
site	Full sun, allow plenty of room for permanent residence
soil	Humus-rich, well-drained

propagation	Fresh seed or by winter root cuttings, 2–3cm ($^3/_4$–$1^1/_4$in) long, to increase particular colour forms
relatives	*P. vernalis*, a choice early plant for the alpine house, bearing upright, smaller, white flowers, with huge yellow stamen bosses. Very hairy buds and finely cut foliage

CYCLAMEN
(Cyclamen coum 'Album'*)*

There is no poor species in this genus, which would be a most rewarding one to collect. There are a few tender species but *Cyclamen coum* is certainly not one; it is very hardy and long-lived and forms colonies by seeding itself (illus, p.116–17). *C. coum* is crimson red.

type	Tuber – sometimes wrongly described as a corm
foliage	Rounded, sometimes somewhat heart-shaped, leaves with silver patterning in varying amounts, sometimes plain dark green
flowers	Many round-petalled, chubby, silken snow-white blooms with dark maroon basal marks. Winter and early spring
height	7–10cm (3–4in)
spread	5–10cm (2–4in)
planting	Plant shallowly from spring until late autumn
site	Sun or partial shade, rock garden, alpine lawn, light woodland or pot
soil	Not fussy, but enjoys humus and dislikes sodden conditions
propagation	Fresh seed sown immediately germinates freely. This can be done carefully in pots or in the open where the plants are wanted
relatives	*C. hederifolium*, is the ever-popular autumn-flowering species that starts blooming before the attractive heart-shaped leaves appear; *C. repandum* is a purple-red, spring species equally hardy and rewarding

PHEASANT'S EYE
(Adonis vernalis)

This genus belongs to the buttercup family; some of the choicer members, such as this, are attractive for foliage as well as blossom.

type	Herbaceous, clump-forming perennial
foliage	Silken bright green leaves, very finely-divided

flowers Open as the clumps stir into life in late winter or early spring. A somewhat limy gold, they are like large celandines and are as highly polished. One crowns the end of each stem and each has up to twenty, outward pointing petals around a boss of darker stamens
height 20–30cm (8–12in)
spread 20–30cm (8–12in)
planting In early spring or late summer
site Semi-shaded, cool, moist spot
soil Humus-rich, well-drained
care Keep moist without drowning
propagation By fresh seed or by division when flowers have faded
relatives *A. amuriensis*, similar in character but slightly larger, blooms in late winter or early spring. *A. brevistyla* is another stylish plant, its leaves divided but more clearly triangular, open flowers beautiful white, buds slightly blue

DIONYSIA
(*Dionysia aretioides*)

A genus of connoisseur's alpines among the elite of the alpine house; forget aubrietas and extrovert friends. Dionysias are hardy plants but winter wet can kill. *D. aretioides* is generally regarded as the 'easiest'.

type Cushion-forming, evergreen perennial
foliage Packed rosettes of small, hairy, grey-green leaves soft to the touch and a magnet to damaging moisture
flowers Five-lobed bright golden flowers are stemless and held just clear of the foliage cushions by long tubes in early spring
height 5–10cm (2–4in)
spread 15–30cm (6–12in)
planting At end of winter or when purchased, in pots with an exaggerated layer of sharp clean chippings around the plant's neck and below the cushion of foliage
site Well-ventilated, alpine house
soil Extremely gritty, well-drained mix
care Water carefully and sparingly, keeping foliage dry and in airy conditions. Keep an eye open for botrytis fungus. This will brown off parts which should be carefully removed and the whole lightly dusted with fungicide
propagation Summer softwood cuttings

relatives *D. tapetodes* with tightly-crowded rosettes of small, grey-green, rounded leaves and bright yellow, early spring flowers might be tried in similar conditions

PRIMULA
(*Primula allionii* 'Marion')

The primula genus is large and varied, with plenty of species for the rock garden, bog garden, scree, alpine lawn and alpine house. *P. allionii* is a hardy European species most often grown in the alpine house where its somewhat sticky foliage can be protected; it makes a marvellous pot plant and many very fine cultivars have been raised.

type Evergreen, tufted perennial
foliage Oval, oblong or narrowly spatulate, light grey-green leaves, totally covered with sticky glandular down. Rosettes form mounded cushions
flowers Masses of singly-borne, wide open, rich pink flowers, with white eyes, held just above the foliage by long narrow tubes can completely obscure the leaves in mid-spring
height 6–8cm (2¹⁄₄–3in)
spread 8–15cm (3–6in)
planting In pots, end winter or when acquired
site Alpine house or frame
soil Very gritty, alkaline mix (the species hails from the limestone ranges of the Maritime Alps) with a layer of grit/chippings below the cushion of foliage
care Watering must be undertaken carefully. The root run needs to be kept just moist; the soil should not be allowed to dry out completely even in winter although this is *the* time, more than any other, to avoid water on the leaves and around the bottom of the cushion. Growing in tufa or in a cleft between two pieces of tufa will help keep the base dry
propagation Take cuttings, as long as possible, after flowering time, insert in a very gritty soil with some lime and keep cool in a covered frame, watering sparingly. Seed sown as soon as ripe
relatives There are a larger number of named cultivars. The better ones are wonderful, although others are poor. Some proven selections are: 'Celia', lilac-toned pink; 'Avalanche', white; 'Apple Blossom', rosy-pink

PRIMULA 'MARION'

DIONYSIA ARETIOIDES

practical project

BUILDING AN OUTCROP

The aim is to create the impression of a natural rocky outcrop which can then be planted up with suitable small plants. There is a certain degree of 'suspension of disbelief' about the whole operation, but it is possible to create something that echoes nature. Having seen natural rock structures up in the hills, a poorly executed bit of rock work will always catch and annoy the eye.

SITE AND PREPARATION

The site should be as much in the open as possible and particularly not dominated by unnatural features. Fences and walls at a distance can be disguised with shrubs and trees. Given the choice between a sloping or a flat site, the sloping one will provide a better chance of a natural effect, but if there is no choice do not worry as flat sites can be made more interesting by tilting rocks so they appear to be pushing their way through the surface. Once the site is chosen, mark out the area designated for the outcrop with hosepiping, rope or string. Leave it for a few days before proceeding so fine alterations can be made. Use a few boxes covered with sacking to suggest high points.

NATURAL APPEARANCE

Achieving a 'natural' appearance is a matter of getting the pieces of rock to look as if they are all parts of one rock formation. Stones with pronounced strata need to have these layers aligned – a rock with its strata lines going a different way to all the others will stick out like a sore thumb.

In nature a small rock outcrop is normally surrounded by grassy turf or low heather scrub; a mown lawn works well, setting off the whole and acting as the frame to the picture. To make grass cutting easier and to prevent a constant invasion of the outcrop by grass, the outcrop area can be surrounded by a band of scree-type chippings, a little lower than the lawn so that an edging can be main-

tained and stones kept out of the way of the grass cutter.

Try to make the outcrop in at least two parts separated with a pathway of scree grit or flat stones surrounded by chippings.

TYPE OF ROCK

Choice may depend on price and, as part of the cost of rock is transportation, local stone is likely to be the most reasonably priced.
- *Limestone* Do not encourage the demolition of natural sites by buying weathered limestone pillaged from nature. Quarried stone may look fresh at first but will mellow surprisingly quickly. Most limestones have a lot of character and clear strata lines
- *Sandstone* There are many forms of sandstone. It usually comes in angular pieces without clear strata lines. Some leading rock gardens have been of sandstone; it is relatively easy to work with and produces lots of ledges, beds and pockets of soil for plants
- *Slate* Although a hard, rather intractable material, it is possible to construct good outcrops using slate especially when combined with running water. Strata are very visible
- *Tufa* This is a soft, often crumbly rock with no strata lines. It is much prized for growing plants directly in the rock, but it is less easy to use to make a visually attractive outcrop. Fairly large pieces are needed to enclose raised areas of soil

HANDLING ROCKS

The larger and heavier the rock is, the more awkward it is to handle and the more likely to cause an accident. Here are a few tips:
- Have rocks delivered close to the site
- Purchase rocks as large as you think you can manage, together with plenty of smaller ones. A few big ones will make a much greater impact than lots of little ones
- Allow plenty of room for moving and working. Remember to allow for wooden planks to take wheel or stack barrows
- Make use of the principle of levers when manœuvring larger rocks (see illustration)
- Keep your fingers clear of two hard surfaces when moving rocks

BUILDING

- Kill off permanent weed
- Dig or rotovate the area to be used

- Arrange drainage if necessary
- With heavy soils work in as much grit and humus as possible
- Rake into desired contours, possibly with two high points and a shallow valley between. On flat ground a contour change of a relatively few centimetres can make a surprising difference
- Make flat sites interesting by tilting rocks
- Choose your 'key' stone, usually the largest, place in position, tilting to whatever degree has been decided, then build back each way until the last rock 'disappears' into the soil. Keep strata lines parallel and ensure that rocks are secure with their backs into the soil and any prominent faces sloping backwards and never overhanging
- Arrange supporting rocks to provide crevices and pockets
- Fill out areas between rocks with a suitable soil mix (see margin) and allow some days for this to settle
- Plant up and then cover the surface with grit/chippings/pea gravel

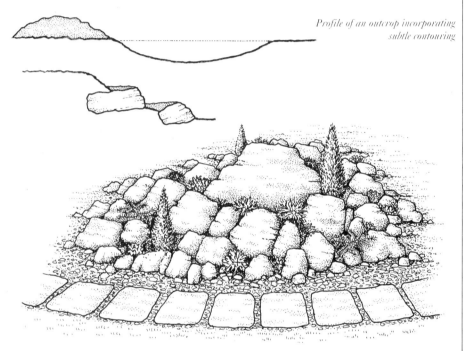

Profile of an outcrop incorporating subtle contouring

SOIL MIXTURE INGREDIENTS

Sand – should be washed free of clay and other small clogging particles

Grit – usually supplied as dust to small pieces of granite waste

Chippings – usually bought as limestone, granite or various sandstone types. Limestone chips can only be used with plants not objecting to lime

Loam – virgin top-soil is rarely offered. Gardeners can make a similar material by rotting down turf

Leaf-mould – clean samples of this are invaluable. Usually made from a wide range of tree leaves, but oak and beech give the best results. Avoid infestation by root aphids

Peat – the most usual kind is coarse. It is a popular good ingredient of soil mixes, but one should consider the ecological costs

Compost – well made material from turned compost heaps is very worthwhile. It should be dark, crumbly and give no clue of what produced it

ROCK TYPES AND COSTS

- *Much of the cost of rock is cartage. It makes sense to collect your own from merchants or the quarries themselves. Obviously, large rocks cannot be managed in the car boot; they will have to be supplied or towed on a trailer*

▪ LIMESTONE, WEATHER-WORN AND QUARRIED
Large pieces rescued from old rock gardens can be very expensive. Newly-quarried pieces will be more reasonable. Garden centres and most merchants rarely offer pieces much bigger than a football and for this type of material the charge is around half or a quarter of the cost of larger pieces

▪ SANDSTONE, VARIOUS COLOURED FORMS
Sandstone comes in various coloured forms; the brightest can be rather garish to start with but normally tone down quickly. Football-sized fragments are usually offered at about half of the price of larger pieces

▪ TUFA
This is a soft, very crumbly material. It needs handling carefully so it is safest to collect it yourself. The choice of sizes may vary according to the supply. Large pieces can be scarce. The cost will normally be 3 or 4 times the cost of other rocks

MARCH

The mountain tops are frozen and covered with deep snow, but in our
gardens the spring has usually sprung before the end of the month. All
is hectic hustle: race-memory urges the plants into getting through their
cycle of flowering, pollination, setting and dispersal of seed before the
winter quickly takes hold again. We are lucky as the season is extended
by many impatient or precocious plants that have been garnered from
all over the world, not necessarily from hilly homes. Now the later
primulas and a multitude of saxifrages come into bloom to accompany
lots of diminutive bulbous beauties.

Dormant buds and almost forgotten plants bestir themselves, and
some will be producing flower almost before leaf. Hepaticas can be
among these, though some strive for evergreen status; they all produce
classy flowers and it is difficult to have too many of them gracing the
rock garden or a woodland area – they are one of a number of dual-
purpose plants. There is also the undeniable and simple joy of the very
easy mossy saxifrages, the aubrietas and alyssums of our alpine world.

Don't listen to the snobs. Just because a plant is easy this does not
devalue its worth! Nevertheless most of us will admit to the special
glow that comes from succeeding with one of the more tricky plants,
however much we may dismiss the success in front of friends.
'Psychotima pusillanimousiana! Can't stop it flowering. Just romps
away.' May we be forgiven.

At his time of the year the sap stirs in the gardener too! There are more
hours of light and the temperature rises a few degrees. There are also a
few challenging jobs to be done: that deep-rooted dandelion that lodged
itself between the two rocks needs spot treating with glyphosate!

tasks
FOR THE
month

PAGES 26–7
The brilliant white heads of
Iberis sempervirens (see p.50)
cheekily pushing through a mound
of Aubretia deltoidea (see p.30)

CHECKLIST

- Planting new alpines
- Spot weeding
- Checking rocks
- Repotting
- Dividing clumpy alpines
- Dealing with vine weevils
- Rooting out aphids
- Removing winter cover

PLANTING NEW ALPINES

With the spring every gardener, young or old, turns to thoughts of garden centres. The sap is rising. There are gaps to fill, there are rock garden extensions to plant and there are always new things to tempt us. No one is immune.

It is a good month for planting. The soil is warming and young plants are likely to grow away quickly giving instant effect and pleasure. There will be plenty of rain, so neither drought nor high temperatures will cause distress.

Tips for new specimens

- Choose healthy-looking plants, not ones that seem to have been struggling too long in too small a pot

- Turn out and examine rooting and check for root aphids and vine weevils (see below)

- If pot-bound with strong roots try to ease some loose before planting

- Plant in a suitable site. Consider: Sunny v. shady; Sharp drained v. extra moist; Humus-rich, acid v. alkaline with lime/chalk. Allow plenty of room for neighbouring plants

- Ensure firm root contact with soil and that neck/top of plant is at same level as in pot. A few things such as heathers, smaller willows and creeping campanulas could be slightly deeper, 0.5–3cm ($^1/_4$–1$^1/_4$in), than in pot

- Top-dress with grit/chipping/ pebbles to match the rest of the rock garden and water thoroughly

SPOT WEEDING

Weeds appear even in the best-regulated establishments. A dandelion seed soon becomes a monster with divided fang-like roots that always seem to dive under substantial rocks. There is no way to remove them physically without leaving behind some roots that will then produce even more recalcitrant opposition. The answer is carefully-targeted chemical warfare. Glyphosate (Tumbleweed, Round-Up) is absorbed through the foliage into the whole plant system and kills all. The choice is between a liquid spray or a painted-on gel. The gel is obviously the safer as it is applied straight on to the foliage, but a small hand-held spray gun is also effective: the jet can be precisely aimed and just enough applied to coat the leaves. A sheet of

newspaper or something similar can be used to protect surrounding plants. The effect is not apparent overnight, but in a fortnight or so it will be obvious.

CHECKING ROCKS

Winter frosts and rain may have loosened rocks. Although they should have been installed with their centre of gravity close to the ground so that movement is unlikely, it is possible that the weather might have caused some erosion and loosening, especially where two or more rocks are closely associated to form a crevice or narrow valley. Small burrowing animals may have aggravated the situation.

Pack compost where needed to stabilise rocks and if need be reposition them. It is important that they are firm because they may be used as stepping stones around the rock garden; a wobbling foothold could cause an accident.

REPOTTING

As plants begin to come into new growth in the alpine house or bulb frame, they may need repotting. Even small alpines can have a whole mass of roots that will eventually exhaust the soil they are in. (See January tasks, p13. See also the notes below on weevils and root aphids.)

DIVIDING CLUMPY ALPINES

Now is the best time to divide clumps of alpines. This can be done successfully until the end of spring; an alternative period would be in early autumn.

- Many campanulas, sedums, sempervivums, thymes, and

semi-creeping, clumpy plants can be lifted and pulled apart to give numerous rooted divisions that can be replanted, watered and grown on quickly

- With some plants it is possible to encourage stem-rooting propensities by top-dressing with a sandy compost a few months before the division is to be made
- For example top-dress in early autumn for dividing now
- Where only one or two extra plants are desired the parent clump can be left almost intact and a small trowel or handfork used to lift as many rooted pieces as necessary
- These can be planted up immediately in good compost (see p12) in pots or in the new sites chosen for them in the open
- All roots, together with stems likely to throw new roots, can be covered with the compost and watered
- If the divisions seem to have a lot of top growth, cut off part of this leafy section to help the new plant get established

VINE WEEVILS

Since the banning of dangerous pesticides the vine weevil has undergone a population explosion. It had been a recognised greenhouse pest for a long time and had been under some control. Over the past decade or so it has spread to many gardens both under glass and in the open.

Often the first sign of trouble is the wilting of a plant that had formerly seemed healthy. Watering has no effect and closer examination shows the plant has been severed from its roots. The grubs of the vine weevil are usually the culprits. These are plump pale cream maggots with distinct brown heads and no legs. They measure up to about 1cm ($^1/_2$in) long and are usually

sickle-shaped. Adult weevils are beetle-like, six-legged creatures about 1cm ($^1/_2$in) long. They are matt-blue-black, dotted or flecked with pale brown and have antennae half as long as the body and distinctly jointed.

Outside, the life cycle starts with adult females laying eggs from sometime in the summer until the middle of autumn. Eggs are less than 1mm; a female can lay over a thousand without needing the help of a male. Being so small they should not be confused with the much larger cases of slow-release fertilisers! Fertile eggs turn from white to brown and hatch into grubs after a fortnight, immediately beginning to feed on plant roots. They continue eating until full grown when they bury themselves deeper and pupate as fat cream darkheaded pupae. These are most prevalent in late spring. Adults emerge in summer and the cycle restarts.

Under glass heat means a continual process of reproduction is encouraged so that all stages of the weevil's cycle are present at all times.

Control is by regular inspection of potted plants and the squashing of any grubs found. Many commercial growers now use Suscon Green, a soil insecticide that works. When this is adopted by all growers the spreading of the pest via garden centres and other outlets should almost die out. The effect of other more widely available insecticides is poor, the best being spraying of foliage and soil with HCH or pirimiphos-methyl, but a more reliable amateur control may be available soon.

Biological controls can be tried. These use cultures of nematodes that work by getting into the body of grubs and releasing deadly bacteria. Nematodes are microscopic and cultures bought at garden

centres contain millions. The culture packs are normally best kept in a fridge and used within a week or so although there are new processed versions that have a longer 'shelf-life'. The culture is mixed with water and applied to the soil. The nematodes work best in moist conditions and with temperatures around the 10–14°C (50–57°F) level. The packs will give details.

For outside use, the optimum period will be that coinciding with the heaviest hatching period – probably late summer and early autumn. Inside the nematodes will work all round the year if moist and warm enough.

ROOT APHIDS

These are grey or soil-coloured pests which are detected by the white waxy powder they exude among roots and soil. Systemic insecticides keep them under control. A badly-attacked plant is best stripped of its old soil and soaked with a solution of malathion. Delicate plants that will resent the extra disturbance of a soil strip should be thoroughly drenched with malathion solution. The waxy white powder around root aphids repels water so a thorough job is needed.

REMOVING WINTER COVER

By the beginning of this month it is normally safe to remove glass sheets or any other artificial cover that has been protecting special plants from excess winter wet.

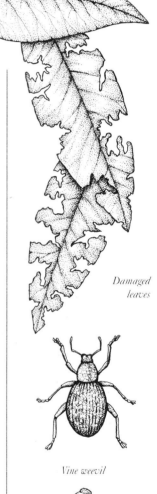

Damaged leaves

Vine weevil

Grub

plants
OF THE
month

PRIMULA
(Primula juliae 'Wanda'*)*

This is one of the most successful early flowering primula hybrids. The species was only discovered in 1900 but for decades 'Wanda' has been widely grown in borders and larger rock gardens. It is extremely easy and hardy. Recently a strain of early flowering pink, mauve and purple-red seedlings has been marketed as Wanda primroses. Only the wild primrose could challenge its popularity in early spring.

type	Evergreen clump-forming perennial with creeping rhizomatous rootstock
foliage	Shiny leaves are heavily suffused with purple red. In winter reduces to tiny clumps
flowers	Rich burgundy blossom covers the plants as a mound of colour, starting before larger leaves expand
height	10–12cm (4–5in)
spread	30–45cm (12–18in)
planting	Best after flowering
site	Sun or semi-shade
soil	Not fussy, but will grow quicker in moist soils
care	Best regularly divided and older parts of rootstock discarded
propagation	Division after flowering
relatives	*P.* 'Tawny Port' is an appropriately named *juliae* hybrid. Others formerly grown seem to have disappeared perhaps because of the huge success of 'Wanda'

BLOODROOT
(Sanguinaria canadensis 'Plena', syn. *S.c.* 'Multiplex', *S.c.* 'Flore Pleno'*)*

A genus of one species, a posh member of the poppy family.

type	Herbaceous perennial with rhizomatous rootstock
foliage	Large, rounded or heart-shaped leaves attractively scalloped and starting purple-flushed become greyish-green, appear after flowers or as later ones are opening. Undersides are glaucous. Very pleasing in leaf
flowers	Large, rounded, much-doubled blooms in shining white produced in succession in early spring
height	10–15cm (4–6in)
spread	30cm (12in)
planting	Place in permanent site, early spring if possible
site	Shady, moist spot in the rock garden or light woodland probably best, but will cope with sun if it has a cool rootrun
soil	Humus-rich, open soil; enjoys leaf-mould
care	Once settled in, plants are probably best left undisturbed. Do not allow to experience drought
propagation	By careful division in midsummer, replant immediately and look after well
relatives	The single form has wide, eight-petalled flowers, four of which are larger giving a somewhat square effect. Ring of yellow stamens around stigma. Buds may be flushed slatey grey-blue or pink. It produces useful seed

AUBRIETA
(Aubrieta deltoidea)

Although this is grown in cultivation most gardeners instal the splendid large, rich-coloured hybrids, some of the showiest with doubled or semi-doubled flowers (illus. p.36–7).

type	Evergreen, trailing perennial forming a compact mound
foliage	Grey-green, slightly tacky, oval or spathulate
flowers	Lilac or lavender-pink in early spring, in short branched heads more or less on the foliage
height	5cm (2in)
spread	15–30cm (6–12in)

PRIMULA 'WANDA'

planting Spring or autumn

site Useful for drier spots, for draping over rocks or walls in sun

soil Unfussy, perhaps best with a meagre diet

care Easy in well-drained soils. After flowering must be clipped back to maintain a compact shape

propagation By green cuttings in early summer or riper ones in late summer. Pieces of the growing plant covered with grit or soil will root and can be detached

relatives The variegated form *A.d.* 'Argenteo-variegata', with clearly-outlined margins, is a whole lot better than many variegated plants

PURPLE SAXIFRAGE

(Saxifraga oppositifolia 'Theoden*')*

The saxifrage family is crowded with rock garden plants of varying types. The species featured is a trailing plant found rarely on the tops of Scottish and English hills as well as more plentifully in the Alps.

type Evergreen, loose mat-forming perennial

foliage Small, tough, oppositely-arranged, oval or oblong, dark green leaves splashed with white along slender trailing stems

flowers Relatively large open cups of rich purple-pink in early spring

height 2.5–5cm (1–2in)

spread 15–20cm (6–8in) but sometimes much more as old specimens root as they go

planting Spring or autumn

site Light, open, moist spot in rock garden, raised bed or trough

soil Humus-rich, gritty mix

care Divide regularly each or every other spring

propagation Division after flowering

relatives Various clones have been named, some with large or richly-coloured flowers, but not all are worth naming; 'Alba' forms are less robust and more suitable in a trough

MORISIA

(Morisia monanthos)

A monotypic genus. One of the huge cruciferae family and useful in several situations.

type Prostrate, tap-rooted evergreen perennial

foliage Rosettes of tough, coarsely-divided leaves, pressed flat against ground

flowers Stemless, relatively large, flat, four-petalled, bright golden blooms. From winter through spring

height 2.5cm (1in)

spread 8cm (3in)

planting Any time

site Open spot in the rock garden, scree or a pot

soil Poor gritty soil

care Best on a starvation diet; richer fare leads to over-large foliage and plants becoming soft and rotting in winter

propagation Fresh seed or 3cm (1in) root cuttings in sharp sand in winter

relatives Only member of genus

MORISIA MONANTHOS

PURPLE SAXIFRAGE

practical project

RENOVATING A ROCK GARDEN

OLD GARDENS

Rock gardens have often been made in the most unsuitable places and, as a result, do not thrive, and are neglected and overrun with weed. If you have inherited such a structure it is not worth renovating. All one can do is to rescue the rock that lies half buried, if it is suitable – some Victorian 'rockeries' were made with quartz and shiny rock quite hideously wrong for a rock garden; these are mostly long gone, but because stone is so permanent, some gardens still house the rocks. Something more can be done about rock gardens that have been correctly sited, but that have been badly neglected by previous owners.

ILL-DESIGNED GARDENS

There are some rock gardens that are in a good site but are simply very badly laid out. For example, the plum-pudding school of rock garden constructors may have created a pile of soil and stuck rocks in at all angles before planting up with rampant spreading

its strata and making the whole look as natural as possible. Only retain those plants that are suitable for replanting and appropriate for a rock garden.

OVERGROWN GARDENS

Badly overgrown gardens that must once have been attractively laid out and well planted will need a lot of renovation work. First, check through the mass of growth to see if any worthwhile plants remain. It is unlikely that many of the smaller more precious plants are left. However, you could find some shrubs and/or trees that are worth preserving and which, as well established specimens, may indeed be useful features.

■ It is best to mark these carefully with bamboos or tall stakes so that they are not inadvertently demolished when tackling the unwanted vegetation

■ Other possible survivors include ferns and bulbs. Smaller ferns may be carefully dug up and moved away temporarily. They are shallow-rooted and can usually be lifted easily and weeds disentangled. Bulbs may be lifted if in clumps and heeled in elsewhere until fresh spots can be found for them or they can be allowed to die down and to take their chance of popping up next season in the right spot

■ The whole area can be treated to a systemic weedkiller, one containing glyphosate or chemical with a similar action. Care should be taken to avoid contact with any of the plants to be saved; shrubs can be wrapped with polythene while spraying

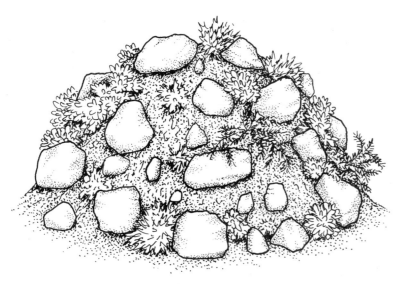

The best solution with a badly designed garden such as this, is to rebuild it, reusing the rocks and some of the plants

plants. If some useful and attractive rocks can be uncovered and rescued from badly designed surrounds that is a good start; at least the rocks will have some of the patina of age. Then the garden has to be fully reconstructed by remoulding the outline to reasonable contours, checking the soil to make sure it is well-drained and healthy, and then reinstating the rock, taking account of

Wrap specimen plants in polythene before spraying weeds

▪ The weedkiller will take ten days to a fortnight to show its full effect and then any parts that were missed will be obvious and will need going over again

▪ When all weed has been killed, remove the dead rubbish and work over the surface of the rock garden. At this stage it will be revealed whether or not the original soil mix was suitable

▪ If unsuitable the top 15–25cm (6–10in) of soil may be replaced by one of the compost mixes recommended on page 12

▪ Rocks can be realigned where necessary then plants can be added and the whole finished with a top dressing of chippings

THE LIGHT TOUCH

Where you have inherited a rock garden in not too bad shape you might proceed as follows:

▪ Remove smaller weeds by hand

▪ Kill deep-rooted perennial weeds (dog's mercury, dandelions, ground elder, bindweed, and so on) with glyphosate, applied with a hand-held fine mist spray. Use a second application on ground elder if need be

▪ Remove unwanted plants and trim back those that look excessively large. Aubrieta, mossy saxifrages, iberis and alyssum can be cut back drastically

▪ Consider whether you can improve the whole by adding an extension with matching stone and if so do this now

▪ Once weed and excessive growth is

removed, redefine its boundaries with a cordon sanitaire of chippings perhaps 30cm (12in) wide

▪ Start restocking if necessary. The range of plants found may give a clue as to the likely soil pH level, but it would be wise to do one or two tests before committing plants to the spruced-up rock garden

▪ If you can be patient it makes sense not to overdo the replanting until you see what bulbs appear. There may be hidden treasure

pH TESTS AND LEVELS

▪ *The level of acidity or alkalinity is measured on the pH scale of 1 to 14. 7 is neutral with the higher figures showing greater alkalinity and lower figures increased acidity. The difference between one number and the next is a major step – 10 times the acidity or alkalinity of the number closer to the neutral 7.*

Most alpines are happy with neutral soils or can tolerate some acidity or alkalinity. Happily most garden soils are not far from neutral. pH readings of 6.5 to 5.5 are somewhat acid and are manageable but lower values become a problem and need dressings of ground chalk or limestone to cancel some of the acidity.

Simple pH soil testing kits are sold in all garden centres. Usually they are of a type where, when sample soil is shaken up with water and chemicals, a colour change indicates degrees of acidity or alkalinity. After the soil has settled you match the colour of the liquid with a chart and read off the pH value ▪

REPLANTING, FINISHING TOUCHES

Before carrying out any major replanting schemes consider the following:

▪ Are any of the existing plants giving the garden a definite character that you do/do not want to retain?

▪ Is it most sensible to add a few additional plants that will be at their best outside the busy spring period?

▪ How about one or two shrubs or small trees to provide focal points and a sense of scale?

LIMESTONE
If you should be lucky enough to inherit old weathered limestone rocks do treasure these. The rocks by themselves are beautiful and scarcely need the addition of plants to make a fine garden.

PLANTS WORTH SALVAGING

Anemone
Bulbs
Cotoneaster, small
Dwarf conifers
Ferns
Geranium
Heathers
Pulsatilla
Sempervivum

APRIL

This is the season of the greatest excitement, the high tide of the spring flood of blossom. Life needs to be organised so that there is a measure of enjoyment as well as work in these months.

In the season of plenteous beauty, we can afford to be choosy. Space is limited and time is precious; neither must be wasted. In the rock garden the collection of plants should be those that give the greatest satisfaction. Everyone has their favourites and as the years pass new friends may replace older ones. Long time interest in a genus or family of plants might have to be shared with a new fascination in a different range.

We can exult in the beauty of all but we can exercise discrimination. Even among humble plants such as aubrietas and sempervivums, there are those that are more obviously garden-worthy than others. They will take the same space and equal care. Once a genus or family has caught the eye it is well worth considering all the relevant species – visit specialist nurseries or, if you have the opportunity, clamber up the hills to see them growing on the top of the world.

There are always some plants, even within one species, with characteristics which make them that much more desirable, and it may not be the obvious things such as floral colour or floriferousness: it may be more pleasing foliage or a neater habit of growth. For example, Primula marginata is loved by all; in fact it is one of the most appreciated of the European species, but, to be truthful, it ranges from a rather ordinary wishy-washy flower to some splendid, large, richly-coloured forms; the foliage, too, may be narrow and ordinary or strikingly toothed and decorated with beauty powder. Only the best is good enough!

tasks
FOR THE
month

PLANTS TO POLLINATE FOR SEED

Those marked * are listed because they tend to hybridise very readily, often without help from the gardener, so care may need to be taken over what they pollinate with.

Adonis species
Aquilegia various*
Crocus various
Dianthus various*
Fritillaria various
Geranium various
Glaucidium palmatum
Iris innominata
I. tenax
Mertensia various
Narcissus bulbocodium
N. cantabricus
N. cyclamineus
Paraquilegia anemonoides
Primula various
Primula allionii
P. marginata
*P. × pubescens**
Ranunculus various

PAGES 34–5
Anemone nemorosa 'Allenii' is a good subject for the peat bed (see p.65)

CHECKLIST

- Maintenance of the trough garden (see Project page 54)
- Weeding
- Top-dressing
- Pollinating for seed

MAINTENANCE OF THE TROUGH GARDEN

See Practical Project page 54 for details on making a trough; that is next month, but this month have a good look at any you see on garden visits or in garden centres. This will give you some ideas about the size and form of the one you want.

Established trough gardens need annual care. They can run short of nutrient so a discreet powdering of fertiliser is sensible early this month; it can be washed in with a thorough watering. There may be one or two plants that have come to the end of their time and died over winter; normally the space will be filled by neighbours but they will need removing and possibly replacing. It could be that some rather too exuberant plants have been introduced. These are best transplanted into the rock garden. Water the trough thoroughly before removing any plants.

Every few years it may be necessary to undertake a thorough overhaul. This means taking out all the plants that you can but leaving established small trees or shrubs that have roots running all round the trough. Replace as much as possible of the compost with fresh and replant the trough, repositioning the rocks and finishing with grit, then water well.

WEEDING

The big weeds — dandelions, thistles, docks and suchlike — are obvious and relatively easily dealt with by spot-weeding as suggested last month. The rock garden has its own pestilential weeds, usually small seedy ones. The following three are often bought in with new purchases:

Allseed (*Radiola linoides*) Annual with repeatedly branching thread-thin stems and narrow leaves. Particularly rampant in wet places.

Hairy bittercress (*Cardamine hirsuta*) Annual with rosettes of pinnate, dark green leaves. Upright stems of tiny, white flowers followed by long pods that distribute seed explosively. Active almost all year.

Pearlwort (*Sagina procumbens*) Low bright green cushions of narrow leaves and tiny flowers, quickly followed by round ripe seed pods. It can make sense to remove the top centimetre of compost from new purchases and replace with your own mix then topped with grit.

Weed control is a matter of regular discipline, of removing weed early before it gets a chance to seed, of raking around the gritty top surface to thwart germinating seed, of using a weed spray where necessary and of top-dressing with fresh grit.

Allseed

Hairy bittercress

Pearlwort

TOP-DRESSING

The aim is to give the rock garden, or part of it, a fillip. We proceed thus:

- Rake off loose top gravel

- Remove weed and unwanted plants and some that have outgrown their sites

- Loosen top 3–7cm (1¹/₂–3in) of soil and if you are unhappy with its quality remove elsewhere, away from rock garden. Rake over the remaining top-soil to provide the desired contours

- Add fresh compost. A mix by bulk might be 2 healthy loam, 1 leaf-mould/sphagnum peat, and 1 grit/sharp sand

- Dust with fertiliser

- Finish by re-covering with grit/chippings/gravel

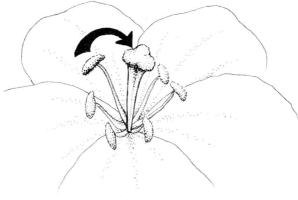

POLLINATING FOR SEED

Nature does not always do all the work unaided; sometimes it is best to help it along with the pollination. This is done by taking a very small water-colour paint brush and with the tip, transferring pollen from anthers to stigmas either of the same plant or another. A particular form of a species may be outstanding and there is the chance that seedlings could be as good or there is the chance of raising something slightly different, maybe a better variation. Sometimes clones have a partial or nearly complete inhibition to produce seed from their own pollen, a mechanism that helps to ensure some genetic diversity. However, if you have two good plants, different clones of the same species, you may be able to cross-pollinate them and thus are halfway to producing your own strain. It is always worth trying.

Once you start pollinating, you may wonder whether it is worth crossing different species. This is anathema to many alpine enthusiasts who would have their treasures just as nature intended; I can appreciate the argument. It is not ideal to lose the individual characters of a species under a flood of look-alike hybrids. However, these puritans may themselves be exercising a law of 'unnatural' selection by choosing to grow only the most pleasing or spectacular forms of a species. For example, a walk around many gardens will reveal the tiny, upright willow *Salix* x *boydii*, a hybrid between the prostrate *S. reticulata* and the silver-leaved bush, *S. lanata*. The hybrid looks like neither and is one of the treasures in many collections.

If you decide to go ahead and try it yourself it is as well to be patient. Some plants can be frustrating when one tries hybridising. Oenotheras, for instance, will produce seed but it is all pure maternal genetic material; all seedlings look like mum! Plants that you may wish to seed might include forms of *Primula marginata*, *P. pubescens*, saxifrages of all forms, *Dianthus* and lewisias, but the opportunities are almost endless.

PLANTS NEEDING POLLINATION TO PRODUCE ATTRACTIVE FRUIT

With some of the following artificial pollination is not normally necessary but will ensure good fruiting, especially on indoor plants with less wind to blow around the pollen. Those marked * have different sexes on different plants and need either the other sex in proximity or artificial pollination.

Amelanchier alnifolia pumila
Coprosma various *
Gaultheria adenothrix
G. hookeri
G. humifusa
G. mucronata
G. nummularioides
G. procumbens
G.. prostrata
G. pumila
G. pyroloides
G. tasmanica
G. trichophylla
Margyricarpos pinnatus
Pernettya leucocarpa
*Skimmia japonica**
Sorbus reducta
Vaccinium angustifolium
V. corymbosum
V. macrocarpon
V. myrtillus
V. oxycoccos
V. praestans
V. vitis-idaea

ROCK ROCK
A few minutes checking that all the rocks in your garden are still stable is time well spent.

CUTTINGS
Start to take these this month. See next month's tasks, page 49, for details.

plants
OF THE
month
1

*ERYTHRONIUM
TUOLUMNENSE*

 DOG'S TOOTH VIOLET
(Erythronium tuolumnense)

A woodland-loving genus from North America; all charming plants. *E. dens-canis* is the European species – the true dog's tooth violet – a name inspired by the likeness of the tubers to a dog's teeth. There are more pleasing names but very few more pleasing plants.

type	Tuber
foliage	Pair of spear-shaped, glossy plain green leaves pointing up and outwards at 45°. These die away by summer
flowers	Stems carry up to ten, hanging, bright golden flowers with reflexed, pointed petals in mid-spring
height	30cm (12in)
spread	15cm (6in)
planting	Autumn (see 'care' below) or summer if lifting your own. Depth about 10–15cm (4–6in)
site	Cool moist root-run and semi-shade. Tubers are best kept cool through summer when without leaves
soil	Enjoys open soil with plenty of leaf-mould or well-rotted compost. Should not be water-logged
care	Plant as early as possible and try not to keep the tubers out of the ground longer than necessary at any time
propagation	Probably best to leave plants for two or three years without

disturbance and then lift and divide the creamy tubers when leaves have died back

relatives	*E.* 'Pagoda' which is a hybrid of the above species but with mottled leaves and somewhat paler more lemony-sulphur flowers. *E.* 'White Beauty' is a distinguished, large-flowered selection with a circle of brownish marks in its centre. Leaves are mottled a purplish-brown

PHLOX
(Phlox subulata)

The border phloxes have quite a number of smaller brethren, both perennial and annual. These carpeting plants are among the most useful and bright of rock garden plants. They are easy and very generous with bloom.

type	Evergreen, mat-forming, perennial
foliage	Narrow, ovate, light green leaves
flowers	Loose clusters of wide, white, pink or purple flowers at end of each of many stems. Short-stemmed and saucer-shaped with overlapping petals. Late spring or early summer
height	7–10cm (3–4in)
spread	30–40cm (12–16in)
planting	Early spring or early autumn
site	Partially shaded rock garden or peat bed
soil	Humus-rich, acid
care	Top-dress with mix of peat and grit in early spring. Replace when looking worn after a few seasons
propagation	Cuttings from shoots without flowers in spring or summer
relatives	*P. adsurgens* 'Wagon Wheel' has pink flowers with narrow outward pointing petals. The many forms of *P. subulata*, purple, lavender, rose and white with darker eyes are easier in rather drier spots and do not need peat-bed conditions

SPRING GENTIAN
(Gentiana verna)

Almost everyone's favourite spring alpine and a true treasure of the Alps.

type	Evergreen, perennial
foliage	Oval, rich green leaves in rosettes
flowers	Five-petalled, upright, rich blue stars with white throats down long tubes
height	5cm (2in)

spread 5cm (2in)

planting Early spring or early autumn

site Trough garden, scree, or pocket of rock garden in open but not quite in the sunniest position

soil Well-drained with leaf-mould and lime

care Easy in suggested soil that is moist without becoming very wet

propagation Best by seed sown as soon as ripe when it germinates freely. Can be sown *in situ*

relatives *G. acaulis* is much larger with large, deep blue trumpets in spring and occasionally in autumn

CORYDALIS
(Corydalis flexuosa)

A wide range of perennials in a genus of tuberous and fibrous-rooted plants. Corydalis are up and coming in popularity.

type Herbaceous perennial with swollen leaf bases acting as storage units

foliage Bright green leaves divided into three leaflets, themselves deeply cut into three lobes

flowers Very bright blue flowers in clusters of 5–15 at the end of each stem. Early to late spring

height 15–30cm (6–12in)

spread 30–45cm (12–18in)

planting Any time

site Some shade, perhaps peat bed

soil High peat content

care Easy

propagation Easy by division in late summer

relatives *C. transsilvanica*, about 15cm (6in) high, with showy glowing pink flowers and finely-cut foliage. *C. wilsonii* has grey foliage and yellow flowers. Beware *C. cheilanthifolia*, which is abundantly self-seeding

ORCHID
(Pleione formosana, syn. *P. pricei)*

These ground orchids are supposed to be frost hardy but are usually grown as pot plants. As such they can be given the attention that can lead to very steady increase and their delicate sculptured flowers are near enough to be thoroughly enjoyed.

type Pseudobulb, deciduous

foliage Light green, pleated lengthwise

flowers Relatively large, 10cm (4in) across.

Like a typical orchid flower such as a cymbidium. All five sepals and petals are a rosy-pink, one points upwards, two are more or less horizontal and two divide the angle below. The central white or pale pink 'trumpet' extends forward with the lower, longer lip curving down. This lower lip is saw-edged and marked with chestnut red spots and lines. Spring flowering

height 7–10cm (3–4in)

spread 10cm (4in)

planting Cover the base

site Alpine house, frost proof

soil Ericaceous compost with an equal quantity of grit

care Repot in late winter or after flowering, using pans with a layer of drainage below. Space pseudobulbs 7–8cm (3in) apart. Allow space in pan for a layer of moss or finely-shredded bark to keep pseudobulb from getting too dried out. Increase watering after a modest start in early spring. Old 'bulbs' shrivel as new ones, usually in pairs, take over

propagation Split when repotting or when pot becomes overcrowded. Late winter or early spring

relatives Many named clones are now established as a result of crossing with the yellow *P. forrestii*. This Shantung grex has produced a much wider range of colours

CORYDALIS FLEXUOSA

PLEIONE FORMOSANA

practical project 1

MAKING A GRASSY ALPINE LAWN

See appendix 1 page 126 for plant list

The aim when making an alpine lawn is to reproduce the effect of the high alpine meadows where grass species are so richly mixed with flowering plants that the whole looks like a brightly-coloured embroidered cover. The grasses form the background and are pretty in their own right but not too coarse or too dominant.

Although the overall effect of an alpine meadow can be obtained in lowland gardens, it is not necessarily the easy option one might imagine, especially as most frequently one starts with a lawn site, which is easier than converting a border, and the main problem, ironically, is that the soil is too rich and fertility needs to be reduced. It is rarely possible to adapt an orthodox lawn simply by letting the grass have its head and planting alpines in it. This is only remotely possible with a poor lawn of weak grass species.

An alpine lawn needs to extend to several square metres to make a viable statement; perhaps half the area of the rock garden. The overall dimension depends on available space and the gardener's choice.

An occasional rock would not be out of place and can be used to provide a sheltered spot for plants that need it. Rocks may also help link the lawn with the rock garden proper. To be properly integrated it will probably have its limits defined by the rock garden on one side; a stone path at the other would be useful. A slightly sloping site may look more interesting than a completely flat one, but a flat one can be somewhat contoured by raking.

SURFACE, SOIL, GRIT

- Remove the top 10cm (4in) or so of lawn or top-soil
- Make good the evacuated space with grit and broken rock, mixing it in with the 10–20cm (4–8in) soil below
- If the site is not well-drained then drainage should be arranged so that the surplus water is taken away. (It is possible to have a boggy alpine lawn but this involves too much labour and, being very much a minority interest, is not dealt with here)

GRASSES

Having eliminated the original grasses, selective reintroduction is needed. Confine choice to the finer kinds such as *Agrostis tenuis* and *A. canina*, together with the fes-

DRAINAGE

■ *Drainage is of prime importance. The use of hardcore and grit below the natural level of the soil will drain water from above, but can form a root-rotting sump unless the water can then get away from the site. It may be necessary to arrange a channel of rubble or field drains falling to a lower level or meeting an existing drain to take away the surplus. In difficult cases seek professional advice* ■

cues such as *Festuca ovina*, *F. tenuifolia* and *F. rubra*. If buying a mix of seed choose the type that is offered for a high-class decorative lawn. For an orthodox lawn one needs 45–50gm per square metre (1¹/₂–2ozs per square yd); this can be drastically cut for an alpine lawn – a quarter or a third of this rate is plenty.

Mix seed thoroughly with dry sand to make it easier to scatter fairly evenly by hand. Lightly rake in.

PLANTING

Planting follows the grass sowing and requires plants that can hold their own with the grass, which grow easily, and which can be cut over at the end of the year. These include perennials that form creeping rootstocks, others that form clumps and yet more that get through their life cycle and disappear such as annuals and bulbs.

Bulbs look best in small groups, while other plants can be grouped or planted randomly. Sometimes a better effect is achieved by having groups of three of a kind fairly close. The site is open, but there may be lower moister spots to suit moisture lovers.

Creeping plants

While there may be room for thymes, it is possible that *T. serpyllum* will be swamped as it likes to see and feel the sunshine. The vigorous bugle, *Ajuga reptans*, is a strong plant able to see off all opposition and in one of its forms has dark burgundy-coloured leaves, which are attractive with the blue flowers. Other creepers include forms of *Anthemis* and *Crepis*, for daisy flowers, and some of the knotweeds, *Polygonums*, and even *Globularias* to add variety. A slightly different effect could be produced by using some mints –

not the rampaging culinary ones – perhaps *Mentha requienii*, the Corsican mint, and *M. pulegium*, better known as pennyroyal. Attractive in moist spots are some of the easy scrophulariaceae, such as the musks, *Mimulus*, in various bright colours, spotted or plain.

Clump-forming plants

It would be a mistake to miss out some of the most obvious choices. Cowslips are lovely in the alpine lawn. They have the good sense to keep their foliage low and can be mown over without damage in late autumn or early spring. Primroses and other primulas are also attractive. (See list of suggested plants in the Appendix.)

Bulbs

The alpine lawn is an ideal setting for many of the early bulbous plants that grow in just these conditions. Hoop-petticoat narcissi (*N. bulbocodium*) look enchanting in grass. *N. cyclamineus* is a must if you have a moist spot, but takes a while to establish. Other slightly later bulbs include the snake's head fritillary and maybe some of its relatives. They can make real magic – one minute all seems grass and suddenly there appear large nodding heads in purples, mauves and whites, all intricately marked.

There are several tulip species that might be tried but pride of place could be given to the latest-flowering species of all, *Tulipa sprengeri*, which opens in late spring or early summer with pointed heads of orange-red. Once established it should produce plenty of seed which can be harvested and easily germinated – or can be left to nature to increase the spread of the species over the years.

MAINTENANCE

One aim is a natural effect, another is to maintain an association of moderate-sized plants without competition from larger invaders. Coarser grasses and weeds such as docks, nettles and thistles will need killing as they appear (see page 29).

To keep all tidy and to allow the early spring bulbs and other flowers to show themselves to their best advantage, the whole lawn can be closely cropped in the autumn and winter. Avoid clumps of ornamental grasses and other specimens you want for winter effect. There should be no need for feeding, and watering is only necessary in times of severe drought.

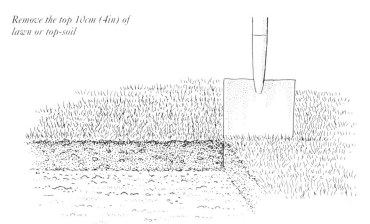

Remove the top 10cm (4in) of lawn or top-soil

Add grit and rock to the soil below and dig in well

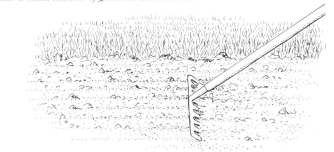

Scatter a mixed selection of grass seed and rake it in

Position a few carefully selected rocks and plant the area with bulbs and perennials

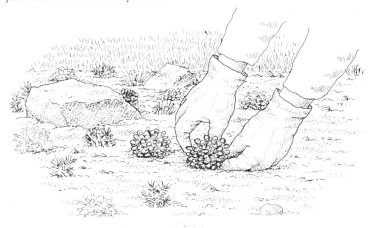

plants

OF THE

month

2

 ### BOG ROSEMARY
(Andromeda polifolia 'Compacta'*)*

Andromeda is a small genus of the large ericaceous family; the species chosen is available in over a dozen forms, but none is tidier or more pleasing than this.

type	Evergreen, compact shrub
foliage	Narrow, pointed, dark green leaves, tough and shiny
flowers	Nodding bunches of pink, three-quarter balloon-shaped bells at ends of stems in spring and early summer
height	15–22cm (6–9in)
spread	30cm (12in)
planting	Early spring or early autumn
site	Light spot but not in full glaring sun
soil	Moist, peaty. Lime-hater
care	No difficulty, provided it is kept clear of lime and is in a relatively moist position
propagation	Semi-ripe cuttings in summer or layers to be detached the following year
relatives	*A.p.* 'Compacta Alba' is a fine white form of the above. *A.p.* 'Alba' with white flowers is around twice the size. *A.p.* 'Nana' only grows to about 15cm (6in)

BOG ROSEMARY

LEWISIA
(Lewisia tweedyi)

Lewisia tweedyi is not very long-lived but its wide starry flowers make it a favourite.

type	Evergreen perennial with tap-root
foliage	Rosette of smooth, succulent leaves

flowers	Branched low stems bear large, wide open flowers with around eight petals in pale dog-rose pink, sometimes with a salmon flush. Spring
height	15cm (6in)
spread	10–15cm (4–6in)
planting	In pot or pan when available
site	Alpine house or frame
soil	Very gritty but with plenty of peaty humus
care	Avoid moisture around neck and in rosette of leaves. Have a few seedlings coming along to take place of those that perish
propagation	By seed sown as soon as ripe
relatives	*L. cotyledon* is one of the easiest species and is parent to a huge tribe of hybrids — bright carnival colours that are almost too gaudy for the rock garden

 ### CLEMATIS
(Clematis marmoraria)

This is an unusual form of clematis forming a neat dome of finely-cut foliage. It is easily grown. Its natural habitat is New Zealand, where it grows in crevices in the hard rocks of mountains on the South Island.

type	Small deciduous shrub with male and female forms
foliage	Divided, dark leaves rather like a buttercup's
flowers	Buds visible in winter but do not open till mid-spring. Male plants have showier flowers, opening greenish but later developing into shining, creamy-white, wide open blooms, each with a conspicuous

boss of creamy stamens. Flowers can hide foliage

height	10–20cm (4–8in)
spread	10–20cm (4–8in)
planting	Early spring or early autumn
site	Sunny
soil	Gritty scree mix with extra humus with rocks or a chipping layer over roots
propagation	Cuttings in summer or fresh seed
relatives	*C. alpina* is a little climber but will scramble over rocks and shrubby plants. Choose a small form with clear blue flowers. *C.a.* 'Francis Rivis' is darker but more vigorous and not really suitable for any but the most monumental rock garden

TULIPA
(Tulipa tarda)

Until fairly recently, the tulip species have often been in the shadow of their big hybrid brothers and the somewhat gaudy but cheerful *T. kaufmanniana* and *T. greigii* hybrids, but alpine enthusiasts cannot resist the individual character of species such as *T. tarda*.

type	Bulb
foliage	Shiny, rich green, long leaves making a jellyfish-like rosette on the ground
flowers	Almost stemless in bud, looking like so many green eggs in the rosette's centre, they open to wide white stars with large golden centres in mid- to late spring
height	10–15cm (4–6in)
spread	20–25cm (8–10in)
planting	Early autumn
site	Sunny, very well-drained
soil	Unfussy, but best in gritty mix
care	If the position is well-drained, warm and sunny, bulbs can be left for several years and only lifted when they become overcrowded
propagation	Bulb division, lift early summer and replant immediately or in autumn
relatives	Of many good dwarf tulips the nearest relative is *T. urumiensis*, which has a similar squat growth pattern and all-gold flowers. This will spread by dropped seed

FRITILLARY
(Fritillaria pyrenaica)

A varied genus with some fascinating plants, many with flowers in unusual colours. This species is outstanding.

TULIPA TARDA

type	Bulb
foliage	Usually narrow, pointed, grey-green leaves, 5–10 per bulb
flowers	Large, nodding, cloche-hat blooms with a small reflex, in spring. 1 or 2 per stem. Colour varies but usually a rich amalgam of chocolate-brown and dark purple, One of the best in this colour range
height	15–30cm (6–12in)
spread	5–7cm (2–3in)
planting	Normally obtained as a dry bulb in autumn. Plant as soon as possible; bulbs do not like being out of the ground. Depth 5–7cm (2–3in)
site	Likes good drainage without too much summer wet
soil	Neutral or slightly alkaline rather than acid
care	One of the easier fritillaries provided soil is not acid
propagation	Bulbs divide regularly. Lift as foliage fails, split and replant immediately. Comes quickly from fresh seed
relatives	There are a number of rather similarly-coloured species. *F. meleagris* is the more familiar snake's head fritillary, approximately the same size but with squarer-shouldered, nodding heads usually noticeably chequered in whites, mauves and pale purples

FRITILLARIA PYRENAICA

practical project *2*

MAKING A GRASSLESS ALPINE LAWN

See appendix 1 page 127 for plant list

The word lawn is usually synonymous with a well-maintained sward of grass, but it ain't necessarily so. In different places, especially on hills, dwarf plants can take over from grass and form a low even growth perhaps more or less dominating an area and creating the effect of a lawn. More often a number of species join forces to create a low patchwork blanket cover. This is the grassless lawn we aim to reproduce.

Grass species need not be completely excluded. There are a number of small, non-invasive kinds that could add their quota to the whole pattern.

REDUCING FERTILITY AND WEEDS

Hills and mountain tops are often places of low fertility with a very limited depth of soil or a scree-type mix. The weather regime is likely to keep all very disciplined. In contrast our gardens are relatively rich and provide soft living. The first job is to reduce this fertility.
- Mark out the area for the lawn and remove the top few centimetres/inches of soil or, if within the rock garden, grit and soil. If the site is grassed cut turves thickly and either use them elsewhere or stack them upside down in an out-of-the-way place where they can be allowed to rot down for using in potting mixes later
- If need be, and the energy is still there, a further excavation of top-soil can take place. The greatest fertility is in this top level – together with the greatest bank of weed seeds
- Half fill the resulting sunken area with grit and hardcore and rotovate or dig it in to incorporate with existing soil
- Fill the remaining space with more of the same grit and hardcore mixture and work it in. This results in a semi-scree, a depth of some 25–30cm (10–12in) of fast-draining, poorish soil

PLANTING

Seeds
The lawn area is now ready for populating. The obvious method is to start introducing grown plants, but some parts at least will be effective if colonised by sowing seed, allowing the seedling plants to do the work. There is a limited number of plants that can be used for this job. One is *Erinus alpinus*, a pretty scrambling plant with lots of pink blossom over a long period, but with white and purple forms; others include some of the drabas, saxifrages, sedums and campanulas. (See appendix list p127.)

Plants
One of the most obvious plants to use is thyme; it is ideal for use as the dominant genus and background to all the remainder. There are lots of prostrate forms which root as they spread so that one plant can soon be divided into several and make the job of planting a wide area not too expensive. *Thymus serpyllum* and its many named forms is the leading prostrate species.

Other prostrate 'lawn' plants include daisy plants such as *Anacyclus depressus* and creeping campanulas such as *C. cochleariifolia*, running around and producing untold numbers of little bells, blue, purple, lavender or white. The most prostrate of carpeters is *Raoulia australis*, so close to the ground with its tiny, round, silvery leaves that it is not really measurable. The plants do not all have to be outstandingly flat or spreading. You can afford to have groups of diminutive species such as the spring gentian, *G. verna*, which are going to be brilliant in bloom but very tidy and self-effacing out of blossom. (Once again, Appendix 1, p.127 gives ideas.)

Bulbs
Extra excitement is lent to the carpet lawn by small bulbous flowers popping up in due season with the added benefit that their less attractive foliage can be disguised: crocuses coming through thyme look splendid and have manageable dying foliage – scarcely noticed. Small daffodils such as the lovely, delicate hoop-petticoats, *N. bulbocodium* forms, and even some of the really small hybrids such as 'Wee Bee' will add a lot to the spring effect. Dwarf tulips will also enjoy the sharp drainage and open aspect.

MAINTENANCE

Looking after the lawn should not be a big chore once it is up and running. The thymes, and perhaps occasional very dwarf heather with other carpeting plants, will act as ground-cover to thwart weed. The excavation of the original soil will have dealt with the original weed and their seed. All that needs to be done is to take out any new colonising weed, especially grass. Then the lawn may require a very light scatter of soil mix once a year.

MAY

*Now we need more hours in the day, even though the light evenings
stretch ever longer. All around gardens are now in their most
luxurious stage; colour has flooded the scene. Shrubs and trees have, or
are busy acquiring, their fresh foliar dress, the forsythias and early
almonds have been replaced by clouds of cherry blossom and banks of
rhododendrons, the alpines that first led the way out of the winter are
still full of colour.*

*The grass is growing apace; perhaps the mower needs to be brought out
more often. This might prompt the thought that some of the more
awkward patches of grass could be dispensed with and paved or made
into gravelled areas which could then be planted with interesting small
plants. A theme could be chosen, perhaps a Mediterranean bed in a
sunny area. Pavings need not be sterile if they are interplanted with
small creeping plants that colonise before the dandelions and creeping
buttercup take hold.*

*The sun should have been making a show and often this month sees the
first threat of drought. After grumbling about continuous wet, we now
are praying for rain. But this need not be too desperate if work has
been done properly in the rock garden and has included an adequate
supply of moisture-retaining humus; alpines may look tiny and
vulnerable above ground but below their roots stretch extraordinary
lengths and can find moisture yards away.*

*Potted plants under glass may be in greater need of water. Ensure that
their needs are being fulfilled.*

*At garden shows all over the country there are spectacular displays by
specialist firms. Although we may go secure in the belief that we are not
going to purchase any more plants, we seldom return without special
new treasures. Maybe it is time to expand the rock garden by adding
a new outcrop.*

PAGES 46–7
Sempervivum pans arranged at the base of an alpine trough, illustrating the wide range of colour, size, leaf form and texture this genus has to offer

tasks

FOR THE

month

PLANTS TO INCREASE BY STEM CUTTINGS

Andromeda polifolia
Aster pappei • *Calamintha alpina*
Campanula various
Daboecia various • *Erica* various
Erodium various
Hippocrepis comosa 'E R Janes'
Iberis various
Saxifraga oppositifolia • *Thymus* various • *Veronica* various

PLANTS TO INCREASE BY ROOT CUTTINGS

Campanula various • *Geranium farreri* • *G. sanguineum striatum*
Mertensia various • *Morisia monanthos* • *Phlox douglasii*
P. longiflora • *P. subulata*
P. triovulata • *Primula denticulata*
Pulsatilla vulgaris
Weldenia candida

CHECKLIST

- Shading
- Tending leggy plants
- Repairing the ravages of pests
- Stem cuttings
- Root cuttings
- Collecting water

SHADING

By now, and possibly even last month, there are periods of bright hot sunshine that may be a little too much for certain plants growing in the alpine house, some of which are used to cool conditions, out of direct sunshine. Ferns, some primulas and smaller woodland plants that are used as 'alpines' benefit from shading. It is a good idea to make part of the alpine house or frame shadier than the rest. Few people now resort to painting the glass with lime; blinds of wooden/plastic slats or, more commonly, plastic-mesh shading are more convenient and can be drawn down quickly as far as required, without hindering the free ventilation which is certainly now needed.

TENDING LEGGY PLANTS

Many alpines are very neat, tight plants but there are some that become leggy, the main stems growing high away from the ground or sprawling across the surface. This is because in nature they are scree dwellers, adapted to a constant adding to their top-dressing of stone chips. *Primula marginata* and others of the Auricula section produce trunks that need lowering into the ground to encourage fresh rooting and keep new growth lively. There may well be a number of good shoots low down. Use a sharp knife to detach upper parts with leaves and some roots; these can be planted to make new specimens elsewhere, while leaving basal shoots to carry on. Sometimes the trunks may be rootless and in this case the excess leaves can be removed and the trunks are used as cuttings. Inserted in an equal mix of peat and grit they should produce new roots after a few weeks. The new plants can be potted up to grow on as specimens or to be planted out later.

Aster alpinus, some *Erigerons* and other creeping plants may benefit from a top-dressing of gritty compost to encourage fresh growth as well as to make them look tidy.

Daphne blagayana growing in a wide pan or in a shaded part of the rock garden needs its wide-reaching branches pegged down with small rocks or grit. The two *Epigaea* species, *E. asiatica* and *E. repens*, are prostrate shrublets that require similar regular treatment at least once a year.

REPAIRING THE RAVAGES OF PESTS

Our world is one of challenge and response. Challenges are plentiful, responses come in sizes from very small to outrageous. A visit to the rock garden may find pests of different kinds have taken their toll. How do we respond?

Moles and rabbits are pests in rock gardens even if you want to encourage wildlife. A single mole can have a very extensive underground system. You might think an army has moved in when the damage is caused by one or two.

Moles

Responses to moles vary. The most drastic, and unlikely, is to sell up and move garden. Do not believe the tale that spurges (*Euphorbia*) remove moles. In fact it is possible that the belief has slipped over from a herbal remedy, the suggestion that 'moles' on the face can be removed by spurge juice. Just as unlikely? I have found smoke-producing anti-mole devices expensive and ineffective. Traditional mole-traps work but must be lowered into runs carefully by gloved hands. There are humane traps which allow you to release the mole into the wild.

WARNING

■ *Worms coated in strychnine is a very very dangerous, unpleasant method of removing moles* ■

Rabbits

Rabbits are a major pest: they concentrate on eating precious plants when surrounded with a choice of lush, juicy weed; they burrow anywhere and often find the elevation of a rock garden and its large stones just the sort of sheltered arena they desire. We surrounded our garden with chicken wire to a height of 1m (3ft) above ground, 15–18cm (6–7in) vertically below the surface and then a similar buried length taken horizontally out from the garden. Any attacking rabbits reach the visible wire, start to burrow and are stopped by the horizontal wire.

STEM CUTTINGS

At this time of year a number of alpines can be propagated by softwood cuttings. Shoot lengths vary according to the plant type; 2.5–8cm (1–3in) long cuttings are easily manageable but are difficult to obtain from some plants. Longer cuttings of many plants can be encouraged by covering part of them with an upturned pot, that has a large drainage hole, or a cylinder. The shoots are forced to grow longer to reach the light; a couple of weeks of this will produce elongated shoots which are easier to cut.
- Cuts should be clean. Nip lower leaves or cut them off and then dust the stem ends with hormone rooting powder before inserting them into a mix of equal parts grit and peat

1)Tip cutting; 2) Heel cutting; 3)Basal cutting

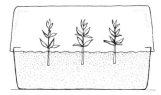

- In a propagator they can be lightly sprayed with fungicide
- In a pot only fill with the rooting mix about half way up so that, with the cuttings inserted, the top of the pot can be covered with glass or polythene and a moist environment maintained
- Alternatively, a potful of cuttings can be enclosed in a polythene bag and then placed in a warmish spot with no direct sunshine
- Check every few days for fungus rot. A mist spray of fungicide will keep this to the very minimum
- Remove dead leaves or failed cuttings
- New growth is usually the signal that rooting has taken place and that cuttings are ready for potting on. The procedure with these cuttings will be familiar to gardeners; the smaller scale makes attention to detail rather more important

ROOT CUTTINGS

A number of alpines are easily increased by root cuttings. Suitable roots are normally around 3mm (⅛in) thick and 2-3cm (1in) long. They need to be firm and fleshy, not thin or fibrous. Slightly narrower roots than those recommended can be cut into rather longer pieces.
 Root cuttings need careful handling so that all sections are correctly orientated top to bottom when they are inserted upright into the pot of gritty compost. Any inserted upside down will die; to avoid this make certain that the base is cut at an angle when taking cuttings.

Compost mix A suitable mix for the cuttings might be 2 parts grit or washed sand to 1 of loam with the bottom of the pot having a layer of normal growing compost. The mix for root cuttings is best grittier than for other types of cuttings; they have no leaves busy transpiring moisture. Too much water may lead to rotting. The tips should be level with the top of the compost, or just below; ends that protrude will dry and will not produce buds.
- Lift plants and detach up to one third of the healthy root system using a clean, sharp pruning knife or razor blade
- Alternatively take advantage of plants growing in pots and remove roots coming through the drainage holes
- This last method can be simply expedited by taking the potted plant and putting it into a plunge frame with some very gritty compost below the fully- or half-sunken pot. A strong plant, finding an unimpeded drainage hole leading into moist compost, will normally produce strong extraneous growth. Lifting the pot carefully some weeks or months after plunging should provide plenty of roots
- Keep the pot of cuttings shaded and just moist in a closed polythene bag
- After a few weeks small rosettes and new fibrous roots begin to develop. As they become large enough to handle comfortably, the little plants can be potted up and grown on
See margin p48 for suitable subjects

COLLECTING WATER

There will be times of water shortage over the next few months. Water butts can be a considerable help. They can be stationed to collect rainwater from the roof of the house, garage or greenhouse.

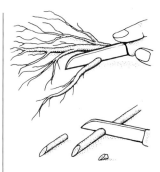

Remove the root from the parent plant. Make a sloping cut at the bottom and a right-angled cut at the top

Insert in compost so the top is level with, or just below the compost surface

Cover the surface with washed grit, put in a shaded place and keep moist

Water and feed once leaves and roots have begun to grow

plants
OF THE
month

PERENNIAL CANDYTUFT
(Iberis sempervirens)

One of the most reliable and worthwhile plants from that family of mixed virtue, the *Cruciferae* (illus. p.36–7).

type	Evergreen sub-shrub
foliage	Oblong, very dark green leaves
flowers	Covers itself with short-stemmed heads of brilliant white flowers in late spring or early summer
height	15–25cm (6–10in)
spread	45–75cm (18–30in)
planting	Any time, possibly early autumn
site	Open spot. Perhaps falling over wall or rock. Useful at path edges
soil	Unfussy
care	One of the easiest of plants, benefits from a trim after flowering to keep it a tight dark evergreen mass
propagation	Seed as soon as ripe or cuttings in summer
relatives	*I.s.* 'Weisser Zwerg' is a more compact form, perhaps two thirds the size. *I.s.* 'Schneeflocke' ('Snowflake') is a vigorous, large, free-flowering clone

PRIMULA
(Primula reidii williamsii)

This is one of the choicer primrose species from the north-western Himalayas – and sometimes, sadly, rather too quick to pine for its homeland.

type	Herbaceous perennial, forming clumps
foliage	Oval, soft, hairy, pale green leaves
flowers	Many-flowered clusters of hanging wide bells of lavender or pale purple with white meal, heavily scented
height	7–12cm (3–5in)
spread	10–15cm (4–6in)
planting	When obtained
site	In pots or a cool sheltered spot in dappled shade
soil	Open, leafy mix, capable of remaining moist but never sodden
care	Easier in cooler areas. Take particular care about root aphids and be sure to avoid constant wet around neck
propagation	Seed, or division in early spring
relatives	*P. reidii*, the type, is white-flowered and more tricky

PRIMULA REIDII

KALMIOPSIS
(Kalmiopsis leachiana)

A single species genus, a member of the heather family.

type	Evergreen, ericaceous shrub
foliage	Small, oval, shiny dark green leaves
flowers	Clustered, wide bells of mauvy-pink at end of shoots
height	30cm (12in)
spread	30cm (12in)
planting	From early spring till early autumn
site	Semi-shade
soil	Moist, humus-rich, acid
care	Robust and easy if without lime
propagation	Cuttings in summer

LADY'S SLIPPER ORCHID
(Cypripedium calceolus pubescens)

Of all terrestrial orchids, this is one of the elite.

type	Deciduous, rhizomatous ground orchid
foliage	Spear-shaped, with longitudinal pleats formed by impressed veins, mid-green, quite hairy
flowers	Typical slipper-orchid flower with bright limey-yellow pouch (slipper)

and purple suffused petals in mid to
late spring

height	50–75cm (20–30in)
spread	20–30cm (8–12in)
planting	Early spring till early autumn, rhizomes just below soil surface
site	Semi-shade, sheltered from wind, or in pots
soil	Drained soils rich in leaf-mould or fibrous peat with some grit, moisture retaining but not sodden. Does not object to lime
care	Try to keep the worst of frost away and protect emerging foliage if frosts threaten
propagation	Careful division of established plants in early spring when growth is just beginning – and when you feel brave enough
relatives	*C. acaule*, similar in form but with a rather bibulous-looking pouch. It may manage slightly drier conditions

WINTER ACONITE
(*Eranthis × tubergenii* 'Guinea Gold')

Why feature these winter-flowering plants in this springtime chapter? It helps highlight when to propagate them, especially this very fine clone. One can never have too many of these midwinter flowers, but it is easy to overlook the dying plants, which ought to be lifted and split now.

type	Tuber
foliage	Deeply-lobed bright green glossy leaves with a healthy bronze cast. Succulent leaf stalks
flowers	Fat, deep golden, buttercup-blooms in midwinter
height	8–10cm (3–4in)
spread	Clumps to 25cm (10in)
planting	Preferably after flowering 'in the green' or now as dying down
site	Semi-shade, moist
soil	Humus-rich, open
care	Easy
propagation	Lift plants a few weeks after flowering and break the knobbly tubers into several pieces each with a growing point. Replant immediately. Repeat every other year
relatives	This is a hybrid from *E. hyemalis* and *E. cilicica*, similar species, with smaller flowers, worth growing and easy to reproduce by division or seed, but not a patch on their offspring

PRIMULA
(*Primula vialii*)

PRIMULA VIALII

The primula genus is very varied; this is one of the most distinct. It is an Asiatic species and looks exotic, but it has proved easy in most gardens.

type	Clump-forming herbaceous perennial, not long-lived
foliage	Long, oval leaves rather upright
flowers	Many, small flowers densely-packed in poker-heads, brilliant red in bud, but pinky-violet when open in late spring. Very distinct and attractive
height	30–45cm (12–18in)
spread	20–30cm (8–12in)
planting	As seedlings or young plants when ready, possibly early summer or early autumn
site	Sun or partial shade
soil	Well-drained with humus and moisture
care	Much the easiest of this group of primulas, and easily raised from seed. New batches should be raised every year or every other year to maintain succession. Individual plants may last two or three seasons
propagation	By seed sown when fresh or from packets in late winter
relatives	*P. muscarioides*, 40cm (16in) high with rich purple-blue, slightly mealed flowers in dense heads. *P. bellidifolia*, 10-24cm (4-10in) high, flowers are rich lilac to violet with a mealy eye. Both have a dozen or more flowers to a head in late spring

practical project 1

THE SCREE GARDEN

Anacyclus depressus

Convolvulus sabatius

In nature screes are often formed on mountainsides where rocks have shattered due to the effect of weather and broken pieces have fallen down to accumulate long slides of various-sized fragments. There may be large rocks of several tons among the smaller ones. Sometimes the scree seems almost unnaturally graded with fairly evenly-sized portions. Screes are not stable; their formation is a more or less continuous process with always the possibility of fresh falls topping them up.

Such an arrangement would not seem to be a very inviting habitat for plants; although drainage is perfect, nutrients are rather sparse and the only shelter is that afforded by larger rock fragments, but it is surprising how quickly such a site is colonised. There are some plants that are particularly well adapted to such sites, happy to get a roothold and maintain their position even if they get a very regular top-dressing of new rock pieces. Their tops give little clue to the long branches that lead down to the original rootstock.

BENEFITS

There is a not inconsiderable number of plants that need scree conditions and are found in the wild in such areas. There are also other small plants that may grow naturally in other sites but in captivity do better in a scree where good drainage and poor nutrient supply encourages them to retain their natural form and shape; they might quickly become out of character in a richer soil and instant drainage goes a long way to counterbalance any tendency to tenderness. A well-made scree, suitably planted, can be a pleasing feature and makes a natural continuation of the main rock garden.

SITES

- Choose an open, unshaded site. The obvious place is against or close to the rock garden, perhaps falling away from part of it. Or it may be more convenient to have it to the side, with a grass or gravel/paving stone path between, or even as a separate bed
- Size may be as little as 1-2 square metres (yds) but could be half as big as the rock garden proper – or even more
- Be sure that it is well-drained or that the lie of the land enables good drainage to be arranged
- Get inspiration from examples of screes in botanical and other large gardens as well as in those of enthusiasts. The scree at the Royal Botanic Garden, Edinburgh, is a particularly fine example

EXCAVATION AND DRAINAGE

- On heavy soils it is sensible to construct the scree so that it is proud of the normal soil level and to hold in the scree mix to a depth of a minimum of 30cm (12in) with a series of rocks. As a first step the site can be dug over and hardcore and other drainage material incorporated into the top-soil. To excavate very deeply in heavy soil may run the risk of making a sump for all surplus water
- On normal and light soils it is acceptable to excavate some 45cm (18in) and, if possible, arrange the soil base to slope away to lower ground
- Dig a generous drainage channel from the base of the scree away to lower ground or to a drain if necessary
- For help in watering during times of

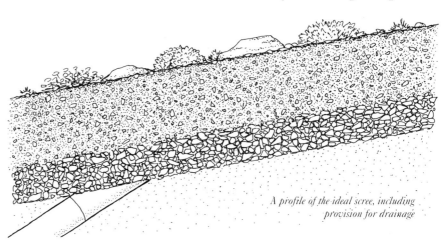

A profile of the ideal scree, including provision for drainage

drought a refinement is to lead a number of polythene pipes with puncture holes into the bottom of the scree. Arrange them to surface at an unobtrusive spot, perhaps behind a rock

SOIL AND ROCKS

Scree mixes are approximately
- 60% grit, crushed rock, gravel, chippings – either as one or as mixed ingredients
- 20% healthy, loamy soil
- 20% leaf-mould or very well-rotted compost

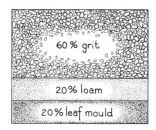

An even more severe mix could increase the proportion of grit to be three quarters by volume. Once the scree mix has filled the area it may look very flat and sterile. It can be improved and made to look more natural by including a number of rocks either in an extension of the natural strata of the rock garden or placed at random, as if they have come to rest naturally. Such rocks should be partially submerged and will not only relieve any uniform flat feeling but also provide some cool shelter for plant roots.

(clockwise from top right) Sedum acre 'Aureum',
Globularia meridionalis, Anchusa caespitosa
and Silene acaulis in a scree bed

PLANTING

It is easy enough to introduce suitable plants into the scree, but remember that established scree plants may only have tiny bundles of leaves above ground but below their roots can travel several yards. The pot-grown plant you are introducing to the spartan fare just arranged will feel high and dry until its roots have delved into their new root run. To help it settle in, its immediate surrounds can be slightly enriched especially below it, but more importantly the area needs to be kept moist. This is vital until the plant has really got its toes dug in. Suggested scree plants are listed in the margin.

MAINTENANCE

- Keep weed free
- In times of severe drought provide extra water
- If plants appear to be struggling after a season or two a light top-dressing of sieved humus, loam and sand can be applied in autumn and/or spring

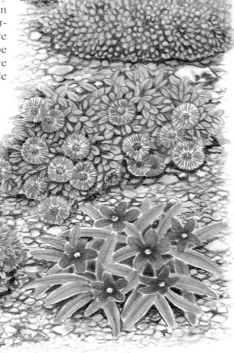

SCREE GARDEN PLANTS

Acantholimon glumaceum
Anacyclus depressus
Anchusa caespitosa
Androsace various
Aquilegia bertolonii
A. flabellata nana
A. scopulorum
Asperula suberosa
Calandrinia umbellata
Callianthemum kernerianum
C. rutifolium
Carlina acaulis
Codonopsis various
Convolvulus sabatius,
    syn. *C. mauritanicus*
Daphne blagayana
Dryas octopetala
Edraianthus various
Epilobium canum
Erinus alpinus
Erodium various
Euryops acraeus
Frankenia laevis
F. thymifolia
Globularia various
Haplopappus brandegeei
Helichrysum bellidioides
H. coralloides
H. milfordiae
Leontopodium alpinum
Minuartia stellata
Myosotis rupicola
Nierembergia repens
Ononis fruticosa
O. natrix
O. rotundifolia
Origanum amanum
O. laevigatum
Raoulia various
Sedum various
Sempervivum all
Silene acaulis
S. elizabethae
S. schafta
Verbascum acaule
V. 'Letitia'
Zauschneria californica,
    syn. *Epilobium canum*

practical
project
2

MAKING AN
'ANTIQUE' TROUGH

PLANTS FOR TROUGHS

Achillea x kolbiana
Aethionema 'Warley Rose'
Androsace carnea
A. hedraeantha
A. sempervivoides
Antennaria dioica
Armeria juniperifolia
Asperula gussonii
A. nitida
Aster alpinus
Campanula various including:
C. raineri
Crassula milfordiae
Dianthus various
Draba various
Erinus alpinus
Erodium cheilanthifolium
E. macradenum
Gentiana saxosa
G. verna
Geranium farreri
Globularia various
Gypsophila aretioides
Helichrysum milfordiae
Iris mellita
Phlox various
Physoplexis camosa, syn.
Phyteuma comosum

Old stone sinks and feeding troughs hewn from rock are collectors' items and have become very expensive. An alternative used to be the old glazed sinks at one time in plentiful supply in builders' yards, the result of the onward march of the stainless steel artefact. These could be coated with a mix to give the appearance of rough hewn rock. However, this coating had a habit of falling away and spoiling the effect. It is possible and much cheaper to fabricate your own trough from scratch and just a few months after completion it might easily be mistaken for the genuine article. The following instructions are for making an ideal trough as good as or better than the original article; better because we can make it to the exact depth we need and improve the provisions for drainage.

BENEFITS

Why bother making troughs? Firstly because they can look very attractive indeed. Secondly because they give an easily manipulated environment for collections of plants that might not manage in the garden proper. Troughs also give gardeners with very limited space or energy the chance to grow a surprisingly wide range of plants.

SIZES

▪ There needs to be sufficient depth for the roots to have a good run
▪ The size should be as large as convenient as a very small trough will be constantly drying out and getting over-hot
▪ The completed trough ought not to be so large that it is immovable – although in these days of thefts of such artefacts from gardens something substantial would be more of a challenge to thieves

As long as these points are taken into account there are no hard and fast recommended dimensions to follow but the depth should not be less than 15cm (6in) and would certainly be better at 20cm (8in). Outside dimensions could be 38–45cm x 60–75cm (15–18in x 24–30in).

MATERIALS

Make the trough out of the following mix by volume,
▪ 2 parts sifted moist sphagnum peat

▪ 1 part clean sand/washed fine grit
▪ 1 part cement
The result of this mix has been dubbed 'hypertufa', tufa being a natural very soft rock without strata, so soft that holes can be easily bored in and plants ensconced.

You will need to buy cement, some grit/sand and some peat; the moulds can be made from waste wood or cardboard boxes.

MAKING THE TROUGH

Either make two moulds in wood, the outer larger than the inner, or use two cardboard boxes, one smaller than the other. Wooden moulds can be used again; cardboard is quicker and cheaper.

Wooden moulds need only consist of the four sides; the base is made by standing the mould on a board, a polythene sheet, a layer of sand or on soil during construction.

Making the mould
▪ It makes life easier if the sides of the mould are screwed together so that they may be unscrewed when the job is complete and removed without damaging the new 'antique' trough. It is also advisable to have the sides sloping slightly inwards to the base
▪ The inner mould should be formed so that between the two moulds there is a gap of 4-5cm (1$^1/_2$–2in) at the base and all the way round. The inner mould must be narrower at the bottom than at the top so that when the hypertufa has set the mould may be removed easily. A piece of wood securely fixed across the top of the inner mould will act as a handle and aid removal
▪ Check that the inner mould does not have any projecting pieces – especially around the base – so that nothing can hinder its removal
▪ The base of the inner mould need not be

NOTE

▪ *The whole trough could be strengthened by reinforcing it with pieces of wire, perhaps chicken netting, before filling the moulds with the mix. Wires coming from the base at least partially up the wall and around the sides will greatly strengthen the whole and is recommended for any large trough. Take care that no wire appears at the surface of the completed trough* ▪

joined to the side; it could be made of two pieces of wood laid side by side and with a piece of wood or projecting screw to act as a handle to lever each carefully away when the mix has hardened

▪ Make four 'plugs' around 3cm (1–1½in) wide and 4–5cm (1½–2in) long out of wood or a cardboard roll stuffed with paper. Place these a few centimetres from each corner of the outer mould to make the drainage holes when they have been removed from the set hypertufa

Making the trough

▪ Mix the ingredients thoroughly, into a wet, but not sloppy, state and put it onto the base of the outer mould. Add enough to reach the tops of the four drainage plugs

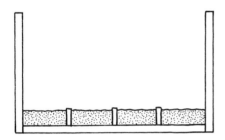

Fill the base of the larger mould with hypertufa. Insert wooden dowels for drainage holes

▪ Place the inner mould on the still-damp base and carefully feed the mix between the two moulds making sure that no air holes are left

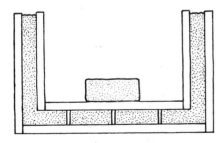

Position the smaller mould inside the larger one and add hypertufa down the sides

▪ Leave for two or three days covered with a damp sack or with polythene sheeting so that the drying is steady, then carefully remove the outer moulding

▪ Rub down sharp edges with a piece of wood, a file or an old brush. A little roughening of very smooth sides may be attempted

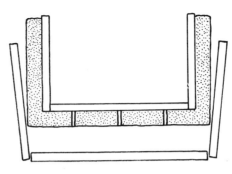

Dismantle the outer mould once the mix has set

Roughen the outside for a more authentic effect

but it is better not to be too elaborate. Recover with damp sacking

▪ After another two or three days remove the inner mould and work the top edges of the trough just sufficiently to dull any sharp edges

▪ Leave for a week or more until fully dry and then knock out the drainage plugs

▪ Move the trough to its permanent quarters and here raise it a few centimetres/inches off the ground on bricks or stones

Cardboard boxes

Using cardboard boxes is cheap but fresh boxes are required for each trough. Some trough enthusiasts prefer to use cardboard which 'gives' in the making so providing a more 'natural' look.

Follow exactly the same procedure as for wooden boxes but prop up the outer mould with sand to prevent it from 'giving' too much.

Planting mixes

Cover the drainage holes with plastic netting or perforated discs and aid drainage by adding a 5cm (2in) layer of broken crocks. Fill the trough with compost (for a suitable mix see p12).

PLANTS FOR TROUGHS

Continued:
Saponaria 'Bressingham'
Saxifraga various
Sedum various
Sempervivum various
Silene schafta
Soldanella alpina
S. pusilla
S. montana
S. villosa
Thymus various
Veronica bombycina
V. fruticans
Vitaliana primuliflora

OTHER TROUGH PLANTS

DWARF CONIFERS
Chamaecyparis obtusa 'Minima'
Juniperus communis 'Compressa'
Microcachrys tetragona
Picea glauca 'Echiniformis'
P. g 'Laurin'
Tsuga canadensis 'Minuta'

DWARF SHRUBS
Andromeda polifolia 'Minima'
Daphne arbuscula
D. cneorum
Genista tinctoria 'Plena'
Hebe many species
Salix boydii

FERNS
Asplenium ceterach
A. trichomanes
Pellaea atropurpurea

GRASSES AND SEDGES
Carex various dwarf forms
C. firma 'Variegata'
Festuca glacialis
Poa alpina

BULBS
Many small bulbs can be suitable; avoid varieties that produce considerable foliage after blooming, eg bulbous irises.

Crocus species
Leucojum autumnale
Narcissus asturiensis
N. rupicola
N. triandrus
Tulipa very small varieties
T. biflora

JUNE

Despite the heat, the rock garden is still a picture, especially if it has a pool and bog garden adjoining where some of the water irises will be in full bloom and the miniature water lilies will be opening buds. Dwarf brooms and low carpeting phloxes create bold splashes of colour; other dwarf forms of familiar plants are coming into their own. An example is the diminutive form of the Ragged Robin, Lychnis flos-cuculi 'Nana'.

Dwarf trees are often mutated forms of giants; the majority of dwarf conifers have arisen from branch mutations of forest trees. A cluster of miniaturised branches create a 'witch's broom' high up a mature tree. Nurserymen can perpetuate a slow-growing clone by using some of this mutated growth. Some are most excellent trees for small-scale landscapes such as a rock garden. There are also a few more natural miniature forms that have been found growing independently, on their own roots. Junipers, for example, are hugely variable, ranging from wide-spreading, flat species to more or less upright trees of varying heights. Good individual plants are propagated by cuttings to become named clones. A word of warning. Take careful note of the probable ultimate height of some of these 'dwarfs' when examining them as neat, pot-grown specimens in garden centres. 'Dwarf' sometimes needs to be interpreted as 'slow-growing' as they eventually make plants twice as high as the planter.

Like last month there is a need to water parts of the rock garden or beds in periods of drought. Enjoy the warmer weather but do not forget to make sure that plants under glass are not flagging in heat. The alpine house will have had all ventilation open for some weeks, and frames will need to have plenty of air too. Now is an ideal time to start thinking about propagating some favourite plants, to increase stock or to provide material for swapping.

tasks

FOR THE

month

PLANTS TO TAKE STEM CUTTINGS

Aethionema 'Warley Rose'
Androsace foliosa
A. lanuginosa
Artemisia various
Asperula suberosa
Cheiranthus dwarf kinds
Cistus various
Cyananthus various
Dianthus various
Gentiana lime-haters
Helianthemum various
Helichrysum bellidioides
Helichrysum various
Phlox various
Polygonum various

PLANTS TO TAKE LEAF CUTTINGS

Asplenium bulbiferum
(bulbils on fronds)
Haberlea ferdinandi-coburgii
H. rhodopensis
H.r. 'Virginalis'
Polystichum setiferum
(bulbils along main stem of frond)
Primula scapigera
Ramonda myconi
R. m. 'Rosea'
R. nathaliae
R. n. 'Alba'
R. serbica
Sedum all kinds

CHECKLIST

- Weeding
- Trimming and dead-heading
- Watering
- Container-garden care
- Stem cuttings
- Leaf cuttings

WEEDING

This regular subheading becomes monotonous. It is not inserted to suggest that anyone with a rock garden is usually found bent double pulling out weeds. Rather it is meant to emphasise the boring commonsense of the saying 'a stitch in time saves nine', or perhaps the more apposite dictum 'one year's seeding, seven years' weeding'. Removing small weeds as they appear will save plenty of work later.

Fortunately rock gardens can be easily kept weed-free provided they start clear of perennial delinquents and they have a good mulch of grit-chippings over the surface.

Anyone who has tackled a rock garden that has really got out of control, a combat ground for ground elder and dog's mercury, will probably have been put off rock gardens for life. (See p32 for the Practical Project 'Renovating a rock garden'.)

TRIMMING AND DEAD-HEADING

Alpines are perhaps not normally thought of as needing trimming and dead-heading – trimming is for hedges and dead-heading is for roses. Alpines are small and do not need to be made smaller – usually, but there are some prostrate plants that

can get a little rampant and do benefit from some discipline. One obvious candidate are aubrietas. Both the species and the hybrids respond well to having a quite severe 'short-back-and-sides' trim. This encourages the plants to produce lively new growth which results in a crowded lot of blossom the following year. Aubrietas belong to the *Cruciferae* family and other related genera are among plants that can be kept young and lively by trimming back to about a third their length; *Alyssum, Iberis* and *Arabis* are three that will take the treatment, even the lovely *Aethionema*, high-class *Cruciferae* that look all quality, can benefit from just a bit of tidying. The daisy family, *Compositae*, also has members that can be neatened when necessary.

Dead-heading, the cutting away of developing seedheads, often leaves good foliage plants distinctly more attractive and not wasting effort on seed production. Aubrietas, saxifrages, and later helianthemums all look the better for having developing seedheads removed with shears, secateurs or scissors. If you are not saving seed and have the time to spare this trimming may be worthwhile, but it is after all a refinement, and not absolutely essential.

There are some plants whose seedheads are usually counted as a second season

of attraction; *Dryas octopetala* and the pulsatillas with their silky tassels are among these, so one must pick and choose when trimming.

WATERING

Through late spring and early summer there can always be a threat of drought. Alpine plants are like icebergs: by far the smallest proportion is visible and their roots can extend very deeply indeed so the plants are normally well provided for. However, in their native conditions a constant supply of water from melting snow is moving through the soil so we must be ready to make good any deficit. As in other parts of the garden it is important to water thoroughly if watering at all. A quick spraying over the surface is next to useless; much evaporates and little gets down to the roots. A plant in real need should be in line for 5 litres (1 gal): we are trying to get the soil wet. If the surrounding soil is dry there is certain to be a levelling process taking place so even the well-watered spot is going to be losing much.

Adequate top-dressings of grit will certainly help rainfall to penetrate the soil and preserve it.

CONTAINER-GARDEN CARE

By early summer the first flush of flowers in our miniature trough gardens or container groupings will have passed, but the activity of the plants will not have slackened; they all have plenty of foliage and this will be losing water to the air. The rusty-back fern, *Asplenium ceterach (Ceterach officinarum)* acts as a quick guide to the surface soil moisture content. This is a pretty little fern which curls up and looks dead when the soil dries out. Fortunately it is

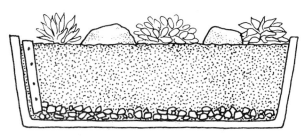

A length of plastic piping inserted into the compost makes watering easier and more efficient

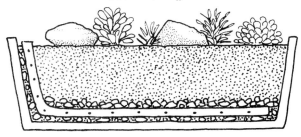

A longer section ensures even watering throughout

growing point. Higher parts of the stalk might root but will normally not make a growing point and so eventually fail
- Carefully insert detached leaves into a rooting compost of an equal mix of grit and peat. A narrow angle is best, with the leaf blade almost flush with the compost; all the stalk and up to a third of the leaf blade should be covered. Ensure the leaves are not touching

resurrected as soon as water is added.

Trough gardens have severely limited soil capacities. Nutrients can run low and in even quite short periods of drought the whole can become dry. It is useful to have at least one spot in each trough where water can be introduced easily without it flowing straight over the side. Insert a piece of plastic piping around 3cm (1¼in) wide and some 7–17cm (3–7in) long into the compost so that water can be led in. The pipe need not be conspicuous, with its rim level with the trough compost surface and disguised by overlapping plants. It will be even more effective if it is perforated down the sides and ends and positioned in a pocket of grit that will take the water quickly.

STEM CUTTINGS

By early summer there are a lot more plants with growth suitable for cuttings. The aim is to get cuttings rooted and established as independent plants before winter arrives.

Most should be rooting within two or three weeks and be ready for potting on within a month. Details about making cuttings are in last month's tasks (p49). A list of plants ready for propagation now is in the margin.

LEAF CUTTINGS

This is a propagation method suited to relatively few plants and only a handful of these are alpines, but there are good plants in this short list. Leading them are the ramondas, especially *R. myconi*. It is useful as one of the finest plants for shaded walls or crevices. Take cuttings now.
- Select a leaf of a rosette that is young but has reached full size
- Gently pull it sideways and at right angles to the main plant centre. The aim is to detach the leaf with the complete stalk (petiole) down to the junction with the main stem
- At the stalk base there is an incipient bud or mass of cells able to produce a new

- Mist spray the pot with fungicide, cover it with polythene and keep it out of the sun in a warm, not hot, place
- Young plants should have developed sufficiently by the end of the summer to be potted up in a peaty mix
- Do not remove the original leaf, which looks very much a pensioner; it is still doing essential work and can be removed when the young plant is fully grown and able to care for itself

Haberleas are related to ramondas and they may be increased in the same way. The young plants of both genera will take twelve months to become fully grown. Sedums are very simply propagated from leaves. The common stonecrop, *Sedum acre*, and its relatives, have fat little leaves that almost too easily detach themselves and root just lying on the soil surface. The more showy and elite species have larger and more safely-attached leaves. These can be removed and inserted in a gritty mix. They will root quickly and soon form full-scale working plants.

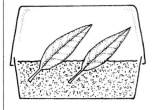

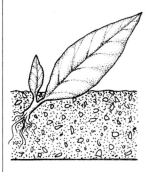

plants

OF THE

month

ARISAEMA
(Arisaema candidissima)

An interesting genus of arum relatives of which this species is one of the most refined – and scented.

type	Tuberous perennial
foliage	Distinctive three-part, arrow-head, bright green leaves appear after flowers
flowers	Large cuckoo-pint spathes, green in bud with broad vertical pale stripes, opening in early summer to pink, divided by narrower white vertical stripes; edges of spathe and its long, pointed hooded end are white. Fragrant. Heads of fleshy red fruits on stems in autumn
height	10–15cm (4–6in)
spread	30–50cm (12–20in)
planting	In spring, plant tubers 15–18cm (6–7in) deep
site	In pots or a sheltered spot in the rock garden, in sun or semi-shade
soil	Humus-lover, moist
care	Easy if not allowed to dry out and planted deep to protect from severe frost
propagation	Sow seed as soon as ripe or remove offsets in early spring
relatives	*A. triphyllum*, narrow, green or purplish spathes. *A. consanguineum* with distinctive palmate leaves, like umbrella spokes; spathes are purplish-cream or green with cream stripes and taper to a very long narrow pointed end almost as thin as fishing lines

ARISAEMA CANDIDISSIMA

DWARF BROOM
(Genista sagittalis)

There are several dwarf tidy brooms, reliable and longer lived than some of their larger relatives. This species is very distinct and an ideal rock garden plant.

type	Procumbent, deciduous shrub of evergreen appearance
foliage	Few, oval leaves. The work is mainly done by the broad flat green wings on all branches
flowers	Tight, pointed clusters of small, pea-like, golden flowers at end of nearly every upturned branch, starting early summer
height	8cm (3in)
spread	30–45cm (12–18in)
planting	Anytime; best as young plants with minimum of root disturbance
site	Sunny
soil	Well-drained, poor, gritty
care	Very easy. Keep on a spartan diet
propagation	Hairy seed-pods follow flowers; sow seed when ripe
relatives	*G. lydia* is a neat domed shrub, 45–60cm (18–24in) high and half as much again across. In late spring and early summer is smothered with golden blossom. Attractive half falling over a wall

RHODOHYPOXIS
(Rhodohypoxis baurii)

A genus of one species from South Africa.

DWARF BROOM

type	Perennial with corm-like rhizomes
foliage	Tuft, almost rosette, narrow, pointed, pale green and hairy leaves
flowers	A succession of very flat flowers of red, pink or white. Six petals meet tightly together in centre
height	5–10cm (2–4in)
spread	2–5cm (1–2in)
planting	Early spring
site	Well-drained, sunny spot, or in pots in an alpine house
soil	Equal mix of grit and peat
care	Easy. Increases rapidly if given plenty to drink through the summer and kept dry in the winter. Hardy in all but the severest winters
propagation	By seed or separating corm-like rhizomes during winter dormancy
relatives	Selected clones have been built up of exceptional individuals – *R.b.* 'Douglas' is a deep red; *R.b.* 'Albrighton' is a rich cerise-pink; *R.b. platypetala* is slightly larger-flowered and comes in pink or white

RHODOHYPOXIS BAURII

practical project

CREATING A PEAT BED

SHRUBS FOR PEAT BEDS

All those listed are evergreen
except ones marked (d) which
are deciduous

Andromeda polifolia
Arctostaphylos uva-ursi
Betula nana (d)
Calluna vulgaris
Cassiope various
Daboecia various
Daphne various (some d)
Empetrum nigrum
Erica various
Gaultheria various
Leiophyllum buxifolium
Leucothoe various
Linnaea borealis americana
Loiseleuria procumbens
Menziesia ciliicalyx (d)
Pernettya various
Phyllodoce various
Rhododendron dwarf forms (some d)
Rhodothamnus chamaecistus
Vaccinium various

*Peat beds can be enclosed by
walls of peat blocks, or logs,
either cut into short sections or
laid lengthways*

There are some very lovely plants whose idea of heaven is the opposite of a scree: they luxuriate in deep masses of peaty humus-rich soil. These include many ericaceous plants and also lots of wonderful woodland plants and some of the very exciting primulas from Asia that would quickly waste away in ordinary soils. So the peat bed is very much a matter of courses for horses!

SITES

The peat bed may be close by the rock garden, but there is more latitude with this feature than with the scree – it could be housed in semi-shade and perhaps in light woodland conditions. What most peat-loving plants enjoy is acid, humus-rich soils in cool areas where their roots can be kept moist at all times without being swamped. Size may vary, but to be viable and reasonably trouble-free to manage, the smallest would be about two square metres (yards).

It should be stressed that a peat bed is unlikely to be a great success in gardens with heavily alkaline soils. There will be a constant conflict of lime with the preferred acid conditions unless you are prepared to take the trouble to make them into raised beds, placing polythene sheeting down first to minimise any alkaline infiltration. This is worthwhile for true devotees but it may be easier to grow any favourite peat-lovers in generous containers where the soil can be properly monitored without trouble.

Most, not all, peat-loving small plants are shade-lovers so it makes sense to have your bed out of the main glare of the sun. An area shaded by the house or trees, but not necessarily overhung by them, is ideal. Leaves falling, and water dripping, from overhanging trees may cause problems.

PREPARATORY WORK

- Clear the ground thoroughly of all weed, especially couch grasses and troublesome perennials like creeping thistle and bracken
- Dig or rotovate the top spit (25cm/10in)
- Work as much moist coarse peat as original soil into this top spit. This will be a very considerable amount
- Introduce some gentle contouring to make the bed more interesting
- Consider enclosing the bed with peat blocks, built like a couple of courses of bricks, logs, railway sleepers or stones
- Make sure any peat block walls are very stable and packed tight with compost. They should not be allowed to dry out
- Dust the surface with a lime-free fertiliser
- Top-dress with pure coarse peat to a depth of at least 5–6cm (2–2¹⁄₂in)
- Arrange a number of wooden blocks or flat rocks as perching places so that you can avoid treading directly on the bed

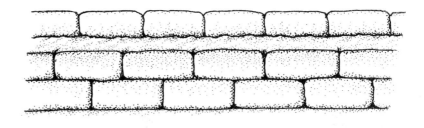

PLANTING

The aim is to create a harmonious community of plants that will be of interest all round the year. This should not be too difficult as many of the plants suitable for growing in peat beds are evergreen so they will provide the background to the flowers.

Plants should be positioned to grow into and over the peat-block walls for decoration and to maintain stability. These will include heathers, together with other small ericaceous shrubs such as *Andromeda*, *Cassiope*, *Gaultheria*, *Phyllodoce* and miniature rhododendrons.

Rhizomatous and bulbous plants can be planted to give winter and spring colour. These range from snowdrops to trilliums and erythroniums. There are a number of rare dwarf summer-flowering lilies if you fancy something unusual, or you could try the orchid family perhaps establishing a clump of early summer-flowering lady's slipper orchids, *Cypripedium calceolus* or *C. reginae*.

Other woodland plants such as wood anemones should flourish as well as the lovely North American and Japanese *Shortia*.

You might consider a unifying theme such as a collection of the smaller ferns, some of which will be evergreen, and this is the place to try growing some of the mouth-wateringly beautiful petiolares primulas such as *P. sonchifolia*, *P. scapigera* or *P. gracilipes*. There are also the lovely autumn-flowering Asian gentians such as *G. sino-ornata* and its hybrids. It is worth building the bed for these alone.

MAINTENANCE

Looking after a peat bed is simply a matter of making sure that it does not dry out and of not allowing any weed to get a foothold. Some weeds can really get very headstrong once in such a spot.

Undoubtedly some of the plants you introduce will grow too much and will have to be disciplined, and bits taken away for planting elsewhere or used for bartering. Such divisions are usually best made in spring.

Loose leaves, twigs and other rubbish needs removing to the compost heap rather than left to attract slugs.

The bed will benefit from an annual top-dressing in late winter to give an extra 5cm (2in) of nutrient-enriched peat or leaf-mould.

PEAT BED PLANTS

Anemone nemorosa
Anemonopsis macrophylla
Aquilegia various
Arnica montana
Astrantia minor
Campanula barbata
Carex fraseri
Codonopsis various
Cornus canadensis
Cyananthus various
Cypripedium various
Dicentra dwarf kinds
Epimedium grandiflorum
Erythronium various
Galax aphylla
Gentiana Asiatic kinds
Haberlea various
Houstonia various
Iris gracilipes
Jeffersonia dubia
Lilium mackliniae
L. nanum
Nomocharis various
Parnassia palustris
Phlox adsurgens
Primula woodlanders
Ramonda all
Ranunculus amplexicaulis
R. crenatus
Roscoea various
Sanguinaria canadensis
Saxifraga cotyledon
S. × *urbium* 'Clarence Elliott'
Shortia various
Soldanella various
Trillium various
Wulfenia various

Also ferns and bulbs

plants
OF THE
month

▼ SOUTHERN MARSH ORCHID
(Dactylorrhiza majalis subsp. *praetermissa)*

A terrestrial orchid of a genus widespread in Europe.

type	Ground orchid
foliage	Lance-shaped, unspotted, mid-green leaves
flowers	Thick spikes on erect dark stems, deep rosy-purple sepals spread out and leaning somewhat forward, like wings; the lip has darker spots and splashes. Early to midsummer
height	30–45cm (12–18in)
spread	8cm (3in) for plant, clumps up to 30–45cm (12–18in)
planting	When available, preferably late winter-early spring
site	Semi-shaded pocket, low in the rock garden
soil	Moist and humus-rich
care	Keep weed-free and without serious competition. Maintain a damp open humus-rich soil
propagation	Division of healthy clumps after a few seasons. Seed under laboratory culture conditions
relatives	*D. incarnata* (Early marsh orchid), slimmer plant with pale green leaves and smaller flowers that can be flesh-coloured or any shade from pink to rosy-red or mauve-purple

ENCRUSTED SAXIFRAGE ▶
(Saxifraga frederici-augustii grisebachii 'Wisley'*)*

The encrusted saxifrages are those that lay down a chalky deposit on their mineral-hard leaves. This is one of the most distinguished in bloom.

type	Evergreen perennial, now usually labelled *Saxifraga* 'Wisley'
foliage	Tight, crowded mounds of rosettes of metal-hard, grey-green leaves encrusted with lime, especially around their margins
flowers	Stems, magnificent with a thick cladding of pink to crimson hairs, arise from the rosette's centre like swan-necked crosiers with smaller leaves. Dark red flowers crowded in dense heads in spring. Very distinctive
height	10cm (4in)
spread	15-20cm (6–8in)
planting	Anytime from early spring to early autumn
site	Full sun in rock pockets, or pots
soil	Well-drained gritty soil with lime and humus
care	Not difficult with good drainage and plenty of sunlight, but should not be allowed to dry out at its roots. Is not over-generous in production of new rosettes
propagation	Division early spring or after flowering
relatives	There are very many encrusted saxifrages producing hard foliage, decorated with extruded lime. Some have almost stemless flowers and others may grow to 15cm (6in) but few are so exciting as 'Wisley'

SOUTHERN MARSH ORCHID

ENCRUSTED SAXIFRAGE

PHLOX
(Phlox 'Kelly's Eye'*)*

The low-growing phlox species and hybrids come into their own after the first flush of spring blossom. This is a particularly neat one.

type	Evergreen perennial
foliage	Small, narrow, oval, prickly leaves making a neat low plant
flowers	Lots of bloom in mid to late spring, flat circles of white each with a tiny cherry-red eye; flowers flush pink with age
height	5cm (2in)
spread	12cm (5in)
planting	Early spring or early autumn
site	Sunny
soil	Well-drained, gritty
propagation	Cuttings in summer
relatives	This hybrid is from *P. borealis*, a very small, tight, cushion plant only 2.5cm (1in) high with lilac flowers. The other parent is presumed to be a form of *P. subulata*, the variable, low scrambling species, which

provides many forms for the rock garden. *P. s.* 'G F Wilson' is an old blue variety, *P. s. brittonii* 'Rosea' is very small and suitable for trough or scree. It has minute leaves, packed in a little hummock, and lovely, pink flowers. *P. s.* 'Temiskaming' is a robust trailing kind in magenta which would look rather unrefined beside some of the smaller varieties

PHLOX 'KELLY'S EYE'

JULY

Spring may be prime time for the rock garden, but there are still some of the later phlox and dianthus forms going great guns in midsummer and dazzling waves of colour are contributed by the rock roses (Helianthemum) – yellows, golds, orange-reds, pinks and golden-centred whites. In a well-stocked rock garden rocks and walls are draped with these sheets of colour.

Summer is also a time for flaxes, some in traditional sky-blues but others in yellows, creams, pinks and white. There are also the more compact evening primroses (Oenothera), their bright yellows and whites often enlivened with chestnut-red buds and bracts. And no summer week is without its quota of potentilla blooms, shrubby or herbaceous. Smaller lavenders and catmints lend cooler colour and low on the ground are carpets of thyme in various tones. Some of these easy plants do their duty with no fuss and it is easy to overlook their value as we peer at a little rarity trying to hang on to life.

Where there is water there are the moisture-loving irises still in bloom and in the pool the marvellous miniature water lilies open their perfect blossoms. In bogs and waterside spots, there are plenty of plants whose foliage is splendid even if they are without flowers.

Thanks to modern horticulture, improved propagation techniques and the work of commercial growers we are fortunate in having new plants made available every year. These often arrive from distant parts and there are some that tend to bloom outside the spring festival. Plants, such as ground orchids, that one would not have thought of buying before as they might have been plundered from the wild, may now be entering the commercial field, thanks to laboratory magic. Other plants are becoming fashionable, for example, the diascias from South Africa. Little wonder as their prostrate branching shoots are covered with blossom, pinks, salmons and reds together with a series of pastel shades that almost defy description.

tasks
FOR THE
month

STEM CUTTINGS

Anthemis biebersteinii
Anthyllis montana
Armeria caespitosa
Asperula arcadensis
Azorella trifurcata
Calluna vulgaris
Jasminum parkeri
Penstemon various
Saponaria various
Saxifraga mossy types
Zauschneria californica
(syn. *Epilobium canum*)

CHECKLIST

- Watering
- Extensions to rock garden
- Shady frames
- More cuttings
- Holiday preparations

WATERING

This is a reminder; the heading has appeared before. What we might consider now is saving rainwater for two good reasons: hosepipe bans come just when we want to use more water; rainwater should be free of lime and, as such, can be used freely on rhododendrons and other lime-haters. If not already organised, consider getting two or more butts, one to collect rainfall from the alpine house/ greenhouse roof,

Water butts are an excellent way to ensure a supply of limefree water for rhododendrons and other lime haters

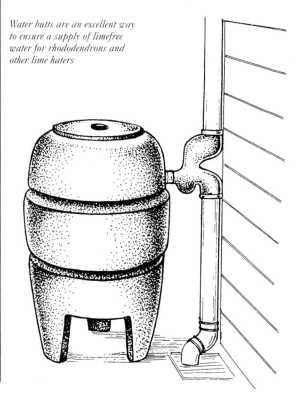

another positioned by the garage, a further one or more to collect from the house.

EXTENSIONS TO THE ROCK GARDEN

Long days and reasonable weather make the execution of major changes in the garden easier and more pleasurable in midsummer. Moving soil and rocks is easier in dry conditions. A rock garden extension was probably not on the agenda when the original was built but after a few seasons, as

the area has got filled with alpines, some extra room can seem an urgent priority.

- Mark out the area of the proposed extension. Try not to make it symmetrical with the existing one and if possible make it obviously bigger or smaller. Try living with the marked outline for a few days to make sure that it seems right. Remember not to extend under trees
- Consider whether there will be a pathway between the old and new sections and, if so, its nature. Will it be sunken, level, stepped, solid or of informal paving stones, or gravelled with stepping stones
- Try to obtain rock of the same type as the original. Sandstone cheek by jowl with limestone will look odd and constantly annoy. If it is impossible to get matching types, consider either making a fresh outcrop/rock garden elsewhere or at least separating the two parts by a fairly wide path and maybe a scree
- With systemic weed-killer kill off grass and weeds on the new area or move plants if annexing a piece of a border
- Remove dead turf and stack it for potting use
- Rotovate or dig over the area
- Arrange drainage if needed
- Rake the soil into contoured forms. Leave it for a while to consider the overall shapes and how they work in with the existing garden. One or two rocks could be placed roughly in position to get a better idea of overall effect
- Make any changes necessary to the contours, remembering not to mirror the form of the original but also not to change the character completely
- Position the rocks and establish them firmly. Try to maintain some sense of continuity with the strata lines of the original rock garden
- Fill in with soil mix as recommended in 'Top-

dressing' (p37)
- Leave to settle for a few weeks. Plant up through late summer and autumn
- Top-dress with grit/chippings/gravel

SHADY FRAMES

Plants that are grown under glass can get very warm and dry without constant attention. It is extremely useful to have a cool shaded area to place some potted alpines during the summertime. Ideally this would be a semi-shaded spot with enough space to enable the construction of a roofless frame of wood, bricks or railway sleepers.

Plants can be evacuated into this shady frame at any time from late spring onwards, their pots plunged into a suitable material, such as weathered ash, sand, grit or peat. Shading with plastic mesh will allow ventilation and rainfall to penetrate.

The frame needs an eye kept on it to make sure it does not get too dry and is not suffering from pests such as aphids or next door's cat.

Plants that might benefit from a holiday in the frame include many primulas, androsaces, saxifrages, and dwarf conifers.

MORE CUTTINGS

Many more plants are providing cuttings. Helianthemums could be dealt with early this month if possible. Techniques are dealt with on pages 49 and 59. A list of other suitable plants is given in the margin.

There are a number of plants now ready for root cuttings. One of these is *Geranium sanguineum striatum (G.s. lancastriense)*, a particularly good low-growing form with low carpets of finely-divided, rich green leaves below wide white flowers, intricately veined with blush-pink. It is an easy plant

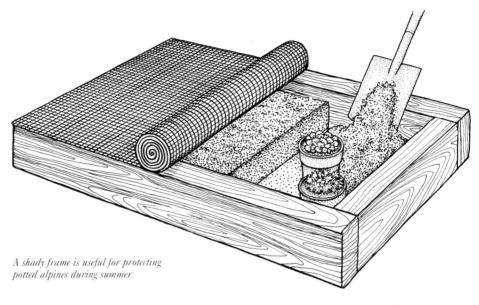

A shady frame is useful for protecting potted alpines during summer

to grow and can be propagated by division or, rather more tidily, by 3cm (1in) root cuttings. (See p49.)

HOLIDAY PREPARATIONS

Holidays loom. The garden needs to be left in a tidy state and with as few plants and projects in a critical state as possible. You may be able to arrange for someone to come in to look over the frames and alpine house and cast an eye over the garden. Any instructions with regards to watering or care are best kept to a minimum and to be simple so they are clearly understood.
- If the period away is only a week to a fortnight most things can be left on hold
- If need be, a lot of the plants can be moved out of the alpine house to the shady frame, plunged and left
- All potted plants can be thoroughly watered before leaving
- If you have the means to allow trickle irrigation of the bench bed then no further attention will be required in your absence
- It is sensible to try to have holidays at times when there

are no pots of important seed germinating or any very fragile seedlings emerging that need extra attention
- In the rock garden commonsense dictates that all should be left well-watered. In dry periods this is the one time when a very thorough application of water by hand or by sprayline is justified
- Hoeing or raking over top-dressings should frustrate any germinating weed in the rock garden and elsewhere
- It is sensible to look all over the garden for any incipient aphid or other epidemic and spray carefully to prevent a build-up
- Cut the grass, pack a book detailing open gardens in your holiday area, cancel the papers and milk and preset the video recorder

BULBS FOR LIFTING

These may already have been lifted last month. If not try to complete in the first half of this one. Lift, check for health, split and replant immediately.

Allium early forms
Chionodoxa
Crocus
Erythronium
Galanthus
Iris small bulbous
Leucojum
Muscari
Narcissus
Nerine
Ornithogalum
Puschkinia
Scilla
Sternbergia
Tulipa

Holiday CHECKLIST

- [ ] Watering
- [ ] Weeding
- [ ] Pest check
- [ ] Cut lawn

plants
OF THE
month
1

CONVOLVULUS
(Convolvulus sabatius,
syn. *C. mauritanicus)*

Having battled with bindweed the gardener may look at all convolvulus with a jaundiced eye. This would be a mistake. The plant highlighted here forms a splendid mat and the lovely silvery shrub, *C. cneorum* mentioned below is also very garden-worthy.

type	Trailing, tap-rooted perennial
foliage	Neat oval leaves, almost stemless
flowers	Perfect, shining violet-shaded, blue trumpets looking upwards just clear of foliage. Midsummer well into autumn
height	15cm (6in)
spread	30–45cm (12–18in)
planting	Early spring
site	Well-drained, warm site with sunshine
soil	Not fussy, from starved to healthy, but should not be wet
care	Not fully hardy in extremely cold spots. Benefits from planting by a warm rock or a brick wall. To ensure plenty of flowering shoots, nip out the point of growing shoots in early spring
propagation	Softwood cuttings from non-flowering shoots in summer. Seed in early spring
relatives	*C. cneorum* is a gem, a small shrub with narrow leaves, made silvery with fine silken hairs, pink buds open to white trumpets, with golden centres. 75cm (30in) high and wide. Care as *C. sabatius*

SATIN FLOWER
(Sisyrinchium idahoense album,
syn. *S. macounii)*

A genus in the iris family with around sixty species, some annuals, but most being herbaceous perennials from North and South America. The species featured here starts blooming late spring but the seed is ripening now and this is worth gathering and sowing immediately.

CONVOLVULUS SABATIUS

type	Tufted, semi-evergreen perennial
foliage	Flat, like miniature iris, relatively long and very narrow
flowers	1-6 white flowers, with blue marked centres, typical rounded flowers, larger than many species of similar stature, late spring-early summer
height	12–30cm (5–12in)
spread	8cm (3in)
planting	Spring to autumn
site	Sunny, open spot, will tolerate some shade
soil	Gritty, well-drained
care	Not difficult if grown in well-drained soil but with moisture
propagation	Seed as soon as ripe in mid to late summer
relatives	*S. idahoense* is rich blue. *S. graminoides* has iris-like, clustered, light to dark purple-blue flowers with yellow flashes in centres, late spring to early summer

SATIN FLOWER

FLEABANE

(Haplopappus brandegeei 'Canary Bird', syn. *Erigeron* 'Canary Bird', *E. aureus* 'Montana'*)*

The Compositae are a huge family containing rapacious weeds and some of our finest garden plants. The erigerons, to which this species was previously allocated, are a very useful lot in borders and rock gardens. The new allocation takes away nothing of the yeoman worth of 'Canary Bird', a plant raised from seed collected in Montana.

type	Clump-forming evergreen perennial
foliage	Shining, spoon-shaped, spathulate leaves with long stalks. Have hairs at margins but are less hairy than the species type
flowers	Borne singly but freely, in midsummer. Large daisies with central bronze-yellow disc, surrounded by two or three layers of overlapping ray florets of canary-yellow. The buds are attractive with silky, purplish bracts
height	5–12cm (2–5in)
spread	15cm (6in)
planting	When available, preferably early spring or early autumn
site	Scree, trough garden, alpine house or warm pocket in rock garden
soil	Gritty, well-drained
care	Easy if not doused with continual wet in winter. Look out for aphids

FLEABANE 'CANARY BIRD'

propagation	Cuttings from unflowered shoots in summer
relatives	*H. brandegeei*, the type, is a tighter plant noticeably more hairy and perhaps even more needful of winter protection

practical project 1

PONDS AND WATERFALLS

WATER PLANTS

These plants will grow fully in water (depths given).

Calla palustris 0–10cm (0–4in)
Hippuris vulgaris 20–40cm (8–16in)
Hydrocharis morsus-ranae 10–30cm (4–12in)
Iris pseudacorus 'Variegata' 0–40cm (0–16in)
Lysimachia thyrsiflora 0–20cm (0–8in)
Nuphar pumilum 40–90cm (16–36in)
Nymphaea such as 'Helvola' 5–10cm (2–4in)
Nymphaea such as 'Aurora' 25–40cm (10–16in)
Orontium aquaticum 5–25cm (2–10in)
Potentilla palustris 0–20cm (0–8in)
Scirpus tabernaemontani 'Zebrinus' 5–20cm (2–8in)
Typha gracilis minima 3–10cm (1¼–4in)

OXYGENATING PLANTS

Callitriche hermaphroditica
Ceratophyllum demersum
Hydrocleys parviflora
Lagarosiphon major, syn. *Elodea crispa*
Mryriophyllum aquaticum
Potamogeton crispus

Water adds magic. In a rock garden it is an especially good contrast to the stony landscape. Making the pond requires work but is well worth the effort.

DESIGN

An informal shape is demanded in the rock garden. The pool can be to the side of the rock garden or could be surrounded by it. On the whole it is normally most pleasing if at least a part of the margin can be approached. Most gardeners are likely to want the pond to be wildlife-friendly. This means that there needs to be easy access for birds and amphibians; a gently sloping side for part of the margin is ideal.

The rock garden should be in the open, an ideal site for the pond as it will be clear of trees and shrubs that otherwise might be constantly dropping foliage into the water causing toxic by-products.

Size depends on personal choice and the overall dimensions of the rock garden. The smaller the pond, the more difficult it is to keep healthy. Surface areas of less than 2 square metres/yards fluctuate dangerously in temperature and chemical content making conditions for plants and animal life difficult.

LINERS VERSUS PREFABRICATED PIECES

Preformed plastic or glass fibre pools are safe and relatively easy to install, but their shapes may not meet your requirements. Treble-laminated polythene or butyl-rubber linings are obviously more flexible and come with longlife guarantees.

Preforms

- Choose pleasing informal preform/s of the size required. Check that the deepest area is around 40–50cm (16–20in) and that there are ledges at approximately 22cm (9in) depth. The ledges need to be at least 22cm (9in) wide, preferably 30cm (12in)
- Excavate the area for the preform allowing plenty of room at the sides. Make sure that when installed the top edges can be safely disguised by rocks, turf or plants
- Introduce the preform and use a spirit-level to check that it lies true
- Ensure good contact at its base and pack soil tightly around the sides

Linings

- Excavate the pond shape and check the bottom is level. Depth is best as recommended for preforms and remember to allow for ledges
- Check the sides are not too sharp, certainly not less than a 20° angle from vertical
- Smooth the sides and base with damp sand or wet newspaper to dull any sharp projections
- Measure required lining.

Longer dimension = pond length + 2 × measurement of sloping side + 2 × margin flap of about 25–30cm (10–12in).

Lesser dimension = widest pond width + 2 × measurement of sloping side + 2 × margin flap

- Lay the lining and cut away surplus after allowing for the margin flap
- Hold margins loosely with rocks or bricks and fill the pond using a hosepipe
- When full, tuck the lining flaps out of sight under rocks, turf, gravel or stones at the sloping entrance for wildlife

WATERFALLS

Two pools at different levels can be linked and, with the addition of a pump, water can be circulated from one to the other, allowing a cascade whenever you fancy by turning on the electricity. The distance between the two pools need not be great; the fall can be shallow and consist of a series of basins either of preformed sections or fashioned out of pool lining material.

Water and pumps

- The two pools at different levels need to have exactly level sides
- The upper, or header, pool must not be used for fish, etc
- The basins or sections of stream between top and bottom pool should be fashioned so that they retain a pool of water when the pump is switched off. There should be no chance of water seeping away along the stream section, something easy to ensure by the laying of a strong polythene base
- Water arriving at the waterfall/cascade will need a sloping rock surface that spills it forward, not over the sides. A suitable rock may be found or two may be abutted and the channel forward made watertight by strong binding concrete
- A submersible pump can be hidden in the bottom pool with a pipe leading under the surface to the header pool. Alternatively an above-ground pump can be hidden in housing behind a rock above the top pool

■ A qualified electrician should install all equipment or at least the safety cutout and check all electrical work

MARGINS

To make the most of the pool/s and waterfall the margins need to be varied. Rocks rising directly from the water look dramatic especially if they are reflected in the water, appearing twice their height. Plants growing up from the water-edge, such as irises or rushes, look soldierly; softer effects can be made by ferns leaning over the water and strong statements can be made by hostas. Parts of the water margins can look pleasing with pebbles linking *terra firma* with the mysterious water world.

MAINTENANCE

You may need to allow your pool a few weeks to find its healthy balance. To help keep the water lively and healthy it is a good idea to introduce one or two oxygenating plants. See margin for list.

PLANTS FOR WATER MARGINS

To be planted by, but not in, water.

Acorus gramineus pusillus
Ajuga reptans
Anagallis tenella
Arenaria balearica
Astilbe various
Caltha palustris 'Plena'
Dodecatheon meadia
D. pulchellum
Dryopteris dilatata
Iris various including:
Iris sibirica
Mimulus various
Osmunda regalis
Parochetus
Primula candelabra types
P. rosea
Ranunculus ficaria named forms
Salix lanata
S. reticulata
Trollius various
Wulfenia carinthiaca

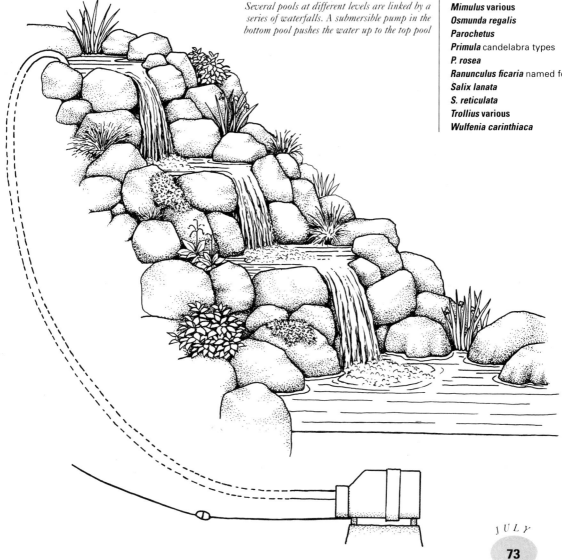

Several pools at different levels are linked by a series of waterfalls. A submersible pump in the bottom pool pushes the water up to the top pool

plants
OF THE
month
2

MOUNT ATLAS DAISY

MOUNT ATLAS DAISY
(Anacyclus pyrethrum depressus)

Another plant from the daisy (Compositae) family and one that almost every enthusiast has grown at sometime either outside or in a pan. It is pleasing enough and young, robust plants are very attractive, although it can look a little less than its best in a wet winter.

type	Prostrate perennial; tap-type root
foliage	Much-divided, dark matt-green leaves

flowers	Purple-red buds open to wide, white daisies with central yellow discs and rather square-ended petals
height	2.5–7.5cm (1–3in)
spread	15cm (6in)
planting	Early spring using young plants and not disturbing root
site	Scree or sunny spot
soil	Not fussy, happy in poor, well-drained
care	Not long-lived and may begin to look a bit tatty when old. To make the most of it ensure good drainage and that it is kept from getting too sodden in winter. Propagate new young plants to be ready to take the place of old ones
propagation	Cuttings from stem ends in spring, or seed in autumn
relatives	Other daisy flowers worth thinking about include *Anthemis cinerea* with silvery, cut foliage and *A. montana*, a cushion-forming, woolly-leaved plant

PENSTEMON
(Penstemon hirsutus 'Pygmaeus'*)*

Penstemon is a surprisingly large genus, mainly from North America. Many species are too large for the rock garden but there are a number that are quite diminutive. They are usually relatively easy plants and grow rapidly in a rather loose-limbed way. The penstemon featured here is one of the neatest for the rock garden, or for trying in containers.

type	Evergreen sub-shrub
foliage	Small, narrowly oval, dark green leaves
flowers	Typical tubular flowers, white usually with blue or purplish suffusions. Long succession of bloom through summer
height	6–10cm (2½–4in)
spread	20–30cm (8–12in)
planting	Early spring
site	Warm, open spot in rock garden or in pot
soil	Need not be rich but should have perfect drainage
care	Easy if not subjected to standing wet. Penstemons are sometimes not very long-lived, so it is as well to have small plants coming along. They quickly mature into semi-bushy plants
propagation	Divide or sow seed in early spring. Take cuttings in summer
relatives	*P. hirsutus*, the type, is attractive but two or three times larger and only suitable for the larger rock garden

FLOWER OF JOB
(Lychnis flos-jovis)

Lychnis is a small genus with a variety of flower forms. Good forms of *L. flos-jovis* add colour and height in rock gardens.

type	Clump-forming, herbaceous perennial
foliage	Oval, grey-green leaves, made silvery by fine down
flowers	Clusters of flat, shocking-pink flowers, midsummer
height	20–45cm (8–18in)
spread	25–45cm (10–18in)
planting	Early spring or early autumn
site	Sunny rock pocket, on a wall, or between stones on a paved area
soil	Not fussy, with or without lime, but should be well-drained
care	Very easy to grow. Where it enjoys life it can become too widespread through self-seeding so it might be prudent to snip off flower-heads as they fade
propagation	Divide older clumps in early spring. Sow seed in spring or save self-sown seedlings

relatives	This is a variable species and some seedlings produce poor-coloured flowers. Obviously the smaller forms are desirable. *L.f-j.* 'Nana' is pink and very compact. There are also pure white ones listed as *L.f-j.* 'Alba'. *L. alpina* has tight, rounded head of pinky-mauve, and has good pink and white forms, *L.a.* 'Alba'. Flowers of *L.alpina* are held 10cm (4in) high above spreading tufts of dark green leaves

FLOWER OF JOB

practical project *2*

MAKING A BOG GARDEN

PLANTS FOR THE BOG GARDEN

Additional to those listed on page 72 as plants for waterside.

Arisaema candidissimum
Arum creticum
A. italicum
Dactylorrhiza elata
D. foliosa
D. incarnata
D. praetermissa
Filipendula ulmaria 'Aurea'
Hosta sieboldiana and others
Houttuynia cordata
Lysichiton americanus
L. camtschatcensis
Matteuccia struthiopteris
Peltiphyllum peltanum
Phormium various
Primula beesiana
P. bulleyana
P. florindae
P. helodoxa
P. japonica
P. pulverulenta
P. secundiflora
P. sikkimensis

There are a number of very attractive plants that need boggy conditions to flourish. As might be expected they are plants of different character to usual rock garden plants: they tend to be more lush and thus make a useful contrast. Quite a number of them bloom later and so keep the complex more alive with interest.

Early blossom could come from the very bright pink *Primula rosea*, the golden marsh marigold, *Caltha palustris* and its double form, *C.p.* 'Plena'. At the same time, in more spacious designs the large unearthly spathes of *Lysichiton americanus* and *L. camtschatcensis* in gold and white, provide a new dimension. The huge leaves that follow the flowers are certainly not alpine-like, but provide a contrast that emphasises the smallness of their neighbours.

In early summer there is a succession of colourful water-loving primulas with candelabras of flowers in whites, yellow, pinks, oranges, reds, purples and pastel shades. There is also a series of irises that bloom through the summer with fine upright sword-like foliage. And it is through the use of foliage plants that we can create a medley of differing forms, colours and textures. The bog garden provides the chance of growing the large royal fern, *Osmunda regalis*, or, if this is deemed too big with fronds up to 2m (6ft) long, the smaller but nevertheless impressive *Dryopteris dilatata*.

SITE AND EXCAVATION

The siting of the bog garden will depend on other features. If you have a pond then it is natural to have the boggy area adjacent, perhaps to the side of the rock garden. Once established one is unlikely to want to go walking through the bog so it is sensible to have secure stepping stones between the rock garden and the boggy area. The size of the area depends on personal choice; it may be restricted to being a smaller feature of perhaps only a couple of square metres/yards. If you are lucky, or clever, enough to have a stream then its course could be margined with wet ground to accommodate the water-loving plants.

Excavation

- Unless you have a naturally damp piece of ground you are going to be forced into excavating the area and making it artificially water-retentive
- Mark out the area then remove the soil to a depth of about 30–40cm (12–16in)
- Lay a sheet of strong polythene over the depression and begin filling, taking the opportunity to increase substantially the humus content. Well-rotted compost is excellent. An ideal is equal parts of humus to soil
- Using a fork, make holes in the polythene so that excessive moisture can drain away.

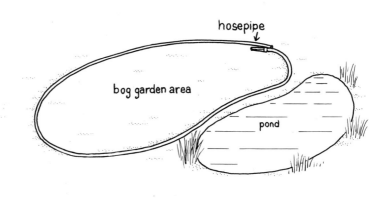

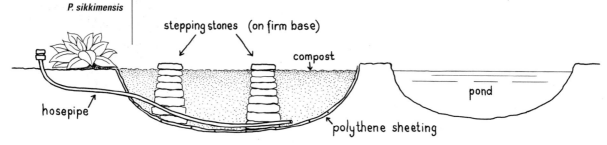

Unless you have other means of supplying water, it is prudent to have a number of punctured pipes leading through the bog. These can be joined and brought to the surface at a hidden point where a hosepipe can be connected and extra water flooded in during times of drought

PLANTING

Planting can be done at any time of year, but the best times are early spring or early autumn. If you complete the construction of the bog area this month, it is best to allow it a few weeks to settle before beginning the planting. You may find that extra compost has to be added to maintain the level after settling. A slightly lower level than the surrounding ground is entirely natural and will help retain moisture.

Irises look well by the waterside; they could be positioned where bog and water meet. Candelabra primulas can be planted rather wide apart on the assumption that they will seed themselves and begin to form colonies. The royal fern or such a huge impressive monster as *Gunnera manicata* can only be introduced if you are working to a very large scale. Lists of suitable plants are given in the margins.

Access stones
A few large flat stones make an informal

KEY
1 Phormium tenax
2 Hosta sieboldiana
3 Iris
4 Phormium tenax
5 Matteuccia struthiopteris
6 Primula bulleyana
7 Lysichiton americanus
8 Iris pseudacorus
9 Primula pulverulenta

stepping-stone path through the mire. They should be secure and could be mounted on brick bases before the evacuated bog area is refilled. If so their tops must be carefully calculated neither to protrude too high or to sink too low; the aim is a few centimetres/a couple of inches above the surrounding bog.

MAINTENANCE

This involves two main considerations: one is to check that there is sufficient water in times of drought; the second is to make sure no rampant weeds get a foothold as they will grow apace with the ready supply of water. Keep an eye open for seedlings of primulas and other plants that you want to encourage. There may come a time, perhaps every two or three years, when a top-dressing of humus-rich compost towards the end of the winter will be welcome, or failing this a sprinkling of a general fertiliser.

SHRUBS FOR WET PLACES

Cornus alba
C. a. 'Elegantissima'
C. a. 'Sibirica'
C. stolonifera 'Flaviramea'
Salix hastata 'Wehrhahnii'
Viburnum opulus 'Compactum'

AUGUST

*Enter the holiday month. Some semblance of peace and order may
reign in a garden seen through a glass of cool white wine. We have kept
apace of the weeds, and judicious, thorough watering when needed has
kept the realm in good heart. Visitors are steered towards favourite
spots; the rock garden not the least of them.*

Polygonum vaccinifolium *and its relatives can be relied on for
months of colour. Some smaller alliums are really quite classy for a
genus so weighed down with domestic responsibilities. Good forms of*
A. beesianum *are only 20-24cm (8-10in) high and are a real joy
with their nodding umbels of bright blue flowers. You may be sold* A.
cyaneum *instead, but this is no real hardship as it is another very
bright and floriferous late-summer flowerer; this time only some 10-
15cm (4-6in) high. There is scope to collect this genus as it boasts 800-
1000 species (see December p124).*

*There are nearly always some small species in genera that we normally
think of in terms of their larger brothers and sisters. The gypsophila
that accompanies summer bouquets is the tall* G. paniculata *'Bristol
Fairy', but there is the creeping species* G. repens *probably best
represented by the cultivar 'Dorothy Teacher', which is so prostrate it
rarely gets above 2-5cm (1-2in) high although spreading more than
35cm (14in). It has mats of narrow, blue-green leaves and covers these
with low sprays of countless small, white flowers, turning pink with
age. The creeping* Erigeron karvinskianus (E. mucronatus), *a slightly
bolder actor, plays the same colour games with its daisy flowers, first
white, then pink before becoming an old-age purple.*

Geranium *and* campanula *species are still in bloom.* Lobelia (Pratia)
pedunculata *carpets moist ground so tightly that its height hardly
registers on a rule but it spreads almost without limit. It is rarely
without blue stars just clear of the green mat. There are plenty of other
flowers: it seems a shame to go on holiday and leave them.*

tasks

FOR THE

month

SEED SOWING

Seed that can be sown as soon as harvested.

Anemone, Aquilegia, Arabis, Arnica, Calceolaria biflora, Campanula, Centaurium scilloides, Dianthus, Crocus, Lilium, Lychnis, Myosotis, Narcissus, Paraquilegia, Primula, Pulsatilla, Saxifraga

PLANT CUTTINGS

Anthemis punctata cupaniana
A. sancti-johannis
Arenaria ledebouriana
A. tetraquetra
Dracocephalum renatii
Erigeron various
Vaccinium various
Viola various

◄ *PAGES 78–9*
This bright pink mossy saxifrage contrasts well with Lithodora diffusa 'Heavenly Blue'

CHECKLIST

- [ ] Trimming and tidying
- [ ] Cuttings
- [ ] Seed sowing – perennials and biennials
- [ ] Dividing plants
- [ ] Repotting bulbs
- [ ] Purchasing bulbs

● TRIMMING AND TIDYING

This time of year will see many plants well past their flowering and possibly their seeding time. Seedheads need removing from many easy alpines otherwise they will fall and the resulting plants could begin to swamp parts of the garden and a lot of plants will look the better for removing dying flower stems. Some dianthus can be so tidied and as helianthemums fade they certainly look better for a hair cut. Remember to save some seed for propagation and to use for seed exchange schemes run by local or national societies.

● CUTTINGS

There is still time to take cuttings of many plants (see pp49 and 59). Root cuttings can be taken of pulsatillas but it is too late to take any from *Primula denticulata* or its relatives; they might not make big enough crowns to come through the winter.

● SEED SOWING

Collected seed can either be stored and sown later, or sown now. Many alpine seeds need the action of frost to trigger germination. However, some will germinate quickly and provide healthy plants before the winter. An example

is the pretty dwarf pink *Lychnis flos-cuculi* 'Nana' – a very squat form of ragged robin.

There is also a considerable number of small biennial plants that ought to have their seed sown early this month if not last.

● DIVIDING PLANTS

Early spring and early autumn are the best times for division and we can make a start at the end of this month. Some that could be tackled late summer and early autumn are shown in the list in the margin.

REPOTTING BULBS

This is traditionally the time for shaking out spring-flowering potted bulbs, sorting them and repotting. My own preference is to do this job earlier by a couple of months as I seem to have more time then and enjoy the feeling that the bulbs have been early-placed, ready to reroot and start into their fresh cycle of growth.

- Prepare the potting compost. Use a suitable mix such as: loam-based compost (John Innes No. 2), coarse grit and peat in parts 3:2:1. Add bonemeal for stronger bulbs
- Turn out pots on to a clear bench
- Scrape away top-soil to reveal bulbs
- Crumble soil away bit by bit, collecting the bulbs as you go
- Check bulbs for disease, clean off loose tunics/scales, detach loose offsets
- Replant bulbs in the fresh compost, large ones in pots for display, small ones in pots for growing on

Many small bulbs can be left for two years in the same pot with only the compost above their noses removed and replaced with fresh.

PURCHASING BULBS

Planting bulbs outside is dealt with next month on page 90, but the bulbs are arriving now in the garden centres and so it is a good idea to keep an eye open for some of the rarer kinds and those that may sell out more quickly. Some rarer, more exclusive bulbs can be found on the stalls of nurseries exhibiting at the autumn shows or may be available from specialist societies.

Look for healthy bulbs that will give a good account of themselves. Check for:

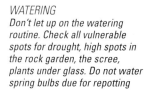

WARNING

- *Some bulbs are very small or have tiny offsets that can easily be lost so be extra vigilant* ■

- Hardiness, make sure that they will grow in your conditions
- Quantity, ensure that you have enough to make a reasonable picture
- Size, larger ones usually have greater reserves of food and therefore perform better. It is still possible to buy bulbs that are too small to bloom, especially of the rarer unusual species. Another reason to buy early – choice is better

- Health, avoid those that are obviously damaged or have some areas of rot. Tulips should have intact tunics, as should colchicums, crocuses, irises and many others. A little blue penicillin mould is normally nothing to worry about unless it is growing over a wide area of damaged tissue
- If bulbs are loose make sure the bags are properly labelled. Other shoppers may not be as careful as they should be and bulbs often get returned to the wrong compartment so the next customer can find a 'cuckoo in the nest' when the bulbs come into bloom – yet another reason for purchasing early
- If bulbs are not planted immediately, store them in cool, dry, airy conditions

GIFT PLANTS

It is best to start early with the preparatory work for gift plants: they will do so much better if well-established when handed over. The obvious gifts are bulbs that are going to come into bloom shortly. A pot or pan of dwarf Narcissi, tulips or something smaller, such as Muscari azureum or Puschkinia scilloides, can be growing nicely when handed over. These could be more imaginative than the more usual hyacinths or poinsettias.

A special friend might be worthy of a pan containing several small plants. To make this look lively and interesting in the middle of winter you will need to have a basic planting of evergreens perhaps with a small group of bulbs also. Suggestions are Raoulia australis as a silver carpet, a colourful Sempervivum, a small Hebe and a group of half-a-dozen Muscari azureum or M. botryoides album.

WATERING
Don't let up on the watering routine. Check all vulnerable spots for drought, high spots in the rock garden, the scree, plants under glass. Do not water spring bulbs due for repotting

PLANTS FOR DIVISION

Acaena, Allium tufted, ***Androsace*** spreading, ***Anemone narcissiflora, A. nemorosa, A. ranunculoides, Anemonopsis, Arabis, Aster, Aubrieta, Campanula*** various, ***Claytonia, Coptis, Cotula, Diapensia, Dodecatheon, Douglasia, Erigeron, Frankenia, Geum*** various, ***Globularia, Inula ensifolia, Linnaea, Mazus, Nierembergia, Oenothera, Omphalodes, Penstemon, Phlox stolonifera, Primula denticulata, P. 'Wanda'*** and other hybrids, ***Pulmonaria, Ranunculus*** various, ***Raoulia, Saxifraga*** Cotyledon and various types, ***Sedum*** various, ***Sempervivum, Sisyrinchium*** various, ***Synthyris, Tiarella, Veronica, Viola, Waldsteinia,***

BULBS TO PURCHASE AND PLANT

Allium various
Brimeura amethystina
B. a. 'Alba'
Chionodoxa various
Crocus
Erythronium various
Fritillaria various
Galanthus various
Iris dwarf kinds
I. bucharica
Leucojum various
Muscari less invasive kinds
M. azureum
Narcissus dwarf kinds
Ornithogalum less invasive dwarf kinds
Scilla various
Sternbergia any
Trillium various
Tulipa dwarf kinds
Zephyranthes various including:
Z. candida

plants
OF THE
month
1

DWARF CAMPION
(Silene schafta)

The campions gathered under the *Silene* banner are a mix of meadow plants plus a few alpines. *S. acaulis* makes wonderful tight cushions but can be difficult to flower freely. *S. hookeri* with large, pink flowers is for alpine house only. *S. schafta* is easier to grow but some may find its vivid colouring tricky to position.

type	Prostrate tufted perennial
foliage	Small, narrow, oval, dark green leaves making wide tufted mats
flowers	Five-petalled, vivid magenta flowers with long tubes holding them just clear of foliage from late spring to late autumn. Petals are like segments of a circle, narrowing towards centre but with airspace between each segment
height	10-12cm (4-5in)
spread	10cm (4in)
planting	Early spring
site	Open spot
soil	Not fussy. Will do well on poor soils. Good drainage is important
propagation	Seed in spring, division or cuttings in summer
relatives	*S. acaulis* makes neat hummocks of tightly-packed, tiny leaves and tiny stemless, pink flowers. Sometimes shy to flower. Likes a cool spot

AUTUMN GENTIAN
(Gentiana sino-ornata)

A leading autumn gentian perhaps showing its first blooms this month but at its best through early into mid-autumn (illus. p.108–9).

type	Herbaceous, prostrate perennial dying back to a crown in winter
foliage	Narrow, pointed, light green leaves
flowers	Huge, upward-facing, brilliant deep sky-blue trumpets, throat and outside of lower tube striped pale green and blue-black

DWARF CAMPION

height	2.5cm (1in), 5–7cm (2–3in) in bloom
spread	30cm (12in)
planting	Plant divided throngs early spring, with crown bud just below soil level
site	Sun or semi-shade, lower rock garden or peat bed
soil	No lime. Humus-rich with grit and leaf-mould
care	Like all Asiatic gentians, must be kept well clear of lime. Keep moist not sodden and split regularly
propagation	Lift and divide thronged roots every two or three years
relatives	Many fine hybrids with the vivid, paler *G. farreri*, grouped under name *G. × macaulayi*, including 'Kingfisher', 'Well's Variety' and 'Kidbrooke Seedling'. The hybrids seem to have a little extra vigour

EVENING PRIMROSE

(Oenothera missouriensis)

EVENING PRIMROSE

There are some very worthwhile *Oenothera* for border and rock garden, as well as some rather weedy invasive ones. The species featured is neat and opens its flowers in the evening – for the bread-winners as they arrive home from a hard day's toil.

type	Spreading, herbaceous perennial
foliage	Oval leaves of mid-green
flowers	Succession of wide, rounded, saucer-shaped, yellow flowers that open for the evening, through the summer. Sometimes marked with red spots
height	10cm (4in)
spread	45cm (18in)
planting	Early spring or early autumn
site	Light position
soil	Not fussy, best in well-drained, rather poor
propagation	Seed in late winter or cuttings in late summer
relatives	Most other oenotheras are too large for the rock garden but *O. acaulis* is 15cm (6in) high with white flowers, turning pink

DITTANY

(Origanum amanum)

A genus including the majorams and some other pleasing plants, good for the border but too big for the rock garden. Many make their floral appeal considerably more potent by the large, rounded bracts as does this species.

type	Frost hardy, tufted, herbaceous perennial with arching wiry stems – almost a sub-shrub
foliage	Small, heart-shaped, pale apple-green leaves
flowers	Two-lipped, pink flowers with conspicuous large, rounded bracts of light green, suffused pink, for a long period through mid and late summer
height	10–20cm (4–8in), some of the most attractive clones are at the lower end of the scale
spread	20–30cm (8–12in)
planting	Plant firmly in early spring
site	Scree, warm crevice of rock garden or alpine house
soil	Gritty, well-drained
care	Needs a warm spot and a dry atmosphere to thrive. A cold wet winter may threaten it
propagation	Cuttings of non-flowering shoots in summer, division in spring, or perhaps more happily by seed in autumn/spring, which avoids any disturbance of attractive plant
relatives	Most origanums are too robust for the small rock garden. *O. laevigatum* is hardy with neat mats of smooth dark foliage. Sprays of reddish purple flowers reach 25cm (10in) over this on daintily branched, wiry stems. It is more robust than *O. amanum*

practical
project

THE ALPINE HOUSE

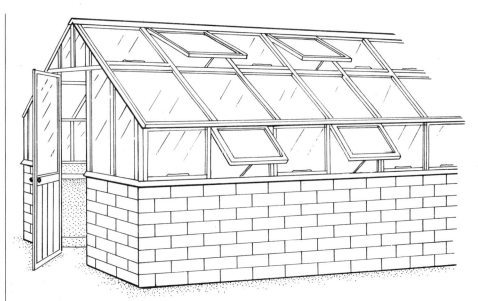

ALPINE HOUSE PLANTS

Androsace various
Aquilegia jonesii
A. laramiensis
Asperula various
Calceolaria darwinii
Campanula various including:
C. piperi
C. raineri
C. zoysii
Convolvulus sabatius syn.
C. mauritanicus
Cyananthus various
Cyclamen all
Dicentra peregrina
Dionysia all
Douglasia various
Draba various
Eritrichium nanum

The alpine house may look like a greenhouse but it is designed to different specifications and for different purposes. The main reason for most greenhouses is to create a much warmer and often more humid climate than in the open. The alpine house is constructed to be as airy as possible while excluding rain and gales. It will often be completely without heating – or will allow for only a minimum winter heating to defeat frost.

BENEFITS AND PURPOSES

An alpine house enables the growing of a whole range of plants that cannot tolerate excessive winter wet, including many of the silvery, rather hairy plants from the Mediterranean and other warm dry areas. It allows us to enjoy winter flowers without them being battered by wind and rain outside. A range of plants that are on the fuzzy borderline of hardiness can be kept happy and safe with the protection of glass; if heating is installed to come into operation when frost threatens, the range of these marginally tender plants expands dramatically.

The idea of tender alpines may seem a contradiction in terms and to an extent it is. Many plants from hills and mountains are covered with deep blankets of snow through the winter and so are protected from biting winds and both excessive wet and cold. In gardens open winters may cause some small plants to be put off guard and become vulnerable – especially to wet, wet and more wet.

The alpine house is just the place for the gardener to shelter in the winter and enjoy plants when nothing can be done outside. There should be a ledge for a cup of coffee, or something stronger, to keep out the cold.

COSTS

It seems that manufacturers have the idea that alpine enthusiasts come from well-moneyed ranks. Prices for alpine houses are hugely higher than equivalent-sized greenhouses, although a proportion is justified for the increased amount of moving vents. Perhaps the lesser demand pushes up the prices.

A very small house is too confined; it is better to have a frame structure.
Recommended sizes might be
2.5 × 5m (8 × 16ft), allowing a central path of 75cm (2½ft)
or perhaps
3 × 5.5m (9 × 18ft), allowing two benches and a central path of similar widths.

Although 1m (3ft) for the central path seems rather generous one does need room to work in comfort and to be able to bring in tools and so on.

To purchase a ready-made alpine house of the suggested size could cost a fortune. It is possible for the handyperson to make a reasonable structure themselves. Once you have read through this section and the second half of this project on page 86 you will be able to judge what your best option is.

DESIGN FACTORS

▪ The aim is maximum ventilation and shelter from rain

▪ Maximum light is desirable, so site the house where it does not get badly shaded

▪ There is no perfect ideal for orientation of an alpine house. If possible, it is helpful to have two doors, although this reduces bench space. Shading is essential from late spring to early autumn

▪ A firm foundation is vital. This can be of concrete or of heavy precast concrete-blocks usually 1m (3ft) long

▪ Access should be easy. Outside a good path is important, door and central path inside should be wide enough for a barrow

▪ Electricity supply is a consideration

▪ Water will be needed. Mains supply can be augmented by rain tanks – or should it be the other way round? There needs to be room outside for the tank that gathers water from the roof and this tank needs to be easily accessible from the house

▪ Ideally there should be room for a frame or frames near the house

▪ If a bulb bed/frame is to be constructed (see p94) then it is sensible to have this near the alpine house

▪ Wood is the more plant-friendly material

and is often visually more pleasing. It will be easier to work than metal

▪ The advantage of metal alpine houses is that they are cheaper and it is easy to obtain additional vents and louvres for them to maximise ventilation

▪ Prefabricated greenhouses may be made of units that could be used slightly differently to make an alpine house. Contact manufacturers or their agents to get prices for parts that your could use. 2.5 × 5m (8 × 16ft) is often a standard overall size

▪ All materials and structures should be safe. Benches and their supports in particular must be strong enough to stand the considerable weight of the bench itself, the gravel or other standing or plunging material plus the potted plants

▪ Vents will be open more often than closed. This will make them vulnerable to wind so the catchments must be of a good safe design and quality

▪ The height of benches is important. The plants want to be well displayed but reached easily. The height should be at an easy working level. While both side benches may be filled with plants, a working bench at the same level can be temporarily fixed across the path with the benches as supports

(*Continued on page 86*)

ALPINE HOUSE PLANTS

Continued:
Globularia repens
Gypsophila aretioides
G. repens and vars.
Helichrysum various including:
H. coralloides
Lewisia various
Myosotis rupicola
Onosma various
Paraquilegia various
Pleione
Primula various including:
P. allionii and hybrids
P. marginata forms
Pulsatilla vernalis
Ramonda various
Ranunculus calandrinoides
Saponaria pumilio
Saxifraga various
Silene acaulis
Telesonix jamesii, syn. **Boykinia jamesii**
Verbascum dwarf forms
V. acaule
Viola various

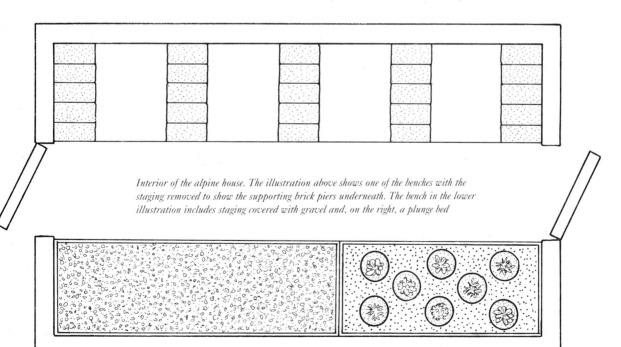

Interior of the alpine house. The illustration above shows one of the benches with the staging removed to show the supporting brick piers underneath. The bench in the lower illustration includes staging covered with gravel and, on the right, a plunge bed

practical project

THE ALPINE HOUSE

continued

ALPINE HOUSE SHRUBS AND TREES

Cassiope various including:
C. wardii
Conifers dwarf
Cytisus ardoinii
C. demissus
Daphne arbuscula
D. jasminea
D. petraea
Forsythia bronxensis
Genista sagittalis delphinensis minor
Hebe various
Hypericum aegypticum
H. pallens
Jasminum parkeri
Rhododendron various dwarfs
Salix × boydii
Salix reticulata
Teucrium aroanum
T. subspinosum
Thymus cilicius
T. membranaceus
Verbascum 'Letitia'

MATERIALS

Materials are probably wood, horticultural grade glass and bricks. Western cedar is the best wood as it is long lasting and can be used without painting. Most amateur houses are built of it. Solid sides, below bench level, can be built of brick or wood.

Fully explore the possibilities of using units made by manufacturers for mass-produced greenhouses. You may obtain sides and ends far more economically than making them yourself. It could also provide you with roof panels, using only those with vented upper halves. The same applies to the glazed sides with opening vents (see below).

DESIGN DETAILS

▪ All sides above the brick base and all upper halves of roof panels should be openable
▪ Side vents need to be approximately 30cm (12in) high
▪ The slope of the roof will rise to a ridge height of approximately 2.1m (7ft)
▪ If using bricks for the base wall these will make twelve or thirteen courses and arrive at a height of 1–1.07m (3–3¼ft) – about 900 bricks

BUILDING

▪ Mark out the dimensions of the house and build a foundation of concrete that is level with the surrounding area or is so after one course of bricks
▪ If using prefabricated wooden sides and ends fix these securely to the foundation, ensuring that the corners are true right angles. Long screws or bolts should hold the wall firmly to the foundation
▪ If using bricks, make sure that true levels are kept and that courses are tidily finished so that there are no small crannies between courses for insects and disease spores to lodge. You could consider rendering the whole interior sides with a strong mix of two sand to one of cement to give a clean smooth wall uninviting to pests, etc. Half a dozen air-bricks each side will be a valuable aid to bouyant air ventilation
▪ Secure side panels – still unglazed – to the wall
▪ Secure panels to one end wall then secure panels to the other end. Remember to have at least one door!

▪ Working from one end secure roof panels in pairs until reaching the other end. Secure the first pair of roof panels to the end and side panels and subsequent pairs to previous panels and sides
▪ Hang the door(s) as a prefabricated unit
▪ Safely secure the ridge pole to complete the structure. If necessary ensure water-proofing of junction of ridge pole and roof panels using bitumastic-type sealant
▪ Glaze
▪ Fix opening vent catchments

THE STAGING

As the benches may have pots plunged 15cm (6in) deep in sand or similar material their weight is considerable and there must be no mistake made about its support. Corrugated iron can be used as the base of the plunge bed. It is not difficult to bend the sides of the corrugated sheets up at vent and central path sides to contain plunge material. The corrugations add substantially to the strength and can be supported on the brick end walls and a series of four walls built at equal intervals at

right angles to the side walls and reaching as far as the path. A similarly secure arrangement could be made with pairs of piers one brick length square (9 × 9in) and this would give better air circulation and access below.

The bench supports should come high enough to just allow the 15cm (6in) depth of the bench to reach the side glazed vents. Air can then play over the plants.

HEATING

Electrical heating is the easiest and most reliable and need not be too elaborate. A good thermostat is necessary and should be fixed so that heating takes place when the temperature falls to within one or two degrees of freezing. At such times the vents should be closed and panels in the house or heaters blowing warm air through the house will not usually involve astronomical power bills. Blower heaters give some air movement and help to create a more lively atmosphere. Purists tend to disapprove of any form of heating but as long as it merely keeps the alpine house frost-free that is acceptable.

SHADING

While through the autumn, winter and early spring we are striving to get as much light as possible in the house by keeping the glass meticulously clean, in the summer the light and heat may become more than some plants want. Gather those that would benefit from some extra shade at one end of the house, the doorless end, if you have only one door, and shade this portion.

The easiest arrangement is to employ slatted plastic blinds. When necessary these can be unrolled from the ridge to eaves and if necessary fixed so they also run down the sides. These are relatively inexpensive, easily put in place, and can be kept clean without much trouble.

PLANTS

A list of some of the plants that you may find interesting to have in the alpine house is given in the margins. There are huge numbers more.

ALPINE HOUSE BULBS

Allium dwarf kinds
Calochortus various
Crocus various
Fritillaria various including:
F. acmopetala
F. camschatcensis
F. pallidiflora
F. pontica
F. pyrenaica
F. uva-vulpis
Galanthus reginae-olgae
Iris danfordiae
I. histrioides
I. reticulata forms
I. winogradowii
Leucojum autumnale
L. nicaeense
L. vernum
Muscari botryoides
M. b. 'Album'
Narcissus various including:
N. asturiensis
N. cantabricus
N. romieuxii
N. rupicola
N. watieri
Romulea various
Sternbergia candida
Tecophilaea cyanocrocus
Tulipa aucheriana
T. batalinii
T. clusiana
T. pulchella
Zephyranthes various including:
Z. candida

STORAGE SPACE
Try to keep the storage space below benches tidy, and not a matter of 'out of sight, out of mind'

SEPTEMBER

*It is a new season; the summer holidays are over. One or two shrubs
and trees begin to turn colour. The sumachs are first to catch fire but
soon all will be change and carnival.*

*The rock garden changes mood. Although there are plenty of summer
flowers still open, they are less exuberant – their play is nearly run.
Autumn's coming is signalled by the cyclamen species;* C. purpurascens
(C. europaeum) *straddles the summer and autumn months and* C.
cilicium *is a pretty autumn creature. Everyone's favourite,* C.
hederifolium (C. neapolitanum) *comes fearlessly centre-stage, its
magical blooms totally unaccompanied by foliage for several weeks. It
is difficult to have too much of this paragon. Flower form and
glowing pink shades are perfect, the corms are hugely generous and
even quite tiny ones will give their quota, delivering without fail for
decades, for this is one of the longest-lived of small plants. The foliage
is a wonderful study on its own, with silvery engraving on heart-
shaped leaves, as intricate as frost patterns on a windowpane. Happily
the seed germinates freely – either taken and raised under supervision
or allowed to fall and letting nature take its bountiful course.*

*Also beginning to open are the autumn gentians, perhaps the first of the
autumn crocuses, and, of course, the colchicums. Crocuses are certainly
due a place in the rock garden; the colchicums are more problematic.
They are all excitement and good sense in bloom but spring brings huge
wide un-alpine leaves. Choose a spot where this excess is masked.
There is a welcome freshness brought into the garden by the autumn
bulbs: the innocence of the vivid white-satin faces of* Zephranthes
candida, *some 15-20cm (6-8in) high among rush-like leaves; the
daintiness of the diminutive little bells of* Leucojum autumnale *hung
from thread-thin stems only 10-13cm (4-5in) high and soon to be
followed by quickly-growing black seed! And here is* Scilla scilloides
with spikes of open pink flowers on stems 24-30cm (10-12in) high.

tasks

FOR THE

month

CONIFERS FOR THE ROCK GARDEN

**Abies balsamea hudsonii
A. b. 'Nana' • A. procera 'Glauca
Prostrata' • Cedrus libani 'Nana'
C. l. 'Compte de Dijon'
Chamaecyparis lawsoniana
'Minima Glauca' • C. l. 'Nana'
C. obtusa 'Compacta' • C. o. 'Nana'
C. o. 'Nana Gracilis'
C. o. 'Pygmaea'
Cryptomeria japonica 'Globosa'
C. j. 'Vilmoriniana'
Juniperus communis 'Compressa'
J. c. 'Hornibrookii'
J. c. 'Depressa Aurea'
J. horizontalis various
J. sabina various
J. virginiana various
Microbiota decussata
Picea abies various dwarf forms
Pinus mugo various
Podocarpus alpinus • P. nivalis
Thuja occidentalis 'Globosa'
T. o. 'Rheingold'
Thujopsis dolobrata 'Nana'
Tsuga canadensis various dwarf
forms including: T. c. 'Minuta**

PAGES 90–1
*(left to right) Arenaria, variegated
thyme, Sedum spathulifolium and
sempervivum*

CHECKLIST

- [ ] Planting out pot plants
- [ ] Planting bulbs outside
- [ ] Loose leaves and debris
- [ ] Free seedlings
- [ ] Bulb frame
- [ ] Shrub planting

PLANTING OUT POT PLANTS

With the early autumn it is time to consider potted plants that need planting in their permanent quarters. These may have been purchased through the past few weeks or even months but have not yet got a niche or they may be plants grown on from seeds, cuttings or divisions that are now ready to be freed from pots. There may also be some recent purchases such as pots of *Cyclamen hederifolium* just showing flower buds.

We proceed:
- Check plant for dead leaves and pests such as slugs

*Position plants in
niches as the rock
garden is being built,
then move rocks into
place above them,
ensuring a natural
finish*

*Fill in soil around
the plant and up to
the same level that it
was in the pot*

- Turn out of pot and check for vine weevil and root aphids. If there are any weevil grubs squash them and saturate plant roots thoroughly in malathion if aphids are present
- Choose a suitable site, and use a trowel to excavate a hole then install the plant with its neck level with the surface as previously in the pot
- Firm compost around the plant
- Firmly stick in a clearly written plant name label especially if fearful of memory lapses
- Top-dress with grit
- Water thoroughly

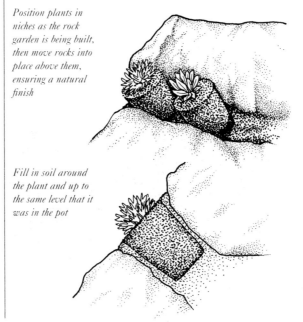

PLANTING BULBS OUTSIDE

If you didn't buy any bulbs last month now is the ideal time to get them for flowering in autumn, winter and spring.

Planting priorities
- First plant up the autumn flowering bulbs, such as sternbergias, colchicums, autumn crocuses
- Follow up with the winter-flowering bulbs – snowdrops (*Galanthus*) species and hybrids, winter aconites (*Eranthis*) and winter crocuses
- Purchase trilliums and erythroniums early and plant quickly for spring display. These sometimes deteriorate when in store – but they should be fine at this time
- Now choose the small spring bulbs. Perhaps give preference to those that bloom in late winter and early spring. For smaller rock gardens it is sensible to grow those with discreet amounts of foliage, so avoid colchicums or larger-leaved tulips or daffodils. See margin for suggestions

LOOSE LEAVES AND DEBRIS

Leaves come tumbling down now and must be gathered up in case they lodge in the rock garden and start to rot. This rot can spread to plants which will also be weakened if they are under leaves and away from daylight. For the next few weeks hygiene is going to be an important concern; a reminder of the sense in the advice to build the rock garden away from trees.

FREE SEEDLINGS

If the ground has been relatively undisturbed beneath seeding plants there is a chance of self-sown seedlings appearing. When these are from a species they are likely to reproduce true to type, unless an insect has brought pollen from another species in which case they may be hybrids. Some very good chance hybrids have arrived this way, gift horses that *can* be looked in the mouth.

If the seed has fallen from a hybrid plant each seedling will be different and there is a good chance of getting interesting, new plants.

Some of these seedlings will be strong enough to weather the winter, but others will not be sufficiently strong in the few weeks' growing time available to be able to get through to the spring. You have the choice between leaving the seedlings to survive if they can and perhaps moving them in the spring, or lifting some, or all, now, potting them up and growing them more carefully, with some protection, until they are ready to be planted out in the spring as fully-established specimens.

BULB FRAME

Things are beginning to happen in the bulb frame. A lot of the small bulbs that respond to the first autumnal rains in their natural homes are flowering now, most of them without leaves. Start watering the frame to stimulate more root growth and all round activity. Many of the bulbs usually grown in a bulb frame are normally hardy but can be battered by continual rainfall and wind. The margin list on p94 indicates those that are coming into bloom now.

Pots of bulbs plunged into the frame will need to be smartened up by removing any weeds along with the top inch or so of compost, which should be replaced and then top-dressed. If the bulb frame is full of compost into which the bulbs are planted to be

BULB PLANTING DEPTHS
Soil surface to tip of bulb

Colchicum 10–15cm (4–6in)
Crocus 5cm (2in)
C. sativus 10–12cm (4–5in)
Erythronium 10–15cm (4–6in)
Fritillaria meleagris 5–8cm (2–3in*)*
Galanthus 5–8cm (2–3in)
Iris reticulata types 5–8cm (2–3in)
I. danfordiae 10–12cm (4–5in)
Muscari azureum 5cm (2in)
Narcissus asturiensis 5–8cm (2–3in)
N. bulbocodium 5–8cm (2–3in)
N. cyclamineus 5–8cm (2–3in)
N. 'February Gold' 10cm (4in)
N. 'Jenny' 10cm (4in)
N. 'Sundial' 8–10cm (3–4in)
N. 'Tête à Tête' 10cm (4in)
N. 'Wee Bee' 10cm (4in)
Scilla sibirica 5–8cm (2–3in)
Trillium 8–10cm (3–4in)
Tulipa batalinii 8–10cm (3–4in)
T. praestans 10cm (4in)
T. tarda 10cm (4in)
T. turkestanica 8–10cm (3–4in)

like a bed or garden, then again it is prudent to weed and perhaps top-dress with grit to give the coming blossom an attractive setting.

Crocuses, tulips and many other bulbs are attractive foodstuff for mice and other rodents. Check for signs of pest attack and bait any traps. Loose bait should be protected from domestic animals and from birds. *Narcissi* are less likely to be damaged as they contain substances that are poisonous to rodents.

SHRUB PLANTING

Dwarf shrubs ought to be planted before the weather turns much colder. The idea is to enable them to make fresh roots in their new homes before the onset of winter. This applies to all shrubs and small trees in rock gardens or in troughs. Any that are intended to form a background to the rock garden or as an adjunct should also be planted now. Consider planting other shrubs some distance from the rock garden to screen unnatural features.

DWARF SHRUBS

Amelanchier alnifolia pumila
Berberis x stenophylla 'Corallina Compacta'
Calluna vulgaris
Cytisus prostrate and dwarf forms
Daboecia cantabrica
Daphne arbuscula
D. blagayana
D. cneorum
D. collina
Erica various
Gaultheria various
Genista various dwarfs
Hebe various
Kalmiopsis leachiana
Margyrcarpus setosus
Moltkia petraea
M. suffruticosa
M. × intermedia
Ononis fruticosa
O. rotundifolia
Rhamnus pumilus
Rhododendron many dwarfs
Rhodothamnus chamaecistus
Salix apoda
S. × boydii
S. lanata
S. reticulata
Sorbus reducta
Vaccinium various

Shrubs and small trees are an excellent way to screen unnatural features

plants

OF THE

month

1

*WILLOW-LEAVED
GENTIAN*

WILLOW-LEAVED GENTIAN
(*Gentiana asclepiadea*)

Gentians can be split into spring- or autumn-flowering species. They are often lime-haters, but some species tolerate some lime. The willow-leaved gentian is one of the easiest and most distinctive.

type	Herbaceous perennial
foliage	Oval, pointed, pale green leaves, opposite pairs arranged stemlessly at right angles up the stems, upper leaves being rather smaller and more pointed; the way alternate pairs bisect their neighbour's angle is very decorative
flowers	Narrow, sky-blue trumpets with purple spots inside and some paler longitudinal striping. Usually two or three stemless blooms to a leaf axil, sometimes single. From midsummer into autumn
height	15–60cm (6–24in) or more when settled
spread	To 60cm (24in)
planting	Early spring
site	Best in a cool spot in partial shade. Peat bed
soil	Can manage with lime but best in moist soils with high humus content
care	Relatively easy provided it is not put in a dry hot spot. A deep root-run is appreciated

propagation	Grows easily from seed sown midwinter and allowed to freeze, but can also be increased by division in early spring

relatives	*G. a. alba* has white flowers and is usually smaller. It makes a good contrast

DIASCIA
(*Diascia cordata*)

A genus that provides a choice of very free-flowering summer and autumn border and rock garden plants. There are fine species and hybrids. They grow easily and can almost become rampant after mild winters.

type	Prostrate, herbaceous perennial
foliage	Neat, heart-shaped, light green leaves
flowers	Many spikes of many tubular and spurred flowers, opening wide at the mouth in a very cheering crushed strawberry-pink. Borne for many weeks through summer and early autumn
height	15–20cm (6–8in)
spread	20–25cm (8–10in)
planting	Early spring
site	Sunny pocket in rock garden, between paving or on the edge of scree
soil	Well-drained soil with plenty of humus
care	Easy in well-drained sunny spots; best tidied up in early spring by clipping back shoots
propagation	Seed as soon as ripe in autumn. Softwood cuttings in spring, riper cuttings in summer
relatives	*D. rigescens* is slightly larger with long, impressive spikes packed with salmon-pink flowers. There is also a range of hybrids

MOUNTAIN AVENS
(*Dryas octopetala*)

A genus of only three species found high up in the hills but also at sea level. They seem to be happiest where they have to battle for a living.

type	Spreading, evergreen sub-shrub
foliage	Miniature oak leaves in dark glossy green, with silver reverses
flowers	Eight-petalled, cup-shaped, white flowers, like small single roses, with golden bosses of stamens. Followed by attractive fluffy seedheads
height	6cm (2–3in)
spread	60cm (24in), or more
planting	Early spring till early autumn
site	Sunny spacious spot with room for

DIASCIA CORDATA

expansion in rock garden, scree or alpine lawn

soil Gritty for good drainage but with plenty of humus; does not object to lime. Blooms more freely on poorer soils

propagation Rooted, layered pieces or cuttings in summer

relatives *D. o. minor* is a half-sized version. *D. drummondii* is very similar but with creamy pale yellow nodding flowers. There is a hybrid between the two called *D. × suendermannii* with pale yellow buds and white flowers

STONECROP
(Sedum cauticola)

Some growers might advise caution here: 'Beware of those bearing gifts of sedums'. There are some that can become weeds and are difficult to eradicate, but there are also good species and this is one of them.

type Procumbent perennial producing stolons

foliage Purplish-red stems hold fleshy oval leaves, three to a short stalk and coloured a greyish-blue-green, becoming burgundy red before dying as the winter arrives

flowers Branched heads of pointed stars in rich purplish-red

height 5cm (2in)

spread 22cm (9in)

planting Anytime

site Open sunny site, perhaps in rock crevice, but adaptable. Will manage in scree and can even grow in a peat bed, although the latter is not deliberately recommended

soil Not fussy, normally best in poor soils with plenty of grit

care Easy and not particularly rampant like some of this genus. The stems can be cut back in the winter

propagation Like most sedums, shoots or leaves taken in summer will root and produce plants for setting out following spring

relatives *S. sieboldii* is rather similar but with pairs of leaves and pink flowers. *S.s.* 'Mediovariegatum' has foliage clearly variegated in cream

SEDUM CAUTICOLA

practical project 1

MAKING A BULB AND PROPAGATING FRAME

BULBS FOR THE BULB FRAME

There are very many – this is a short list!

AUTUMN

Allium callimischon mid-late autumn

Crocus cancellatus early-mid autumn

C. goulimyi mid-late autumn

C. hadriaticus early-mid autumn

C. kotschyanus early autumn

C. medius mid autumn

C. niveus late autumn

C. ochroleucus mid-late autumn

C. tournefortii mid-late autumn

Leucojum autumnale early autumn

Scilla autumnalis early autumn

Zephyranthes candida early autumn

Z. citrina early-mid autumn

Z. grandiflora early autumn

Why should bulbs be given special treatment? The answers are that many attractive species bloom at the time of year when they are likely to be ruined almost as soon as they appear; others wobble a bit on the margin of hardiness but with just a little help are splendid. Another important reason is that in the frame bulbs can go into overdrive and produce massive increases. How pleasant to plant one bulb and raise a cluster!

DESIGN

This frame is a cross between a normal frame and a small greenhouse. The aim is to provide drainage, protection from inclement weather and the possibility of a more or less controlled soil environment. The frame needs siting in a light position but some shelter from the stronger winds would be welcome. While manufacturers do produce such frames it is a relatively simple matter to make one of your own that is exactly the size you want.

It can be a simple one using railway sleepers for the walls and the top being some of the better-made cloches with removable glass. Such cloches can be permanently secured to the wall or held down with a plastic clip or wire tied over the top and secured to the walls.

Sizes

Normally the width is no more than can be easily reached from one or two sides.

Brick can be used to form the walls. The height is whatever is convenient, perhaps three or four courses. Some growers may like to have them closer to working level, perhaps table height 75cm (30in). The diagram shows a popular height with walls 30cm (12in) high. Length is what need dictates.

MATERIALS

- Walls of brick, precast blocks or railway sleepers
- Framework above of wood, aluminium or bought as prefabricated parts
- Glass of horticultural grade – not lighter
- Wire mesh

CONSTRUCTION

- Walls should allow for drainage
- Framework above should be securely fastened to walls
- Glass should be movable. The glass sides could be arranged on double tracks of metal or strong plastic. You may be able to utilise some kinds of curtain track
- Glass on the top can overlap the ends and sides so that end or side glass panels can be opened for ventilation without allowing rain in
- Roof glass should be removable so that rain can be allowed when needed
- All parts should be secure. If wind can get in make sure it can get out as well
- It is imperative to make the whole as rodent- and mole-proof as possible. This means covering the inside – bottom, sides and ends – with strong wire mesh of a grade small enough to keep out the smallest mice, which seem able to squeeze through something not much bigger than the eye of a needle. No gaps should be allowed. Without such precautions the frame can form luxurious homes for small, furry inhabitants

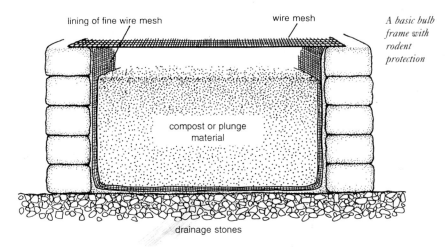

lining of fine wire mesh

wire mesh

A basic bulb frame with rodent protection

compost or plunge material

drainage stones

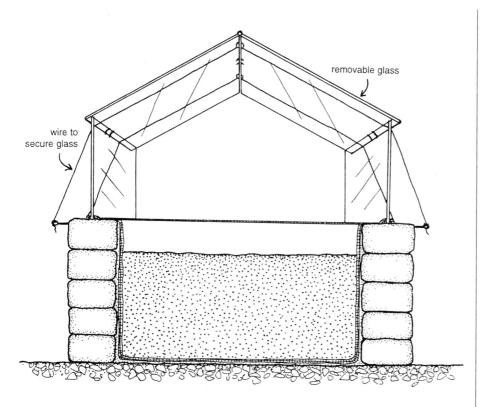

removable glass

wire to
secure glass

BULBS FOR THE BULB FRAME continued:

WINTER

Crocus laevigatus late autumn-midwinter
C. sieberi mid-late winter
Iris danfordiae late winter-early spring
I. histrioides mid-late winter
I. reticulata forms late winter
I. winogradowii late winter
Narcissus asturiensis mid-late winter
N. cantabricus early-midwinter
N. cyclamineus late winter
N. romieuxii midwinter
Scilla bifolia mid-late winter
S. mischtschenkoana midwinter
S. siberica late winter
Tulipa turkestanica late winter

SPRING

Arisarum proboscideum early spring (may be invasive)
Bulbocodium vernum early-mid spring
Calochortus albus mid spring
C. luteus late spring
C. venustus late spring
Crocus imperati mid spring
C. minimus mid spring
Fritillaria acmopetala mid spring
F. camschatcensis mid-late spring
F. pallidiflora mid spring
F. pontica mid spring
F. pyrenaica mid-late spring
F. uva-vulpis mid spring
Narcissus rupicola mid spring
N. watieri mid spring
Romulea bulbocodium early-mid spring
R. ramiflora early-mid spring
Tecophilaea cyanocrocus early-mid spring

• FILLING THE FRAME

Soils

The frame used for direct planting will be filled with various layers.

- Add a layer of rough drainage 7–10cm (3–4in) deep
- Cover the drainage level with fine plastic netting to prevent all the compost washing down
- Mix compost (see p12 for a suitable combination). Good quality loam may take the place of the JI potting compost
- Fill with main compost to a depth of 20–25cm (8–10in)
- After bulbs are planted finish with 1cm (¹/₂in) of grit/chippings

(*Continued on page 96*)

Profile showing the ideal structure and contents of a bulb frame

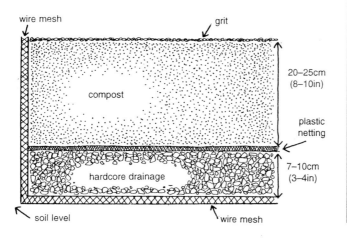

wire mesh

grit

compost

20–25cm
(8–10in)

plastic
netting

hardcore drainage

7–10cm
(3–4in)

soil level

wire mesh

practical
project
2

PLANTING
THE BULB FRAME

PLANTS FOR BULB FRAME

Anacyclus depressus
Crassula milfordiae
C. sarcocaulis
Hebe various small forms
including:
H. buchananii 'Minor'
Helichrysum bellidioides
H. coralloides
H. frigidum
H. milfordiae
H. selago
Jovibarba various
Teucrium various small forms
including:
T. aroanum
T. subspinosum

Protecting plants

One of the favourite genera to plant up in frames is *Crocus*. These are also a favourite food of rodents. After planting it is wise to cover the surface with wire mesh to prevent any animals getting in. Perhaps make a wooden frame and cover it with wire mesh so that it can be lowered over the bulb frame securing it on a temporary basis. As long as it fits the sides without holes this frame can be proud of the soil level and so allow for perennials below. Small slats of wood could be fixed to the wall for the wire frame to rest on.

Tulips, fritillaries and small lilies are also rodent fodder; Narcissi and *Galanthus*-types seem less palatable.

Propagated plants

The bulb frame makes a useful stop-gap spot for planting up propagated pieces of various alpines. Some tend to grow on better here than in pots because they are less vulnerable to fluctuating temperatures and moisture content.

COMPLETE BED VERSUS PLUNGE BED

Is the bulb frame going to be a complete bed of suitable compost with bulbs planted direct or are the bulbs going to be planted in pots and plunged in sand or peat to be kept sensibly cool and moist? For only a few bulbs/corms it may seem sensible to have them safely in a pot, but usually a somewhat faster rate of increase can be attained by planting out in a bed. Perhaps the answer is a compromise, to have part a plunge bed and part a direct planting bed.

SOIL MANAGEMENT

The main feature of the bulb frame is that it is well-drained and the water content of the compost can be carefully controlled. The rough hardcore drainage below should ensure surplus water moves away. The compost will be approximately as recommended on page 12. The food in the compost can be augmented by periodic waterings with a high potash liquid feed – such as tomato fertiliser. Alternatively slow-release capsule fertilisers can be incorporated in soil mixes.

PLANNING AND PLANTING

A direct planting bed can be organised with bulbs in rows and everything neatly labelled, or there can be some attempt at a less formal planting. Introducing a few prostrate plants will help a more natural approach.

Bulbs

Different bulbs need to be kept distinctly apart if they are not to be muddled when lifting; an unintended miscellany is all too easy to achieve. As bulbs and corms grow they move – sometimes quite surprising distances. Secure clear labels will help, so will wide separation. Better still plant them up in the type of lattice pots used for submerging plants in pools but with netlon netting around the perimeter enclosing the compost. (Netlon netting is the material often used as bags for packing citrus fruits in shops.) For peace of mind an additional label can be enclosed within the pot – even tied to it – so that any movement of the label stuck into the ground is not so tragic.

Pots unlikely to be lifted for the whole growing cycle can be plunged so that their rims are just below the surface; those you may want to handle are best with the rims in view and easy to grip.

Pots are easy to lift in summer and the netting ensures that all is safely gathered in. The bulbs can be shaken out, split and replanted in fresh compost. You will be surprised how quickly some increase. With rarer kinds, it may give the option to use the surplus in trial spots in the rock garden.

When to plant

The sooner bulbs are planted the better they will grow. Your own bulbs can be lifted and replanted the same day – while bulbs are easy items to handle and keep stored, their home is in the ground. A predominant number of small bulbs start growing strongly in the autumn and bloom in winter or spring. There are of course some that flower in the autumn. This means that there can be bloom for two-thirds of the year! Lists are in the margins on pages 94, 95 and 97.

As a plunge bed

The frame can be kept exclusively for bulbs with only a few perennials to add foliage and flower contrast, especially through the summer. Any gaps could be used as a plunge bed for pots you want to remove from the alpine house for one reason or another. Consider allowing for this when building the frame and perhaps make it a third larger than originally planned.

MAINTENANCE

• Removal of glass lights when it is raining is beneficial
• Return the glass lights when bulbs are coming into bloom to protect those bulbs with the temerity to bloom at times when the weather is likely to damage performance
• Normal check for weeds. They are likely to be of low incidence and more wind-borne annuals than pernicious perennials

• Lift bulbs either from the open frame or in pots after they have died down, usually in early summer. If this is left until late summer the bulbs may have started rooting strongly and are less amenable to disturbance
• Bulbs left unpotted in the frame can be dusted with high potash fertiliser in early autumn and late winter
• Water as needed. In the absence of late summer- or early autumn-rainfall, the frame can be given a thorough soak at this time to encourage strong rooting activity

DANGER CHECKLIST!

Watch out for:
All mice and rodents
Moles
Rabbits
Cats
Insecure glass panels
Birds removing labels

Don't forget to:
Water once autumn rooting starts

OCTOBER

Trees and shrubs of the garden and countryside are turning into a hundred bright colours and it is not wrong to hope for the same colour in the rock garden. There is that provided by the small shrubs and trees; there are also the grasses and sedges, which can be very bright in greens, golds, silvers, rusts and bronzes. Alongside the foliage of some are the fruits of autumn of others. In the peat bed Gaultheria, Vaccinium and Pernettya are distinguished evergreens with spring and summer flowers followed by conspicuous fruits. The leaves of some make 'evergreen' a misnomer by turning vivid red shades in autumn. Certain berried shrubs will be decorative well into winter.

In a rock garden small trees need planting with some care. If they are next to large-leaved plants all sense of scale is lost. In the wild the higher up the hills the shrub or tree is found the more likely it is to be low or even prostrate. The upright Juniperus communis compressa or erect forms of the variable J. communis itself can be planted effectively at the base of the rocks.

The stronger heathers can almost take over a small rock garden but a larger site may happily accommodate some of the more prostrate forms of Erica carnea to provide good foliage colours from gold to the deep green that is almost black in E.c. 'Vivellii'. 'Foxhollow' is strong with golden-yellow foliage, tipped orange in spring. 'Eileen Porter' is early: its red and pink flowers will be opening this month.

Again autumn highlights some of those plants that look good through the year but tend to be taken for granted. Now they can come into their own. The sedges are a fine example. Carex oshimensis 'Evergold' makes tufts 15-20cm (6-8in) high and arching as wide with leaves brilliant gold, edged with green. Dwarf forms of Carex buchananii may only reach 10cm (4in) high and wide, with narrow copper-bronze leaves. There are dozens of others from which to choose.

tasks

FOR THE

month

SEEDS FOR SOWING

Allium various
Alyssoides utriculata
Alyssum various
Anthyllis various
Calceolaria biflora
Gentiana various – they
germinate more freely after
frosting – including:
*G. corymbifera, G. gracilipes,
G. kurroo, G. septemfida
Lilium formosanum pricei
L. mackliniae
L. nanum
Lobelia angulata* (syn. *Pratia*)
*Paris polyphylla
P. quadrifolia
Primula* various as soon
as seed ripens
*P. clusiana
P. frondosa
P. secundiflora
Scutellaria alpina
Trifolium* various
Viola various

PAGES 98–9
*The robust Persicaria affinis
'Donald Lowndes' is an eye-
catching plant which flowers well
throughout summer and autumn*
(see p.102)

<cb> C H E C K L I S T

☐ Frost and winter protection outside
☐ Pruning
☐ Pond care
☐ Seed sowing
☐ Potting up rooted cuttings
☐ Alpine-house hygiene

FROST AND WINTER PROTECTION OUTSIDE

The majority of alpines are not strangers to cold, but in their natural habitats they often have the benefit of a thick blanket of insulating snow and are not usually subjected to excessive amounts of free water in the winter months. Attention for these is directed towards lessening the effects of persistent wet in soil, particularly around the necks of plants. Many mountain plants need little or no extra care – provided soils are well-drained.

Often the plants that need looking after more carefully are not truly mountain dwellers but ones adapted to rather hot dry conditions. Some with silver foliage from Mediterranean-type climates appear to be silvery because of the layer of silken hairs that reflect the light and are an aid to conserving the plant's moisture. The hairiness can work against them in wet winters by becoming saturated, which encourages rotting.

Protective measures are:
■ Ensure perfect drainage around the neck and below the cushion of foliage. This may mean renewing the gritty top layer of the soil
■ Removing any loose detritus around the plant and any dead foliage
■ Plants that die down to a resting bud and which may be vulnerable to persistent cold can be covered with grit and/or dead bracken
■ For herbaceous plants that die down completely a square of polythene can be used for protection but must be watched for condensation if used over plants with persistent leaves. Anchor it with grit
■ Those plants with winter-persistent foliage are better protected by a sheet of glass securely fixed over them some 5cm (2in) clear of the topmost leaves. As the glass is to remain for some months use strong wires to hold it in place and make sure they are firmly embedded. For even more security position a rock or brick on the lower end of the glass. Run a wire tie from this, over the top of the propped sheet and tie it to a similar brick or rock on the other side. In areas where there will be plenty of testing wind, ties running at right angles across the glass might be prudent
■ Small flat-topped cloches may also be used. Avoid tent-shaped cloches with a gap at the top which will allow wet to drip over plants

*Dead bracken can be used a
protection against frost for plants
that die down to a resting bud*

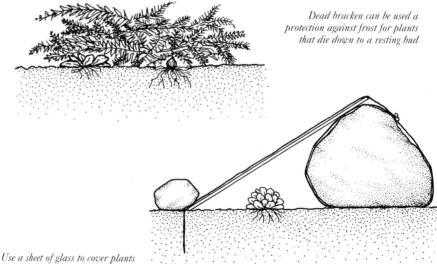

*Use a sheet of glass to cover plants
with winter-persistent foliage*

You may wish to consider whether any such plants should be outside for the winter as these protective arrangements do not add to the attractiveness of the rock garden. The plants might be better in a frame or alpine house

PRUNING

Pruning rock garden plants? It may seem odd but it makes sense to wander round the rock garden and check plants to see if a surgeon's knife is needed. Some exuberant specimens may need cutting back, while others may just need stray pieces trimming to make a better shape. Shrubby or sub-shrubby plants may have damaged branches that need cutting away. Although heathers are often better for a haircut they are normally dealt with later – the winter-flowering ones in spring, and the summer-flowering ones later in the winter.

POND CARE

At this time of year the pond seems to attract fallen leaves like a magnet and these will eventually poison the water. With a small pond a regular clearing of rubbish will not take more than a few seconds. A few leaves do not matter but substantial numbers can cause trouble. A child's fishing net will make a useful tool to collect sodden . leaves from the water. Although spreading net over the surface of the pond may seem a thorough job it looks unsightly and it is a danger to any frogs and to birds coming for a drink.

Towards the end of the month waterlilies and other aquatic plants gradually cease any lively activity. Dead foliage can be removed if necessary, but the rusty brown leaves of some irises, sedges

and other plants can still look attractive and provide wildlife with a better environment.

SEED SOWING

While late winter or early spring is traditionally the time that most seeds are sown, it can be an advantage to get some in now to save time later and to ensure that seed which loses its vitality quickly is in the right place – the soil. There are also some seeds that need the action of one or two frosts to trigger their germination.
- Sow in pots of John Innes seed compost or any other proprietary mix
- Label carefully and place outside, or in a cold frame or alpine/greenhouse
- When any germinating activity starts pots may be brought from outside under glass
- Don't discard pots too quickly; while most seed will have germinated by the spring, there are some seeds that may take two or even three seasons!
- Pack unused seed in an airtight container and keep in the refrigerator until required

POTTING UP ROOTED CUTTINGS

If you have cuttings that have rooted by the beginning of the month they are best carefully potted up.
- Gently prise the cutting from the rooting medium
- Using the compost recommended earlier (p12) tuck the plants into small pots

- Add a layer of grit to the soil surface, water and be particularly careful to keep moist – not sodden – for the next few weeks
- Towards the end of the month it may be prudent to leave any more recently-rooted cuttings *in situ* until the end of the winter. They are not going to be growing very actively until then. The lightest dusting of a general fertiliser easily meets any nourishment needs they have

ALPINE-HOUSE HYGIENE

The alpine house can collect pests and diseases although not so easily as the greenhouse. Clean cultivation and clean habits will help to ensure that there are fewer places for pests and diseases to lodge. Follow this cleansing routine:
- Wash inside all glass and rub down struts
- Thoroughly clean glass outside and stop any build-up of algae
- Clear pots and bench tops of fallen leaves and other debris
- Wash below benches and up walls and check and tidy any stored material
- Wash the pathway
- If there is evidence of pests or fungus, cover the plants with sheets of polythene while the house is sprayed with pesticides and fungicides. The plants are covered so that excessive moisture is not allowed on them; if need be they can be given a light spray when the polythene sheet is removed

Carefully pot up rooted cuttings into individual containers

AUTUMN TIDYING
Remain ever vigilant against leaf and detritus litter among the rock garden population.

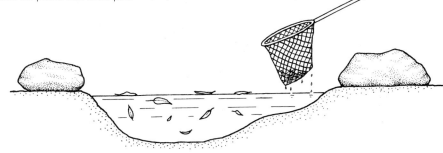

plants
OF THE
month

STERNBERGIA
(Sternbergia lutea)

This species is the leading garden member of a small bulbous genus, allied to daffodils although the flowers look like crocuses.

type	Bulb
foliage	Strap-like, dark green leaves, rather like small daffodils, appearing before the flowers
flowers	Crocus-like, very bright golden-yellow, flowers low to the ground in autumn
height	7–15cm (3–6in)
spread	7–10cm (3–4in)
planting	Early autumn. 10cm (4in) deep
site	Warm, well-drained spot that gets summer sun to 'ripen' bulbs. Perhaps at base of a warm rock, facing the sun, where it will flower earlier
soil	Not fussy but good on chalk
care	Given the site recommended, bulbs grow easily and thrive on neglect. Do not allow their sites to become too overgrown in summer; the bulbs are best 'baked'
propagation	Easiest by normal bulb division. Lift after a few years and divide clumps in summer
relatives	*S. sicula* is probably only a variety of *S. lutea* with narrower leaves but is possibly more free-flowering than some clones of the type. *S. candida* is a choice late winter-flowering species with snow-white flowers

KNOTWEED
(Persicaria affinis,
syn. *Polygonum affine)*

The species featured is one of the easiest rock garden plants; relatives can be useful border and bog plants while some are wretched weeds (illus, p. 98-9).

type	Mat-forming perennial
foliage	Oval, shiny, dark green leaves that turn warm rusty-brown for winter, stems are pressed to ground so the plentiful foliage makes a thick carpet
flowers	Individual flowers are small and pink, but many are gathered in poker spikes and are red in bud. Flowers through summer and probably through autumn as well
height	15cm (6in)
spread	75cm (30in)
planting	Anytime
site	Rock garden, edge of scree, between paving – anywhere that its widespread hardy cover can be accommodated without crushing less extrovert plants
soil	Not fussy
care	So easy you will soon be giving it away or using it on awkward banks and 'waste' areas
propagation	Remove rooted pieces in early spring or early autumn
relatives	*P.a.* 'Donald Lowndes' is one of the most robust clones. *P. vacciniifolia* is similar but very much smaller in leaf and flower, which may be preferred in a smaller rock garden. It is still a strong, spreading, low plant

STERNBERGIA LUTEA

COPROSMA
(*Coprosma* 'Indigo Lustre')

Coprosmas are interesting fruiting and foliage plants from New Zealand. They are not fully hardy but can be grown successfully in pots. Two plants are required to produce berries – one of each sex.

type	Prostrate, mat-forming, evergreen shrub. This hybrid is female, the species plants are either male or female
foliage	Small, very narrow, lanceolate, dark green leaves
flowers & fruit	Late spring flowers are minute and make little impact, but when fertilised by a male plant, freely develop into highly-decorative autumn fruits. These are shining, translucent, ovoid berries – like pearls – veined and flushed with blue, a colour that strengthens with age becoming deep blue purple
height	7–9cm (3–3¹/₂in)
spread	30–45cm (12–18in)
planting	When obtained
site	Best not in full sun
soil	Well-drained, acid
care	On borderline of hardiness. To ensure fruiting display, pollen needs transferring from a male plant of *C. petriei, C. brunnea* or similar species and dusting over the tiny flowers when they open. Males produce plenty of pollen
propagation	Cuttings and layering in late summer
relatives	This plant is a seedling from 'Blue Pearls' which was itself from *C. petriei × C. brunnea.* The hybrids are more satisfactory plants than the parents, though these are also attractive

CROCUS
(*Crocus goulimyi*)

There are crocuses of one kind or another in bloom from early autumn till mid-spring – more than half the year. It is surprising that more is not made of them especially as this is a period when we can be starved of flowers.

type	Hardy corm
foliage	Typical narrow crocus leaves, dark green with central silvery strips. Unlike most naked autumn-blooming crocuses, these appear

COPROSMA 'INDIGO LUSTRE'

with the flowers in autumn

flowers	Clean-cut more or less uniform, soft lilac or pinky-mauve flowers, with white throats, sometimes the inner three segments are a half shade paler than the outer three. Pale long tubes holding flowers produce a light floating effect. Mid-autumn
height	8–10cm (3–4in)
spread	4–8cm (2–3in)
planting	Late summer or earlier if you have your own corms. Depths 5–8cm (2–3in)
site	Best in a well-drained sunny spot in the rock garden, scree, in pots or the bulb frame
soil	Not fussy, provided it has good drainage
propagation	Corms will double or treble their number each season. Lift as soon as foliage has died down, split and replant immediately
relatives	*C. speciosus* has larger, heavier flowers in rich lilac, purple or white. *C. kotschyanus* (syn. *C. zonatus*) may open a few days earlier than *C. goulimyi* and is lilac-pink, with a golden throat and white stamens. It is best in a somewhat cooler, moister spot where it will increase rapidly. These species wait till spring to produce leaves

CROCUS GOULIMYI

practical
project

PAVED AND
GRAVELLED AREAS

LIME-HATING PLANTS

Achillea moschata
A. nana
Androsace carnea
A. hedraeantha
A. imbricata
A. obtusifolia
Calluna vulgaris
Campanula excisa
Cassiope all
Dianthus glacialis
D. microlepis
Dicentra cucullaria
D. eximia
Douglasia all
Erica, except *E. carnea* and
E. erigena and *E.* × *darleyensis*
forms
Gentiana sino-ornata
G. Asiatic hybrids
Haplopappus brandegeei, syn.
Erigeron aureus
Helichrysum frigidum
Houstonia various
Leucanthemopsis alpinum
Lewisia all
Lithodora diffusa
Lychnis alpina
Penstemon various
Potentilla aurea
(contd right)

Paving and gravel and their planting are often an important element in the garden.

GRASS VERSUS PAVING OR GRAVEL

Grass as lawn has been a hugely important part of garden design for centuries, it will be for more centuries, but it is not a necessary element in the small scale gardens that are becoming more numerous every year. In these small gardens it just does not make sense to use precious square metres/yards on grass which then demands a mowing machine, and then there is the problem of housing this machine.

Judged on a severely practical level, properly laid paving wins as an all-weather surface, it can be safer underfoot and is much cheaper in the long run; maintenance is minimal. Gravel is cheaper than paving and lends itself to formal and informal use.

It can be restricted by firm margins of curbs, bricks, boards or manufactured edgings or used in sweeping masses, echoing a dried-up river bed, with the occasional decorative large rounded boulder, shrub, or strong perennial. It can also be used as the background material for an informal pathway of stepping stones providing a very good contrast to the growing plants.

Judged aesthetically grass has colour in its favour, but paving or gravel can be planted up with small alpines that will make it lively and of more varied interest than grass.

PREPARATORY WORK

Having made the decision to lay paving and/or gravel there are four main considerations – costs, appearance, safety and maintenance.

Costs

Covering a given area with paving stones is several times more expensive than laying gravel to a 7–10cm (3–4in) depth, but in the long run paving is far cheaper than lawn. Genuine York stone has become extortionately expensive, so it is sensible to use imitation stone blocks, which are now manufactured to a high standard and wear and weather well.

Washed pea gravel and larger grades are not normally expensive, especially if you have a locally-produced supply; it is much cheaper from the producers than bought in small quantities from garden centres.

Appearance

Manufactured blocks that mimic worn natural stone are visually almost on a par with the genuine article. Where a considerable area is to be laid out, perhaps a patio, a terrace or a wide path, the worn natural stone appearance is very much more pleasing in the garden than the completely flat paving stones of the kind used in public streets.

Gravel is not a uniform product. Some garden centres show over a dozen different kinds with fancy colours and names. If your most locally-produced product is a pleasing mix of colours you are in luck and will not be involved in the charge for extra cartage. It makes sense to bring a small quantity home and lay it down to view it *in situ* and to take account of its colouring both wet and dry.

Safety and maintenance

So long as it is not wet for long periods, well-laid paving is one of the safest walking surfaces. Imitation stone slabs are very much easier to lay than the genuine article as their bases are flat and this can make them more secure and safe. Gravel laid over a drained hardcore base runs the paving a close second.

Maintenance is merely a matter of keeping paving or gravel free of weed by hand weeding or spot spraying. Gravel can be raked occasionally or topped-up as needed.

SITE

The plan is to lay an attractive area of slabs or gravel that may be walked upon easily and also provide the home for a series of small plants. Therefore one of the first considerations is the state of the soil. It must be well drained; the paths must not be subject to standing damp and if soaked by rain should dry out quickly. Sodden or very heavy soils must be lightened with the introduction of plenty of grit and gravel and drained with land drains to lower ground, sumps or drains. Trenches dug from the area away to low ground and half-filled with rubble covered with plastic netting before refilling may also serve.

LAYING STONES AND GRAVEL

▪ Decide whether you are going to use paving alone, paving with gravel and margins, gravel alone, or gravel with stepping stones
▪ Clearly mark the area to be covered, using string or hosepiping. Leave this for a day or two, coming back at intervals to see whether

ADVANTAGES OF GRAVEL

- *An all-weather surface that looks attractive*
- *Weed is contained very easily*
- *It makes a quick-drying walking area*
- *It can be easily topped up when necessary*
- *It acts as a good contrast to the plants*
- *Where it is laid around plants it works as a mulch, keeping roots cool and moist*

you still like it, whether it gets enough sunshine, and whether modifications are needed
- Decide on the margins (see below)
- Take off turf or the top few centimetres/inches of soil
- Excavate further if extra drainage is required
- Rake level so that the completed area will be more or less flush with the surroundings or just a bit proud of them. If near the house, a slight camber from the house will take rain water away
- If the area is going to take a lot of traffic, a hardcore base needs laying and ramming hard before spreading sand, but a patio or terrace of modest proportions is not likely to be bearing heavy traffic

Paving
- Cover area with 5–6cm (2–2¹/₂in) of washed sand as a base for paving stones
- Paving stones can be laid flat quite easily on the sand without any wobbling. A full trowel of mortar at each corner will assist stability

Gravel
- If laying gravel over all, excavate 10–12cm (4–5in) and introduce hardcore which can be rolled flat and compressed
- Pea gravel can be used to a depth of approximately 8cm (3in)

MARGINS

Paved areas usually look best if they have clearly defined margins, even if these are subsequently softened with some plant growth over the edges. The margin could be just the clean smart edge of paving but might be given extra emphasis with a row of bricks or imitation Victorian terracotta rope edging.

Wide areas of gravel can merge more softly into the garden borders. Some plants grow well within the gravel and they will help link the growing area with the promenading area.

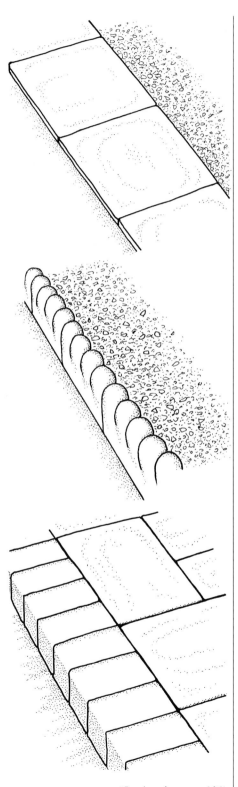

(Continued on page 106)

LIME-HATING PLANTS

Continued:
Pulsatilla alpina
P. vernalis
Saponaria pumilio
Saxifraga cortusifolia
S. cotyledon
S. lilacina
Sempervivum montanum
S. wulfenii

PLANTS TOLERANT OF OR NEEDING LIME

Achillea ageratifolia
A. clavennae
Acantholimon all
Acanthus all
Adonis, except **A. brevistyla, A. pyrenaica**
Aethionema all
Alopecurus lanatus
Androsace lactea
A. chamaejasme
Aubrieta all
Callianthemum kernerianum
C. rutifolium, syn. **C. anemonoides**
Carlina all
Cyclamen all
Cypripedium calceolus
Dianthus all except **D. glacialis, D. microlepis**
Dryas octopetala
Gentiana clusii
G. dinarica
Globularia all
Gypsophila all
Haberlea all
Hepatica all
Leontopodium all
Potentilla nitida
Primula auricula
P. clusiana
P. marginata
Pulsatilla all, except **P. vernalis, P. alpina**
Saxifraga except those on lime-haters list. It is important to have lime for lime-encrusted species

practical
project

PAVED AND GRAVELLED AREAS

continued

KEY
(to illustration on this page)

1 Thymus
2 Sedge
3 Siyrinchium graminoides
4 Dianthus alpinus
5 Armeria pseudarmeria
6 Thymus
7 Dianthus alpinus
8 Sedum lydium
9 Campanula cochleariifolia
10 Sedge
11 Sempervivum tectorum
12 Sedum

KEY
(to illustration on page 107)

1 Juniperus procumbens
2 Iris tectorum
3 Dianthus
4 Iris tectorum
5 Juniperus scopulrum
6 Hebe cupressoides 'Boughton Dome'
7 Dianthus
8 Convolvulus sabatius
9 Hosta
10 Convolvulus sabatius
11 Dianthus

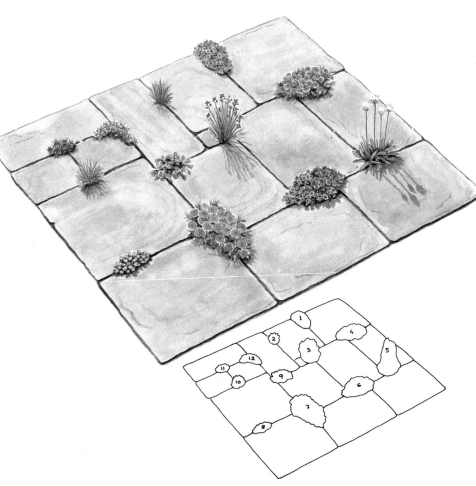

Wide areas of gravel can merge more softly into the garden borders. Some plants grow well within the gravel and they will help link the growing area with the promenading area.

PLANTING

Paved areas in constant use can be planted with some creeping thyme but even this will not put up with unrelieved trampling. With wide areas of paving a selection of the plants listed in the margins can be tried and an occasional gap can be left for a slightly larger plant, perhaps hebe or dwarf lavender.

Wide areas of gravel in warmer climes are not tortured by clinging wet after rainfall. Some of the smaller-leaved bulbous plants also flourish in gravel and may end up seedling themselves. They will help to give a seasonal flavour to the scene.

For anyone with a preference for simple sculptural artefacts, areas of gravel or paving could be the ideal background. Bird baths and sundials or even a living sculpture, in the form of a trimmed bush either growing through gravel or installed in a substantial container, can be very effective. One, or perhaps two, large planted containers or trough gardens will form a focal point.

Position a few evergreen shrubs in larger areas of gravel. *Brachyglottis* 'Sunshine', with silvery foliage, will look right but you need some darker green plants to contrast with the gravel, for example cistus species and hybrids can look very effective. Pinks, flaxes, poppies and helichrysums also look well growing in gravel, and there are many other plants suggested in the margins. Daisy-flowered species such as *Anthemis* and *Erigeron* are effective, but you can also afford to start a small collection of sempervivums and sedums here. It could be one of the most effective parts of the garden.

PLANTS FOR PAVED AREAS

Acaena affinis
A. microphylla
A. novae-zelandiae
Antennaria dioica
Anthemis biebersteinii
A. nobilis (Chamomile)
Arenaria balearica
A. montana
Campanula various small kinds
including:
C. cochleariifolia
C. pulla
Cotula squalida
Cymbalaria aequitriloba
C. hepaticifolia
Dianthus various small pinks
Erinus alpinus
Erysimum linifolium
Euphorbia myrsinites
Frankenia thymifolia
Globularia various
Gypsophila cerastioides
G. repens
Helichrysum various
Hieraceum villosum
Iberis sempervirens
Linaria alpina
Lithodora diffusa
Lychnis alpina
L. flos-jovis 'Nana'
Mentha requienii
Minuartia stellata
M. verna
Oenothera acaulis
Papaver alpinum
Polygonum affine, syn. *Persicaria*
affinis
P. vacciniifolium
Sagina glabra 'Aurea'
Saxifraga various
Sedum various dwarfs
Sempervivum many
Thymus serpyllum forms

NOVEMBER

*Even this late in the year there may still be a bit of colour outside.
Look for flowers on* Gentiana sino-ornata *and the small* Allium
callimischon, *which has been in bloom since early autumn, is not
giving up yet although a second lot in a pot are more comfortably
enjoyed in the alpine house.* Allium callimischon *is an unusual plant.
Its leaves grow in the autumn, a flowering stem of 8-30cm (3-12in) is
produced in the spring and appears to waste away with the leaves, but
it comes back to life in the autumn to produce clusters of white bells
with chestnut veining..*

*Plants flowering in the alpine house or in the bulb frames will be
perfectly hardy and are responding to autumn waterings – the
equivalent of the end of the summer droughts in their native haunts.
The benefit of the cover is that we can inspect these beauties in comfort
and the flowers last much longer without damage. The winter-
flowering hoop-petticoat daffodils from the Atlas mountains and
southern Spain are a great joy. Hybrids between* Narcissus romieuxii
and N. cantabricus foliosus *open in succession with a mass of pale
cream and white flowers. 'Nylon' is the name under which several
similar clones are offered; they flower now and carry on well into the
winter.*

Most gardeners tend to bracket Crocuses *with spring. If crocuses are
in bloom can spring be far behind? But the alpine enthusiast knows
there are plenty of autumn and winter crocuses. The most robust,* C.
speciosus, *made a brave show last month and is still here for part of
this. The same applies to the sturdy little* C. ochroleucus *with white
flowers opening to show a yellow throat.* C. tournefortii *from Greece
blooms now, its soft lilac-blue flowers with very showy much-divided
brilliant orange stigmas and white anthers. It produces leaves
alongside the flowers so is a real autumn-winter treat. And there are
many others.*

tasks
FOR THE
month

LATE AUTUMN FLOWERS OUTSIDE

Calluna vulgaris forms, such as
'H. E. Beale'
Crocus banaticus
C. goulimyi
C. laevigatus
C. niveus
C. ochroleucus
C. tournefortii
Cyclamen hederifolium
Daboecia forms
Epilobium canum, syn.
Zauschneria californica
Erica carnea forms
E. × darleyensis forms
Galanthus reginae-olgae
Parochetus communis
Persicaria affinis
Sedum cauticola
S. sieboldii

◄ *PAGES 108–9*
The vibrant, deep blue blur of
Gentiana sino-ornata
(see p. 82)

SEED LISTS AND CATALOGUES

The making of lists seems to be an almost universal pleasure and certainly one in which most gardeners indulge. We make lengthening columns of plants and seeds that we woud like to try. Then add up the cost and start again. This does help to focus attention on to some special project – to start a collection of a particular type of plant, maybe. New seed lists begin to be sent out now from commercial sources; later specialist societies circulate theirs to members. One of the most valuable features of many of these societies is to publish a list of seed available, usually only for the cost of distribution.

Society seed lists depend on the members saving seed, cleaning and labelling it and sending it in to the society in good time. To encourage members to do this, those who donate seed are usually allowed to choose extra packets so it is a good idea to join in this activity. One major advantage of society lists is that you will have a choice of seed of plants that are rarely offered for sale.

It can be an exciting time making a list. Once you have decided what you want, do get your order sent away quickly. In the case of specialist societies there may be only limited amounts of some of the choicer items and requests are usually dealt with on a first-come first-served basis.

The large commercial seed houses may have some alpines but usually these are left to more specialist firms whose names and addresses are found in the pages of the magazines published by national and international societies as well as commercial magazines.

Plant catalogues are likely to follow seed lists. They are in preparation in the summer and autumn and usually published in the winter so that they list all the plants available for the late-winter early-spring rush of orders as well as the later ones through the year. The expense of producing these catalogues and posting them is often very heavy so the modest price that some firms charge is understandable and, besides, is often recoverable with your order. There is often a rich vein of information to be mined from these publications.

UNDER GLASS

Plant hygiene

Under glass the atmosphere is likely to be less buoyant for the next few weeks and months (see Ventilation). Condensation on glass and lack of air movement could make conditions less crisp and encourage mildew and other fungus types that still work in the lower temperatures. Combat this by quickly removing any leaves or parts of plants that may have rotted and using a fine spray to treat the surrounding parts to a mist of fungicide.

Apart from opening vents there is little that can be done to improve air circulation unless an electric fan heater is used with the thermostat turned down.

Watering

During the coming weeks transpiration and evaporation is not massive, but nevertheless there is a continual loss which must be made good. For pots sunken in a plunge bed or standing on capillary mats or beds the supply of water should be easily maintained; the pots will be taking up moisture as they need it. However, it is as well to check pots on a random basis as it is easy to be deceived into thinking that a surface is moist when in fact something close to drought conditions pertains. Some plants in a specially gritty soil mix may well need extra water.

The range of plants that are more active now includes dwarf bulbs, and they can be given plenty of water provided that drainage is good. Miniature narcissi, especially, are very active now and will even manage a dilute liquid fertiliser to encourage fattened bulbs and quicker increase. A high potash tomato fertiliser usually proves beneficial and while you have some mixed the other growing bulbs will enjoy a boost.

Ventilation

Under glass it is important to maintain as airy an atmosphere as possible. All vents could still be fully open, in fact; unless you are growing frost-tender plants, the vents can be kept open all the time. When gales are forecast the side vents could be closed to stop everything inside being blown to bits. Ensure all vents have safe catches so that they do not bang about, resulting in broken glass on plants and benches. If particularly powerful gales and rain are due it is advisable to close the roof vents to prevent rain being driven in and to keep all secure; for a limited time all vents and doors could be closed – it could be dangerous to have one entrance for wind without a parallel exit.

In periods of severe cold a battening down of the hatches is also advisable so that electrical heating triggered by the thermostat is not going straight out of the vents.

CARE OF WINTER FLOWERS OUTSIDE

Most winter blossom outside will look after itself, but there are a few improvements that can be made. If your rock garden is on a sufficient scale to allow you a clump of *Iris unguicularis*, this is often made more pleasing by removal of the old brown foliage – cut, not pulled: only the oldest dead leaves come away with a tug.

Although too large for the rock garden proper, the periphery may have clumps of hellebores of *H. orientalis* breeding coming into bloom any time from mid-autumn onwards, well into spring. They can look better if old foliage is cut away and this helps prevent the spread of leaf diseases that may build up if you have a number of hellebores. *H. niger*, the Christmas rose, comes in clones that all behave differently – some blooming mid- to late winter but some starting now. Keep the flowers clean by ensuring that the surrounding surface is clean grit, not soil.

OUTSIDE FOLIAGE EFFECTS

Foliage can be used to provide colour and interest through

the autumn and winter. Some of the winter-flowering heathers take on especially good leaf colourings as cooler weather arrives. *Erica carnea* 'Foxhollow', growing to about 15cm (6in) high, is a neat plant with golden foliage that becomes tinged with red through the winter. 'Ann Sparkes', 8cm (3¹⁄₂in), is orangey-yellow with red tips in the winter. 'Westwood Yellow', 15cm (6in), is shining yellow at all times but seems more luminous now through the darker days. Some of the tiny grasses and sedges are splendid now. *Carex*

buchananii makes tufts of very narrow leaves of a copper-bronze colour. While usually up to 50cm (20in) high, there are smaller clones making attractive little tufts sometimes as little as 5–7cm (2–3in) high. *Carex oshimensis* 'Evergold' is a popular plant with arching tufts 15–20cm (6–8in) high of leaves brilliantly striped in gold. A collection of these very easy colourful sedges is easily accommodated in corners and adds very considerably to the effect in winter – as well as at other times.

Parochetus communis

Cyclamen hederifolium album

Erica carnea 'December Red'

AUTUMN AND WINTER FOLIAGE

Asplenium ceterach, miniature green fern
A. trichomanes, small evergreen, dark green fern
Carex buchananii, thin-leaved, evergreen, copper sedge
C. firma 'Variegata', green and gold, evergreen sedge
Erica carnea 'Foxhollow'
E. c. 'Westwood Yellow', dark golden-foliaged heather
Gaultheria procumbens, polished green turning red in winter
Hedera helix 'Congesta', miniature ivy, dark green with paler veining
Saxifraga moschata 'Cloth of Gold', mossy, golden foliage
Sedum spathulifolium, silvery-grey suffused mauvey-red
Sempervivum all, greens, reds and purples

SILVER-LEAVED PLANTS

Artemisia schmidtiana 'Nana', ferny, silver-green foliage
Celmisia coriacea, evergreen rosette of silver swords
Helichrysum coralloides, evergreen, dark green and silver leaves
Leucogenes grandiceps, neat evergreen silver leaves with hairs
Raoulia australis, evergreen, ground-hugging carpet of tiny grey-green leaves
Raoulia hookeri albo-sericea, evergreen rosettes of tiny round silver leaves
Tanacetum argenteum, evergreen, precisely-cut, bright silver foliage
Tanacetum densum amani, evergreen, ferny, silver-grey foliage

plants
OF THE
month

SHORTIA
(Shortia uniflora)

This genus is composed of evergreen woodland plants from North America and Japan. They are all desirable classy items worth taking some trouble to keep happy.

type	Evergreen perennial, steadily making wide mats
foliage	Tough, rounded, serrated, glossy dark green leaves, taking on red shades in winter
flowers	Borne singly on 15cm (6in) stems in early spring, earlier in pots under glass. There may be a good number of these decoratively fringed, large bells of pale blush-pink
height	8cm (3in)
spread	25cm (10in)
planting	Early spring or early autumn
site	Needs cool and shade. A shady spot in the peat bed is ideal. The roots should not be subjected to any drought
soil	Deep well-drained, humus-rich soil. Leaf-mould is relished
care	Take note of its need for cool, shady conditions and if it gets growing

SHORTIA UNIFLORA

well outside leave it alone. If flowers are produced early and are threatened with frost it is wise to offer a little temporary protection

propagation	Fresh seed when available will germinate but seedlings take time getting to flowering size. Divisions can be made in early spring or after flowering, in early summer, once your plant has got to a size to allow taking a rooted piece away. Remove some of the leaves then pot up carefully in leaf soil and keep moist under shaded glass. Once new roots are being produced and roots and fresh leaves are growing, plant out
relatives	*S. soldanelloides* is a smaller plant of similar character but with very fringed flowers of rich pink

NARCISSUS
(Narcissus cantabricus)

Along with the large-flowered hybrid daffodils, the genus *Narcissus* possesses a number of small species, ideal for the rock garden.

type	Bulb
foliage	Narrow, rush-like upright and then arching leaves
flowers	Wide, white or milk-white crowns with stamens held upwards. Petals are six narrow strips behind the crown, late autumn-early winter
height	8–10cm (3–4in)
spread	5–8cm (2–3in)
planting	Summer or late spring if you have your own bulbs. Depth 5cm (2in)
site	Alpine house or bulb frame to protect flowers from bad weather
soil	Normal soil mix (see p12), good drainage
care	Easy pot plant. Water in early autumn to start bulbs into growth and then keep moist until leaves begin to die back in mid- to late spring. Allow them to dry out then lift, divide and replant immediately
propagation	By division when foliage dies down mid to late spring. Seed is freely produced and, sown as soon as ripe, germinates freely. Seedlings should bloom by third season
relatives	*N.c. foliosus* has somewhat more milk-white, narrower flowers; grows easily. *N. romieuxii* has sulphur-yellow flowers, spun out to wider form. There are hybrids between the

two species. *N.* Nylon is a mixture of white-flowered hybrid clones

GAULTHERIA
(Gaultheria trichophylla)

A genus grown for its evergreen foliage, flowers and fruit; in all these this species distinguishes itself.

type	Low, evergreen shrub, spreading by means of gently creeping underground stems
foliage	Small, tough, shiny, oval leaves
flowers & fruit	Typical bell-shaped ericaceous flowers in pink in early summer. Followed by unusual, attractive, egg-shaped shiny turquoise-blue fruits. Fruits last a considerable while
height	8–15cm (3–6in)
spread	20–25cm (8–10in)
site	Moist, sun or part shade, peat pocket or peat bed
soil	Acid, humus-rich, which does not dry out
care	Not difficult in acid, peaty soils
propagation	Cuttings in summer, or divisions early spring
relatives	*G. procumbens*, probably fastest-grower, is a ground-coverer with white flowers and shining red berries. Leathery, oval leaves turn purple and red in winter. *G. nummularioides* is another tight, neat shrub with tough oval or heart-shaped leaves, globular, white or blush-pink flowers in late spring or early summer, and rather sparse, very dark blue-black berries

RETICULATE WILLOW
(Salix reticulata)

There are over 200 species of willows. They range from giants to scrubby shrubs and some delightful little plants. The smallest is *S. herbacea*, which grows in the Arctic, the Alps and on the tops of some Scottish mountains. Its branches usually run under rocks or just below soil level and poke up just enough to wave a small leaf or two like flags. *S. reticulata* is often a neighbouring plant in the wild but is considerably more noticeable with lovely foliage from firm branches running over the soil's surface. Like other willows, specimens are either male or female. The males have much the showier catkins.

RETICULATE WILLOW

type	Deciduous prostrate shrub
foliage	Round glossy dark green leaves with an impressed network of veins
flowers	Upright catkins in early spring, the females are narrow and green, while the males are bushy and red, turning golden when the stamens display their pollen
height	5–8cm (2–3in)
spread	30cm (12in) or more with branches pressed to the ground
planting	Early spring or anytime
site	Moist cool spot; will grow over moist rock
soil	Not very fussy if moist but probably best in humus-rich soils
care	Easy where soils do not dry out. Aftercare is minimal, only a matter of cutting back pieces needed for propagation or stopping it moving out of its allotted space
propagation	Cut off rooted pieces of branches and grow on
relatives	*S. × boydii* is a hybrid of *S. reticulata* with *S. lanata*. This charming plant is very upright with rounded, grey leaves. A good shrub or small tree for a rock garden

practical project

PLANNING AN EXPEDITION

BOOKS ABOUT HOLIDAY PLANT FINDING
Several good publications are available; a few are listed in the Further Reading section, p142.

One of the joys of rock or alpine gardening, once the bug has got you, is to travel in search of the plants in their native habitats. This is a marvellous opportunity to see the plants in their own setting and gives keen gardeners a chance to increase their understanding of growing habits and cultural requirements.

Should you plan to go on an expedition make sure you go armed with the facts. For example, it is vital to understand fully the conservation aspect. Long gone are the parties of marauding holidaymakers stripping bare the alpine pastures in search of plants for their gardens; today, the seeker of alpine plants is more likely to be armed with a camera than a trowel, and is very careful where he or she places walking boots and tripod. The importance of preservation cannot be overemphasised: we must not deprive future visitors of the enjoyment we experience.

THE ALPS

Switzerland, in particular the area known as the Bernese Oberland, is a good place to start a search for alpine plants. The very comprehensive public transport provisions, including bus, train, cable car, chair lifts and rack railways, can be used in a number of different permutations, offering easy methods of reaching the plants.

Lauterbrunnen is to be recommended as a centre. It is reached via plane to Basle or Zurich, then by train to Interlaken, where you change for BOB – the Bernese-Oberland-Bahn, which speeds you up the valley where the Jungfrau and the Eiger dominate the landscape. The area is rich with flowers such as the Trumpet Gentian, *G. acaulis* and the later-flowering *Campanula barbata*. The higher-growing alpines are found on the slopes of the Schilthorn, where *Androsace alpina*, *Ranunculus glacialis* and *Soldanella* grow. Other treasures in the area include the Alpine Columbine, *Aquilegia alpina* and the Lady's Slipper Orchid, *Cypripedium calceolus*.

Further south, this time in the shadow of the Matterhorn, lies Zermatt, another excellent destination for alpine plant hunters. The speciality of this area is the Queen of the Alps, *Eritrichium nanum*, whose forget-me-not flowers are difficult to register as a true blue on film. Nearby, to the east, is Saas Fee. Until the 1950s, the only method of ascent was by horse; now

shiny charabancs zoom up the new road but, like many Swiss mountain resorts, private vehicles are not allowed. The flora of Saas Fee is similar to that of Zermatt.

Way over in the east is the Engadine, with the Bernina Pass lying to its south as a gateway to Italy; St Moritz is not far away, but the best place to stay is Pontresina. Primulas are abundant in the area and a week here, with another slightly to the north in Arosa, is a very pleasant interlude.

Hopping over the Alps into Italy at the eastern end, there are the lakes, charming in themselves, but back west the Dolomites begin around Cortina, with resorts at the head of most of the valleys providing beautiful scenery and a bounty of plants. In Cervinia, you see the other side of the Matterhorn, and, in fact, if you ski, you can cross over from Zermatt. To the south of Cervinia lies Aosta and south of that is the Gran Paradiso, worth exploration.

Continuing back west and crossing the French border, the Savoy Alps are reached. This area is not as well-endowed with public transport as the Swiss mountains, but from centres like La Grave one can reach Lauteret, where *Eritrichium nanum* can be found again and also *Campanula rupestris* (syn. *C. allionii*), and the Galibier Pass, where *Geum reptans* abounds. Lanslebourg is a useful jumping off point for Val d'Isère, more famed for skiing than plants, but with some plants of interest, one speciality being *Petrocallis pyrenaica*. Nearby is Mont Cenis, which has given its name to a number of species, perhaps the best known being *Campanula cenisia*, happy in a sink or trough.

If you like orchids, then the Dordogne region is rewarding. If it is your desire to see *Primula allionii*, then visit the Alpes Maritimes in May.

THE PYRENEES, SPAIN AND PORTUGAL

On the border between Spain and France lie the Pyrenees, which possess a very rich and varied flora. Gavarnie is a recommended venue, but it is rather crowded with pilgrims from Lourdes, so on the French side quieter resorts are favoured both east and west.

Crossing over into Spain, the climate changes to drier and warmer, with an altered flora. There are several pockets of alpine interest in Spain and Portugal, particularly if you are interested in dwarf *Narcissus*. For these you have to go early in the year, even as soon as February. Further south in Spain, the Sierra Nevada has its own flora, with one or two interesting violas to tempt you. *Viola cazorlensis* is a beauty. Andalucia has enough flowers for a book to have been devoted to it (*Andalusian Flowers and Countryside*, Lt. Cdr. C.M. Stocken DSC. RN, 1969, now out-of-print) and the Picos de Europa to the north-west is a popular destination. In Portugal, the Algarve makes the bulb enthusiasts happy.

FORMER YUGOSLAVIA AND GREECE

Tragically, at the time of writing, former Yugoslavia is a no-go area. But in its mountains there are many plants that have attracted plant hunters in the past. Of them possibly *Campanula zoysii*, with its strange blue flowers is the most outstanding. It also happens to be quite easily grown in a trough.

For those in search of bulbs or orchids, the Mediterranean islands offer a veritable feast, almost all the year round. Greece in autumn is a dream, particularly in the Peloponnese, where cyclamen and crocus abound.

OTHER DESTINATIONS

The Rocky Mountains of Central USA, the Canadian Rockies along the border, and the Cascade Mountains of Washington offer an easy way of seeing wild flowers, while enjoying the advantages of decent roads and comfortable lodgings. Lilies and Lady's Slipper Orchids are easily found and sometimes acres of colour can be seen.

A Himalayan trek might appeal to the really adventurous. For those who are able to spare four weeks and who are prepared to walk a hundred miles up, say, the Marsyandi Valley in Nepal, and then walk a hundred miles back again, this is the holiday for you. Timing is all important and, unfortunately, the peak time for flowers falls within the monsoon period of July and August. These trips are not for the faint-hearted.

The Drakensberg Mountains of South Africa, whence a number of now widely grown alpine plants have emanated, are well worth a visit at the beginning of the

CONSIDERATIONS

Simple and reasonable preparations will enhance your enjoyment of the mountains and their floral treasures.

GUIDED OR DIY?

Unless you are an experienced traveller, with a thorough knowledge of the area to which you are going, it is prudent to go with an organised group. There are many tour operators who specialise in field trips and study holidays. The Alpine Garden Society run holidays each year and these are led by experts who have a knowledge both of the plants and the locations.

READING AROUND THE SUBJECT

Before booking up, it is as well to read carefully about each trip. Some can be quite arduous so make sure your health and fitness are up to the challenge. Be sure that you are prepared to go out in all conditions, or that there are alternative activities on 'days off' if required.

CHOOSING AN AREA

Check that the destination you choose has the flora you are interested in and offers the exploration opportunities you require. It is hopeless to go to one place if you are interested in alpines or plants that are indigenous to another.

WHAT TO TAKE

Clothing should range from light and airy to warm pullovers and windcheaters. You must take your own medication if you need it. Above all sensible footwear is essential – boots that have been thoroughly worn-in, not bought a week beforehand.
As the plants are to be looked at but not removed, take your camera, or perhaps borrow one, to record what you see; if you have a choice of cameras, remember that on steep climbs weight seems to increase, so the lighter it is the better. A good guidebook, both to the area and the flora, will be useful. It is better to get books before travelling, they may be difficult to obtain at your destination and choice will certainly be limited.

WHEN TO GO

In general, a journey to the European mountains should be undertaken from mid-June to August, which is the ultimate time; however, the autumn is pleasant and, where permitted, seed gathering is useful. South Africa offers a pleasant variety of flora in January and February. The peak time to visit the Himalayas is July and August – the monsoon period.

year. Helichrysums are abundant, as is *Rhodohypoxis baurii*, a small tuberous plant in a range of colours from deep pink through to white, tinged pink. And, of course, there are Red Hot Pokers and *Agapanthus* galore.

Further possibilities include Northern Europe, the Kosciusko Mountains in Australia, the Alps of New Zealand, and Japan, not to mention China, Eastern Russia and the Andes in South America.

DECEMBER

The winter rock garden can look well, stripped down to its bare design essentials, the rocks, the evergreens, and the strategically placed mini-trees and shrubs. Rusted vacciniums and tufted small grasses add some colour and there are occasional flowers, some like crocuses belonging to this time but others winking open flowers out of season playing the same ill-fated role as the swallow that failed to make a summer.

Inside the alpine house things are different; all around stirring activity can be seen. There are winter crocuses, Cyclamen coum forms and snowdrops in proper splendour, Reticulata-type irises are ornate. Small daffodil species and miscellaneous bulbs like Scilla and Muscari are moving forward. Other things are stirring too. Pots of Hepatica are showing signs of growth and flowers will not be long coming; Adonis too will soon be minting golden many-petalled buttercup flowers. There is already a potful of the very high-class buttercup, Ranunculus calandrinoides, with silken white flowers just very lightly blushing pink. It should bloom for weeks. As yet its lovely blue-green, undivided leaves like miniature hostas are not in evidence.

The festive season is coming and it is time to think of presents. Gardening friends and relations will enjoy any garden-related item – books, gardening gloves, plants, a packet of useful labels.

In our household it is a bit of tradition to have a vase on the festive table with bits of all the flowering plants from the garden. It is usually a sweet-scented posy with winter-flowering honeysuckles, winter sweet, witch hazel, Viburnum 'Dawn', Mahonia 'Charity' and a host of others. Also I try to have one pan of small things in bloom. More often than not it is one of the hoop-petticoat narcissi – an enchanting picture to contrast with the festive decor.

tasks

FOR THE

month

PLANTS IN THE OPEN THAT MAY NEED PROTECTION

Artemisia glacialis
A. schmidtiana 'Nana'
Celmisia argentea
C. bellidioides
C. coriacea
C. spectabilis
Eriogonum umbellatum
Helichrysum species
Leontopodium alpinum
L. haplophylloides
Meconopsis species
Parochetus communis
Primula edgeworthii
P. reidii
P. scapigera
P. sonchifolia
Soldanella alpina
S. montana
S. pusilla
S. villosa

PAGES 116–17
The ever-popular Cyclamen
coum 'Album' (see p.22)

CHECKLIST

- Winter protection
- Rock garden check
- Alpine house check
- Cleaning pots, tools and tidying
- Catalogues
- Gift ideas
- Societies

WINTER PROTECTION

Most gardeners are keen to have the earliest possible display of flowers outside. Snowdrops, crocuses, winter aconites and cyclamens such as *C. coum* are always popular. So too are the little bulbous irises such as *I. danfordiae* and *I. histrioides* hybrids. Adonis species push up early and so will the lovely hepaticas. In many gardens these early birds can manage perfectly adequately by themselves without any fuss but in harsher climates they may need extra protection, such as cut branches of fir or pine laid over areas where they are due to perform. Done at the beginning of this month the branches should provide a useful amount of cover to deflect a lot of the effect of extreme cold. As soon as the plants start to come into bloom the branches can be taken away. Dry fronds of bracken or other ferns could serve a similar purpose on a smaller scale.

Plants with hairy rosettes such as some of the meconopsis could do with an umbrella through the winter. If not already attended to (see p100) provide protection now. This can be provided by surrounding the plant with a ring of twigs, bracken or pine needles and then laying a piece of glass or better still a sheet of rigid transparent plastic across. It should be large enough to cover the plant comfortably and is prevented from moving by placing a number of stones or brick pieces on top. It is best if the sheet is at somewhat of an angle so that water runs off and it should be held firmly some 5–10cm (2–4in) clear of the leaves.

ROCK GARDEN CHECK

- Look to see that all rocks are secure
- Make sure that there are no places where rainfall has caused the washing away of soil mix or grit from plants. Check the crevices especially. Secure plants that may be loose. Pack in fresh compost and cover with grit
- Take the opportunity to review the grit layer over the rock garden and scree. Soil can build up through the grit and it may be the time to give the whole a face-lift by the addition of a shallow layer all over
- Remove loose leaves and plant debris

- Take a look at all the labels — if you no longer need them remove them, if they are becoming illegible get them rewritten. Make sure they are pushed in firmly at the right position

ALPINE HOUSE CHECK

- Sort all potted plants and remove any that are dead or redundant
- If necessary rearrange pots to give a better visual effect and to have plants that need similar watering requirements in proximity
- Check labels and align them so they can be read easily

- Remove late weeds and where necessary re-top pots with grit

CLEANING POTS, TOOLS AND TIDYING

There may be an accumulation of dirty pots from plants that have gone to new quarters or from seed raising.
- Clean pots/trays
- Discard broken pots, used fertiliser cartons and so on
- Arrange pots/trays by sizes

and shapes so that they are easily taken from stock when wanted later

■ Clean tools – mend or discard broken ones

■ Take unused tools to charity shop

■ Arrange tools as you had meant to keep them throughout year

■ Discard unwanted seed packets

■ Check fertiliser levels and replace any if necessary

■ Check compost reserves so that ingredients can be purchased for mixing a fresh stock

CATALOGUES

Send for any catalogues that you may want to study. In Britain the book 'The Plant Finder' lists the nurseries that grow particular plants and gives details of any catalogue they publish. Specialist alpine nurseries tend to have a common block of plants that they all supply but each is also likely to have quite a number that are less often found; the owner's interests are reflected in the plants grown.

It is not too early to study the catalogues and place an order. The number available of any one plant will be limited, perhaps severely so. If you have an interest in a plant or group of plants that you find difficult to locate in catalogues it may help to list these when requesting catalogues; many nurseries have stocks of plants that are too limited to justify listing in their catalogue.

GIFT IDEAS

Gardeners are relatively easy to please. Suitable presents range from a packet of labels to a planted-up trough garden. Here are some other suggestions:

■ Labels together with a good

indelible pencil

■ Hand tools, such as a trowel or fork, a very narrow trowel for removing deep rooted weeds, tweezers for removing dead foliage from special plants or for using when pollinating flowers

■ Books varying from old treasured titles such as Reginald Farrer's two volume *The English Rock Garden* to the latest glossy coffee table book. See Further Reading page 142

■ Seeds. A few interesting packets of seed will always intrigue the recipient

■ Plants in all sorts and sizes. If you do not know exactly what to get you can always give a gift voucher to be spent at nurseries or garden centres

■ Membership of a garden

society is a long lasting gift for the enthusiast. See below and page 141

SOCIETIES

The alpine garden enthusiast is well served by specialist societies. A list of the main ones is given on page 141. They usually have a regular magazine and some also publish books and pamphlets. They hold shows and provide advice. An annual seed list is eagerly awaited and can be a huge treasure store of all kinds of plants from the relatively easy and common to exceedingly rare specimens. Subscriptions are not high – the seed list alone is a bargain at the cost of joining.

HEATING ALPINE HOUSES

Although many owners do not provide any heating in their alpine houses, some warmth is useful for growing frost-tender plants or to encourage others to grow on without undue checks through the worst weather. Heaters can be set to come on when the temperature falls to within a degree or so of freezing. Except in prolonged severe winters the expense is low and well repaid by the health of the plants.

DWARF FERNS

Adiantum capillus-veneris
A. pedatum
A. venustum
Asplenium adiantum-nigrum
A. ceterach
A. ruta-muraria
A. trichomanes
Athyrium filix-femina 'Congestum'
A. f-f. 'Congestum Cristatum'
A. f-f. 'Frizelliae'
Blechnum penna-marina
B. vulcanicum
Cryptogramma crispa
Dryopteris erythrosora
Polypodium australe
P. a. 'Cambricum'
P. vulgare 'Cornubiense'
Polystichum setiferum
 'Congestum'
P. tsus-simense

plants
OF THE
month

VARIEGATED SEDGE
(Carex firma 'Variegata'*)*

Grasses and sedges are just beginning to creep sufficiently high up the popularity charts to force gardeners to look afresh at their claims for admission into our gardens. There is a wide range of small grasses and sedges of considerable decorative appeal. The evergreen sedges are particularly good. They are usually easy plants and not invasive

type	Evergreen, clump-forming sedge, grown for its bright foliage
foliage	Pointed, arching leaves make tidy tufts that are bright through the year. The centre of the blade is green and is edged by margins of creamy-yellow
flowers	Stems arise with club-shaped spikelets of male flowers at the top and two or three female spikelets below, all brownish. Shy to flower
height	8cm (3in)
spread	8cm (3in)
planting	Early spring or early autumn
site	Rock garden pocket, trough garden, perhaps between paving stones
soil	Moist with some humus, yet well-drained
care	Easy if not allowed to dry out
propagation	Division in early spring
relatives	There are a range of species, many

of which vary in size. *C. buchananii* can be 60cm (24in) tall but there are tiny clones only 7–8cm (3in) high. They all have thin, wiry, copper-coloured leaves

RUSTY-BACK FERN
(Asplenium ceterach, syn. *Ceterach officinarum)*

From a major genus of widely differing ferns, this is a delightful, useful small plant for crevices, between steps, on walls or in troughs.

type	Evergreen dwarf fern
foliage	Fronds, light green above and orange-brown underneath, have looped margins. In times of drought the fronds curl up and look dead until fresh water resurrects them as good as ever
flowers	None
height	10cm (4in)
spread	15cm (6in)
planting	Early spring until early autumn
site	Sunny or part-shaded site
soil	Well-drained soil. Found growing on walls especially in old mortar, will be happy with some lime
care	Remove dead fronds
propagation	Division in spring just as more active growth begins. Has extensive surface roots, try to avoid losing too many. Silvery scales on the frond backs house immature spores, the scales turn orangey when ripe. Spores can be distributed on the surface of a pot of peat/grit mix sterilised a few minutes before with boiling water; cover with clingfilm to protect from moss and other airborne spores
relatives	*Asplenium trichomanes* (Maidenhair spleenwort) has black-stemmed, narrow fronds with pairs of somewhat square pinnae. Height to 15cm (6in), spread 15-30cm (6–12in). Any soils including limy

MINIATURE IVY
(Hedera helix 'Congesta'*)*

Not every alpine enthusiast would include an ivy but, while it is obviously not an 'alpine' plant, this small ivy is useful for keeping the rock garden alive through the winter months and is not rapacious, taking a number of years to reach its given height and spread.

VARIEGATED SEDGE

type   Evergreen sub-shrub
foliage   Typical ivy foliage but in miniature. Tough, good rich green leaves and clustered but neatly and closely held by sturdy branches
flowers   None in my experience
height   30–45cm (12–18in)
spread   45–60cm (18–24in)
planting   Available in pots; plant any time
site   Rock garden corner in sun or shade, in larger trough garden, edge of paving or pathway
soil   Very tolerant, useful in poor soils and sites
propagation   Cuttings summer, or layered pieces
relatives   Most other smaller ivies are very much larger. H. h. 'Conglomerata' is rather similar with small curled leaves. It will scramble over rocks or walls to a height and spread of 1m (3ft) given time

DONDIA
(Hacquetia epipactis)

A monotypic genus, a distinct and classy small member of the Umbelliferae family, which is not normally noted for its daintiness. Useful as one of the late winter and early spring flowers, it is included here as you may be able to find potted plants in time to enjoy them in a few weeks' time.

type   Rhizomatous perennial that forms neat clumps
foliage   Tripartite, rounded leaves appear as flowers fade
flowers   Small, rounded flowerheads of clustered, tiny, lime-yellow or primrose flowers surrounded by wide collars of six or seven, rounded, bright green bracts, in late winter or early spring
height   6cm (2¹/₄in)
spread   15–25cm (6–10in)
planting   Best in spring or early autumn
site   Moist, shaded or semi-shaded spot
soil   Humus-rich
propagation   Careful division in spring after flowering, by seed in autumn, or root cuttings in winter. It really resents root disturbance so seed is best
relatives   None

NOAH'S-ARK TREE
(Juniperis communis 'Compressa'*)*

The juniper genus is one of the most useful

DONDIA

coniferous ones for the gardener and this neat tree is almost an obligatory member of any rock-garden enthusiast's collection.

type   Dwarf, evergreen tree
foliage   Typical blue-green juniper needles, closely-packed
flowers   None
height   75cm (30in), grows approximately 2.5cm (1in) a year
spread   7–15cm (3–6in)
planting   Can be planted any time as is always offered for sale growing in pots
propagation   Take cuttings in early summer, dip in hormone-rooting powder, insert into a grit/peat mix and keep just moist in a shaded propagating frame. Slow but moderately sure rooters
relatives   Other junipers are much larger as columnar or spreading plants. For other dwarf conifers look to the dwarf *Chamaecyparis* such as *C. obtusa* 'Nana Gracilis', a slow-growing variety, eventually reaching 1.5–2m (5–6ft). *C. o.* 'Nana Pyramidalis' is smaller, getting to 60cm (2ft) high and wide after ten years or more

practical project

CREATING SPECIAL COLLECTIONS

A very short time after taking to the cult of alpine growing; favourites will start to capture your extra special interest and then the desire to grow more of a particular group of plants quickly takes hold. Within the immense 'alpine' diversity you may find yourself growing more and more of one type – the collecting bug has claimed another victim. Some expertise within a restricted range may help us appreciate all plants more and there is a lot of fun to be had in perusing specialist interests. Have you seen our aspidistra collection?

GENERA VERSUS GROUPS

The expression of mounting obsession can take many shapes. The most obvious will be to start amassing forms of a particular genus. Alternatively you may find it irresistible to collect groups such as scree dwellers or silver-leaved plants or maybe, like me, you will discover a lifetime's fascination in all things bulbous.

Another manifestation of this desire to focus on particular plants is a concentration on the flora of a particular region. This can be quite absorbing and means that one can build up a collection of quite disparate species, dwarf trees and shrubs together with evergreen perennials, small herbaceous plants and bulbs.

Some floras seem very distinctive: probably due to its relative geographical isolation, New Zealand has a particularly unusual set of plants that are unknown elsewhere, and very close attention has recently been given to the flora of the high mountains of South America: these too have a character of their own, the Himalayas, Japan, and other Far Eastern countries also possess a wealth of fascinating species. One does not need to go to the ends of the earth for interesting groups. you could concentrate on plants of the Pyrenees or the Dolomites; I am determined before long to make a rock garden inhabited by plants only found in Britain.

WARNING

■ *Plants must not be taken from the wild at home or abroad. Seed found when holidaying should not be plundered. While it may not seem too heinous a crime to take a small pod if there are tens of thousands, the rules and regulations of a number of countries forbid its collection, so take care. If it is allowed it should still be done with careful thought – a single pod may suffice for several persons: a whole pod need not be taken as it may be possible to shake a few ripe seeds into a packet or twist of paper. Make sure it is labelled* ■

Viola 'Jackanapes'

Viola 'Irish Molly'

Viola calcarata

Viola 'Maggie Mott'

SOURCES

Finding plants that interest you may mean exploring several fields. Alpine nurseries will often hold collections that make the offerings of garden centres seem rather thin – though it does not do to ignore this ready source. In Britain specialist nurseries are listed in the book The Plant Finder which is constantly being updated and covers almost all plants in commerce in Britain, listing the nurseries growing each. Specialist nurseries publish lists and catalogues but may also have smaller stocks of species that they can supply to the interested person.

Fellow enthusiasts are usually only too pleased to do a little bartering and will exchange information about where certain plants can be obtained. Membership of a specialist society and taking part in its local and national activities will help your social life and discover unexpected plants.

SEED

Societies often publish extensive seed lists available to members. There are also commercial seed collectors and growers in many parts of the world who may advertise in society magazines. Seed is easy to transport and is relatively cheap and is an important potential treasure store, especially once the offerings of nurseries have been exhausted – or maybe before. Sometimes individuals and organisations make special trips to far parts with the idea of collecting seed; the trips are sometimes partially subsidised by enthusiasts who stake a relatively small amount of money in order to have a share of the seed that is collected.

When you have raised your plants from seed they seem especially yours. Labels with names giving collectors numbers mean that you are really deep into the alpine cult. Sometimes only the generic name is given followed by the cryptic 'Sp nova?'

Using seed to select the best forms of a species is very worthwhile and might lead to an interest in hybridising. Some enthusiasts regard this as taboo, but there is always the chance of producing some easier and more attractive cultivars: there are two sides to the argument. *(Continued on page 124)*

SCOPE AND DANGERS OF COLLECTING?

■ *It hardly needs saying that the scope is virtually limitless. But just a short word of warning – specialising is fun but keep it fun; do not become too obsessive and thus be blinded to the beauty of any other very popular or easy alpines. There is no place for snobbery in gardening* ■

SOME COLLECTABLE PLANTS

Primula. Over 1000 forms in commerce, and many other species not commercially available. Their classification runs to thirty sections of which Auricula covers attractive European species and Vernales plants such as cowslip and primrose.

Saxifraga. Around 800 forms in commerce, a varied lot, split into 14 sections. The popular, easy 'mossy' kinds are grouped under the formidable section name Trachyphylloides. A good job there is no need for the gardener to know anything of the botanists' machinations.

Viola. 600 forms in commerce. Many are delightful little hybrids but perhaps for the viola fancier rather than the alpine gardener. Nevertheless a genus with many very attractive species.

Sedum. Nearly 300 kinds in commerce. A genus with an image problem, but even the most expert growers are likely to have some in their garden. There are interesting and beautiful ones that suffer for the reputation of the weedy few.

Sempervivum. Approximately 600 forms in commerce. Succulent plants that are varied in colour, size and a surprising amount in leaf form and texture. Invaluable for holding the fort with their evergreen masses through the months when herbaceous alpines die down. Much used as trough and container plants.

Viola tricolor

Viola odorata

practical project

CREATING SPECIAL COLLECTIONS

continued

The scope for making collections is unlimited. Take care where your eye alights: if you spot sempervivums, be warned that at present there are in commerce 600 forms and another 100 of the closely-related Jovibarbas. On the other hand you might like to hold the national collection of Parochetus or perhaps Galax – you will not need acres: they are genera with a single species. The following review may give some ideas of where to start.

BULBS

There are a lot of alpine growers who have a special relationship with bulbs. One reason is the magic way they grow, out of sight one minute, growing strongly next and always looking newly-minted in bloom. The larger number that bloom in winter and the darker days is another reason for their popularity. Bulbs as a group could be a special interest, or you could refine this to one of the bulbous genera.

Galanthus After some decades of maintaining that a snowdrop is a snowdrop, I am rather shame-facedly beginning to start a collection and even hybridising different forms. Perhaps I shall never get quite to the state of some sharp-eyed aficionados who can see differences between very similar plants and almost approach that finely critical state of seeing two forms when viewing the same flower from different angles! However, there are plenty of species, forms and hybrids to collect and one real benefit will be to extend the snowdrop season to as early as mid-autumn, finishing up in early spring – flowers for six months of the year!

Crocus (Following the usual pattern of including corms under the heading of bulbs.) With over 200 forms in commerce the range is considerable – especially as there are many species not in cultivation and of those that are available there are still other forms of different colours and sizes that are not. Like snowdrops they have the great virtue of blooming from autumn well into the spring. Some species blooming in the middle of the winter are very attractive grown in the alpine house or bulb frame. One corm usually produces more than one replacement corm and can yield three or four. Seed germinates freely and can be grown into flowering corms within two or three years.

Alliums You know your onions? Relatively few growers have taken this diverse genus to heart – 800–1000 species is perhaps a little daunting! However, there are very many mountain species that are tiny and very attractive giving plenty to engage your interest without getting beguiled by the big ones such as *A. giganteum* with stems 80–200cm (30–80in) high.

Allium cyathophorum

Allium caeruleum

Allium moly

| *Fritillaria meleagris* | *Fritillaria cirrhosa* | *Fritillaria pudica* |

COLLECTABLES

Apart from those listed on page 123, these are some of many genera that would form the basis of a fascinating collection:

Allium
Androsace
Anemone
Campanula
Carex
Cassiope
Coprosma
Crocus
Daphne
Dianthus
Diascia
Draba
Fritillaria
Geranium
Gentiana
Hebe
Hepatica
Iris
Narcissus
Origanum
Phlox
Phyteuma
Raoulia
Rhododendron
Thymus

Fritillaries There are a large number of species scattered through the northern hemisphere. Many are small, even smaller than *Fritillaria meleagris*, the snake's head fritillary which is 20–30cm (8–12in) tall, but very slender in stem and leaf. Many are also somewhat tricky and offer the challenge that many growers relish; some are best grown in containers in the alpine house or bulb frame, as much to protect their fascinatingly-coloured flowers as to give them the touch of protection that they may need.

Tulips There are a number of very attractive small or smallish species readily available. These are usually selected clones of the species. If collectors test the boundaries of each species they may find to their satisfaction, or perhaps bewilderment, that the rigid picture of a tulip species hides a potential for wide variation. So wide is this variation that one suspects that the 'tidy' specific names provided by botanists and bulb growers can often be used to label parts of an 'untidy' nature's florally diverse single species. Confusing, fascinating and always attractive in growth and bloom. Collected seed may still reveal further species as yet unnamed.

FERNS

There are a large number of small ferns, both deciduous and evergreen, that might be grown in various parts of the rock garden or in pots. As a readily recognisable group with a particular character they can make a refreshing change to surrounding plants.

CYCLAMEN

The beauty of these plants is very obvious: flowers and foliage delight. There are plenty of species to give flower from early autumn until spring is well advanced and, even without any flower, a fascinating collection of foliage plants is easily made. Within many species the silver-green patterning of the leaves seems as varied as frost patterns on window panes. There are some species that are somewhat tender; they are worth extra care. The value of the genus is recognised by a cyclamen society (see p141).

GENTIANS

There are some gentians that flourish on limy soils but most of the Asiatic species demand acid conditions so if your soil is of this order you have the chance that many would like of growing a wide collection of species and hybrids of this genus. They are especially lovely from the late summer onwards to winter.

appendix
1

PLANTS FOR A
GRASSY ALPINE LAWN

Primula vulgaris

plant	season	colour	height x spread
Ajuga reptans	spring	blue	10cm (4in) × 60cm (24in)
Alchemilla alpina	summer	lime	15cm (6in) × 30cm (12in)
Anthemis biebersteinii	summer	yellow	22cm (9in) × 45cm (18in)
Anthyllis hermanniae 'Compacta'	summer	yellow	25cm (10in) × 40cm (16in)
Aquilegia various	spring/summer		various
Campanula rotundifolia	summer	blue	20cm (8in) × 30cm (12in)
Crepis aurea	summer	orange	10cm (4in) × 20cm (8in)
Crepis incana	summer	pink	22cm (9in) × 35cm (14in)
Dianthus deltoides and various	spring/summer		2–12cm (1–5in) × 10–30cm (4–12in)
Festuca glauca	all year	blue-green leaves	20cm (8in) × 20cm (8in)
Linum perenne alpinum	summer	blue	15–30cm (6–12in) × 15–30cm (6–12in)
Lotus corniculatus	summer	yellow, orange	10cm (4in) × 40cm (16in)
Mentha various	summer	lilac-purple	varies considerably
Polygonum various	summer/autumn	pink, red	10–18cm (4–7in) × considerable
Primula juliae	spring	magenta	7cm (3in) × 25cm (10in)
Primula veris	spring	yellow	25cm (10in) × 25cm (10in)
Primula vulgaris	late winter/spring	pale yellow	10cm (4in) × 30cm (12in)
Thymus various	summer/autumn	pink, white	2 × 40cm (1 × 15in) or 15 × 15cm 6 × 6in)
Viola various	spring		various

HARDY GROUND ORCHIDS

Bletilla striata	summer	lilac purple	30cm (12in) × 20cm (8in)
Dactylorrhiza foliosa	late spring-midsummer	pink, purple	60cm (24in) × 15cm (6in)
Dactylorrhiza fuchsii	summer	pink, purple white	30cm (12in) × 15cm (6in)
Dactylorrhiza majalis	late spring-midsummer	lilac, maroon	50cm (20in) × 15cm (6in)

BULBS

Allium moly	summer	yellow	15cm (6in) × 25cm (10in)
Allium narcissiflorum	summer	white	20cm (8in) × 25cm (10in)
Allium sphaerocephalum	summer	red, purple	40cm (16in) × 7cm (3in)
Brimeura amethystina	late spring	blue	20cm (8in) × 15cm (6in)
Brimeura a. 'Alba'	late spring	white	20cm (8in) × 15cm (6in)
Crocus ancyrensis	late winter	yellow	7cm (3in) × 7cm (3in)
Crocus speciosus	autumn	purple blue	10cm (4in) × 10cm (4in)
Crocus tommasinianus	late winter	silver lilac	10cm (4in) × 10in (4in)
Eranthis hyemalis	midwinter	yellow	10cm (4in) × 20cm (8in)
Fritillaria meleagris	late spring	white, mauve	25cm (10in) × 7cm (3in)
Galanthus various	winter	white	10–25cm (4–10in) × 10–25cm (4–10in)
Leucojum vernum	spring	white	20cm (8in) × 15cm (6in)
Narcissus bulbocodium	spring	yellow	15cm (6in) × 10cm (4in)
Narcissus cyclamineus	early spring	yellow	15cm (6in) × 10cm (4in)
Ornithogalum various	late spring, summer	white	10–40cm (4–16in) × 10–20cm (4–8in)
Tulipa saxatalis	spring	pink	30cm (12in) × 20cm (8in)
Tulipa sprengeri	early summer	orange	40cm (16in) × 20cm (8in)

appendix 1

PLANTS FOR A GRASSLESS ALPINE LAWN

These are listed as additional to those already listed for the grassy alpine lawn

plant	season	colour	height x spread
Acaena buchananii	summer	lime-green	2cm (1in) × 75cm (30in)
A. glaucophylla	summer	steely-grey	5–7cm (2–3in) × 30–40cm (12–16in)
A. microphylla	summer	red	5cm (2in) × 15cm (6in)
A. novae-zelandiae	summer	mauve	5cm (2in) × 45cm (18in)
Antennaria dioica	late spring, early summer	pink	2cm (1in) × 25cm (10in)
Anthemis bierbersteinii	summer	yellow	22cm (9in) × 45cm (18in)
A. carpatica	summer	white	8cm (3in) × 30cm (12in)
A. sanctijohannis	summer	orange	60cm (24in) × 60cm (24in)
Carlina acanthifolia	early summer	white	60cm (24in) × 60cm (24in)
Coprosma various	late summer	white, purple	8cm (3in) × 90cm (36in)
Crepis incana	summer	pink	22cm (9in) × 35cm (14in)
Cymbalaria aequitriloba	summer	purple	2cm (1in) × 25cm (10in)
C. hepaticifolia	summer	lilac	2cm (1in) × 20cm (8in)
C. muralis 'Nana Alba'	summer	white, yellow	5cm (2in) × 25cm (10in)
Festuca glauca	grass		20cm (8in) × 20cm (8in)
Frankenia thymifolia	summer	pink	2cm (1in) × 60cm (24in)
Globularia cordifolia	summer	pale blue	5cm (2in) × 10cm (4in)
G. reptans	summer	pale blue	2cm (1in) × 8cm (3in)
G. trichosantha	summer	blue	20cm (8in) × 30cm (12in)
Lobelia angulata (syn. Pratia)	late spring	white	1cm (½in) × 60cm (24in)
L. pedunculata	summer	rich blue	1cm (½in) × 60cm (24in)
Mazus reptans	spring	purple	5cm (2in) × 30cm (12in)
Mentha requienii	summer	mauve	1cm (½in) × 60cm (24in)
Polygonum various	summer/autumn	pink, red	10–18cm (4–7in) × considerable
Primula various	spring/summer		7–30cm (3–12in) × 7–30cm (3–12in)
Raoulia various	summer	creamy-white	1cm (½in) × 30cm (12in)
Sagina boydii	evergreen foliage plant		1cm (½in) × 20cm (8in)
S. glabra	summer	white	5cm (2in) × 30cm (12in)
Thymus serpyllum	summer	pink, red, white	5cm (2in) × 45cm (18in)

BULBS

plant	season	colour	height x spread
Allium oreophillum	early summer	deep pink	15cm (6in) × 7cm (3in)
Chionodoxa various	spring	blue	10cm (4in) × 8cm (3in)
Crocus asturicus	autumn	lilac	7cm (3in) × 7cm (3in)
C. banaticus	autumn	lilac blue	7cm (3in) × 7cm (3in)
C. chrysanthus	early spring	white, yellow, blue	7cm (3in) × 7cm (3in)
C. etruscus	spring	lilac	10cm (4in) × 10cm (4in)
C. sativus	mid-autumn	purple	7cm (3in) × 7cm (3in)
Fritillaria various	spring		
Muscari azureum	late winter, early spring	pale blue	5–7cm (2–3in) × 5cm (2in)
Narcissus 'Wee Bee'	early spring	yellow	10cm (4in) × 7cm (3in)
N. 'Jumblie'	late winter	yellow	12cm (5in) × 7cm (3in)
N. 'Tête à Tête'	late winter	yellow	10cm (4in) × 7cm (3in)
Ornithogalum balansae	early-mid-spring	white	10cm (4in) × 7cm (3in)
Puschkinia scilloides	early spring	pale blue	10cm (4in) × 7cm (3in)
Scilla bifolia	late winter	blue	10cm (4in) × 7cm (3in)
S. sibirica	early spring	blue	12cm (5in) × 10cm (4in)
Sternbergia lutea	autumn	yellow	10cm (4in) × 7cm (3in)
Tulipa humilis	early spring	magenta pink	15cm (6in) × 12cm (5in)
T. tarda	spring	white, yellow	12cm (5in) × 20cm (8in)

DRYAS OCTOPETALA
Late spring, early summer cream flowers, height 10cm (4in), spread 90cm (36in)

IRIS HISTRIODES and hybrids
Late winter, deep blue flowers, height 5–10cm (2–4in), spread 5cm (2in)

appendix 2

CHECKLIST OF PLANTS

The following plants have been mentioned in this book and are listed here in tabular form for easy reference. They are divided into sections according to their season of flowering or greatest effect with a separate category for conifers and plants grown chiefly for foliage. Many plants overlap seasons; these are listed in the season they start flowering. Plants that are interesting both for foliage and flowers are usually included under their flowering season.

e = evergreen
s/e = semi-evergreen
d = deciduous

IBERIS SEMPERVIRENS

CONIFERS AND FOLIAGE PLANTS

plant	type	season	colour	height	spread
Abies balsamea hudsonii	conifer	all year		60cm (24in)	60cm (24in)
A. b. 'Nana'	conifer	all year		60cm (24in)	1m (3ft)
A. procera 'Glauca Prostrata'	conifer	all year			
Adiantum capillus-veneris	s/e fern	all year		30cm (12in)	30cm (12in)
A. pedatum	s/e fern	all year		30cm (12in)	30cm (12in)
A. venustum	d fern	all year		20cm (8in)	30cm (12in)
Asplenium bulbiferum	e fern	all year		15cm (6in)	30cm (12in)
A. ceterach	e fern	all year		5cm (2in)	20cm (8in)
A. ruta-muraria	e fern	all year		5cm (2in)	10cm (4in)
A. trichomanes	e fern	all year		8cm (3in)	20cm (8in)
Blechnum penna-marina	e carpeting fern	all year		15cm (6in)	45cm (18in)
B. vulvanicum	e fern	all year		15cm (6in)	40cm (16in)
Carex buchananii dwarf forms	sedge	all year	brown foliage	8cm (3in)	8cm (3in)
C. firma 'Variegata'	sedge	all year	yellow foliage	15cm (6in)	15cm (6in)
C. oschimensis 'Evergold'	sedge	all year	yellow foliage	20cm (8in)	20cm (8in)
Chamaecyparis lawsoniana 'Minima Glauca'	conifer	all year		90cm (36in)	90cm (36in)
C. l. 'Nana'	conifer	all year		90cm (36in)	90cm (36in)
C. obtusa 'Minima'	conifer	all year		60cm (24in)	70cm (28in)
C. o. 'Nana'	conifer	all year		90cm (36in)	1.5m (5ft)
C. o. 'Nana Gracilis'	conifer	all year		2m (6ft)	1.5m (5ft)
C. o. 'Nana Pyramidalis'	conifer	all year		60cm (24in)	60cm (24in)
C. o. 'Pygamea'	conifer	all year		40cm (16in)	60cm (24in)
Cotula squalida	e carpeting perennial	all year		8cm (36in)	40cm (16in)
Cryptogramma crispa	d fern	all year		12cm (5in)	20cm (8in)
Cryptomeria japonica 'Globosa'	conifer	all year		45cm (18in)	60cm (24in)
C. j. 'Vilmoriana'	conifer	all year		90cm (36in)	90cm (36in)
Empetrum nigrum	e shrub	all year		25cm (10in)	40cm (16in)
Erica carnea 'Foxhollow'	e shrub	all year	pink flower; yellow/orange foliage	20cm (8in)	60cm (24in)
E. c. 'Westwood Yellow'	e shrub	all year	lilac flower; yellow foliage	20cm (8in)	45cm (18in)
Festuca glauca	grass	all year	blue/green foliage	10cm (4in)	10cm (4in)
Hedera helix 'Congesta'	e climber	all year		40cm (16in)	50cm (19$\frac{1}{2}$in)
H. h. 'Conglomerata'	e climber	all year		90cm (36in)	90cm (36in)
Juniperus communis 'Compressa'	conifer	all year		70cm (28in)	12cm (5in)
J. c. 'Hornibrookii'	conifer	all year		50cm (19$\frac{1}{2}$in)	2m (6ft)
J. c. 'Depressa Aurea'	conifer	all year		40cm (16in)	4m (12ft)
J. horizontalis	conifer	all year		40cm (16in)	4m (12ft)
J. sabina	conifer	all year		20cm (8in)	1m (3ft)
Microbiota decussata	conifer	all year		50cm (19$\frac{1}{2}$in)	1.5m (5ft)
Muehlenbeckia adpressa	shrub	summer	white	30cm (12in)	70cm (28in)
Matteuccia struthiopteris	d fern	all year		90cm (36in)	90cm (36in)
Osmunda regalis	d fern	all year		1.2m (4ft)	1.2m (4ft)

plant	type	season	colour	height	spread
Pellaea atropurpurea	s/e fern	all year		30cm (12in)	30cm (12in)
Picea glauca 'Echiniformis'	conifer	all year		50cm (19^1/$_2$in)	1m (3ft)
Pinus mugo 'Mops'	conifer	all year		1m (3ft)	2m (6ft)
Polypodium australe	e fern	all year		20cm (8in)	45cm (18in)
P. a. 'Cambricum'	e fern	all year		20cm (8in)	45cm (18in)
P. vulgaris 'Cornubiense'	e fern	all year		20cm (8in)	45cm (18in)
Polystichum setiferum	e fern	all year		50cm (19^1/$_2$in)	90cm (36in)
P. s. 'Congestum'	e fern	all year		15cm (6in)	25cm (10in)
P. tsus-simense	s/e fern	all year		30cm (12in)	30cm (12in)
Raoulia australis	carpeting perennial	summer	yellow flower; white foliage	0.5cm (^{1}/$_4$in)	25cm (10in)
R. hookeri albo-sericea	e perennial	summer	yellow flower; white foliage	1cm (^{1}/$_2$in)	25cm (10in)
Sagina boydii	e carpeting perennial	all year	dark green foliage	1cm (^{1}/$_2$in)	20cm (8in)
S. glabra	e carpeting perennial	summer	white flower; yellow foliage	1cm (^{1}/$_2$in)	15cm (6in)
S. g. 'Aurea'	e carpeting perennial	all year		1cm (^{1}/$_2$in)	15cm (6in)
Salix x boydii	d shrub	all year		30cm (12in)	20cm (8in)
Sarcococca hookeriana humilis	e shrub	late winter	white flower	60cm (24in)	90cm (36in)
S. ruscifolia	e shrub	late winter	cream flower	90cm (36in)	90cm (36in)
Scirpus tabernaemontani 'Zebrinus'	grass	all year		4m (12ft)	60cm (24in)+
Sedum sieboldii	e carpeting tuber	all year	pink flower; blue/green foliage	10cm (4in)	20cm (8in)
S. s. 'Mediovariegatum'	e carpeting tuber	all year	pink flower; blue/cream/red/green foliage	10cm (4in)	20cm (8in)
S. spathulifolium	e carpeting perennial	all year	yellow flower; silver/red/green foliage	5cm (2in)	30cm (12in)+
Sempervivum montanum	e carpeting perennial	all year	red flower; dark green foliage	8cm (3in)	20cm (8in)
S. wulfenii	e carpeting perennial	all year	yellow flower; brown/green foliage	10cm (4in)	25cm (10in)
Skimmia japonica	e shrub	all year	white flower; red fruit	4m (12ft)	4m (12ft)
Thuja occidentalis 'Globosa'	conifer	all year		90cm (36in)	90cm (36in)
T. o. 'Rheingold'	conifer	all year		1.5m (5ft)	1.5m (5ft)
Thujopsis dolabrata 'Nana'	conifer	all year		90cm (36in)	1.2m (4ft)
Typha gracilis minima	water plant	late spring	brown flower	50cm (19^1/$_2$in)	30cm (12in)

FLOWERING PLANTS
Spring

plant	type	season	colour	height	spread
Adonis vernalis	herbaceous perennial	early spring	yellow flower	15cm (6in)	20cm (8in)
Aethionema 'Warley Rose'	e shrub	mid-spring-midsummer	pink flower	15cm (6in)	15cm (6in)
Ajuga reptans	e perennial	mid-spring	blue flower	15cm (6in)	60cm (24in)
Alyssoides utriculata	e shrub	mid-spring	yellow flower	30cm (12in)	30cm (12in)
Amelanchier alnifolia pumila	d shrub	late spring	white flower	60cm (24in)	60cm (24in)
Anagallis tenella	carpeting perennial	spring	pink orange flower	1cm (^{1}/$_2$in)	15cm (6in)
Anchusa caespitosa	e perennial	late spring	blue flower	3cm (1^1/$_4$in)	25cm (10in)
Andromeda polifolia 'Alba'	e shrub	mid-spring-early summer	white flower	45cm (18in)	60cm (24in)
A. p. 'Compacta'	e shrub	mid-spring-early summer	pink flower	20cm (8in)	30cm (12in)
A. p. 'Minima'	e shrub	mid-spring-early summer	pink flower	18cm (7in)	25cm (10in)
A. p. 'Nana'	e shrub	mid-spring-early summer	pink flower	15cm (6in)	20cm (8in)

plant	type	season	colour	height	spread
Androsace carnea	e perennial	all year	pink flower	5cm (2in)	5cm (2in)
A. hedraeantha	e perennial	all year	pink flower	1cm (¹/₂in)	10cm (4in)
A. lactea	e carpeting perennial	late spring	white flower	4cm (1¹/₂in)	20cm (8in)
A. sempervivoides	e carpeting perennial	all year	pink flower	2cm (³/₄in)	30cm (12in)
A. vandellii, syn. *A. imbricata*	e cushion-forming	all year	white flower	2cm (³/₄in)	10cm (4in)
Antennaria diocia	e carpeting perennial	late spring-early summer	pink flower	2cm (³/₄in)	25cm (10in)
Anthyllis montana	herbaceous perennial	late spring-early summer	pink flower	30cm (12in)	30cm (12in)
Arenaria balearica	carpeting perennial	late spring-early summer	white flower	1cm (¹/₂in)	75cm (30in)
A. tetraquetra	cushion-forming perennial	late spring	white flower	2cm (³/₄in)	15cm (6in)
Arisarum proboscideum	tuber	all year	brown flower	10cm (4in)	25cm (10in)
Armeria juniperifolia, syn. *A. caespitosa*	e shrub	late spring-early summer	pink flower	10cm (4in)	25cm (10in)
Arum creticum	tuber	spring/autumn	white/yellow flower	40cm (16in)	30cm (12in)
A. italicum	tuber	all year	green/cream foliage	20cm (8in)	30cm (12in)
Aubrieta deltoides	carpeting perennial	all year	pink-mauve flower	5cm (2in)	20cm (8in)
Berberis x stenophylla 'Corallina Compacta'	d shrub	late spring	orange flower	25cm (10in)	25cm (10in)
Betula nana	d shrub	all year	yellow flower	30cm (12in)	45cm (18in)
Boykinia jamesii	herbaceous perennial	late spring	red flower	12cm (5in)	18cm (7in)
Brimeura amethystina	bulb	late spring	blue flower	18cm (7in)	12cm (5in)
B. a. 'Alba'	bulb	late spring	white flower	18cm (7in)	12cm (5in)
Bulbocodium vernum	bulb	spring	purple flower	3cm (1¹/₄in)	5cm (2in)
Calceolaria biflora	e perennial	late spring	yellow/brown flower	8cm (3in)	10cm (4in)
Calla palustris	s/e perennial	all year	white flower	25cm (10in)	30cm (12in)
Callianthemum kernerianum	carpeting perennial	late spring	lilac flower	8cm (3in)	15cm (6in)
C. rutifolium (syn. *C. anemonoides*)	carpeting perennial	mid-spring	white flower	8cm (3in)	15cm (12in)
Calochortus albus	bulb	spring	white flower	30cm (12in)	8cm (3in)
C. luteus	bulb	late spring	yellow flower	35cm (14in)	8cm (3in)
C. venustus	bulb	late spring	white/yellow/purple/red flower	35cm (14in)	8cm (3in)
Caltha palustris	herbaceous perennial	all year	yellow flower	50cm (19¹/₂in)	50cm (19¹/₂in)
C. p. 'Plena'	herbaceous perennial	all year	yellow flower	25cm (10in)	25cm (10in)
Campanula pulla	herbaceous perennial	late spring-early summer	violet flower	2cm (1in)	10cm (4in)
Cassiope wardii	e shrub	all year	white flower	15cm (12in)	20cm (8in)
Celmisia coriacea	e perennial	all year	white flower; silver foliage	30cm (12in)	30cm (12in)
Chamaemelum nobile	e carpeting perennial	late spring-early summer	white flower	10cm (4in)	60cm (24in)
Chionodoxa lucilliae	bulb	early spring	blue flower	8cm (3in)	5cm (2in)
Clematis alpinas	climber	all year	white flower	2m (6ft)	1.5m (4ft)
C. marmoraria	shrub	late spring-early summer	white flower	10cm (4in)	10cm (4in)
Convolvulus cneorum	e shrub	late spring-early summer	white/pink flower	75cm (30in)	75cm (30in)
Cornus canadensis	carpeting shrub	spring-early summer	white flower	10cm (4in)	40cm (16in)+
Corydalis flexuosa	herbaceous perennial	spring	blue flower	20cm (12in)	40cm (16in)
C. pumila	tuber	late spring	purple/red flower	10cm (6in)	20cm (12in)

plant	type	season	colour	height	spread
C. transsilvanica	herbaceous perennial	all year	pink flower	15cm (6in)	30cm (12in)
Crocus ancyrensis	corm	early spring	yellow flower	5cm (2in)	3cm (1¹/₄in)
C. corsicus	corm	mid-spring	lilac flower	8cm (3in)	8cm (3in)
C. etruscus	corm	early spring	blue flower	10cm (4in)	8cm (3in)
C. imperati	corm	early spring	cream/violet flower	11cm (4¹/₂in)	8cm (3in)
C. minimus	corm	early spring	lilac flower	7cm (3in)	7cm (3in)
C. sieberi	corm	early spring	white flower	8cm (3in)	8cm (3in)
Cyclamen repandum	tuber	spring	red/purple flower	10cm (4in)	12cm (5in)
Cypripedum calceolus	orchid	late spring-early summer	yellow/purple flower	75cm (30in)	50cm (19¹/₂in)
C. reginae	orchid	late spring-early summer	white flower	90cm (36in)	60cm (24in)
Daboecia cantabrica	e shrub	late spring-early autumn	white, purple, mauve flower	40cm (16in)	60cm (24in)
Dactylorrhiza foliosa	orchid	spring-summer	purple, pink flower	70cm (28in)	45cm (18in)
Daphne arbuscula	e shrub	late spring	pink flower	12cm (5in)	50cm (19¹/₂in)
D. blagayana	s/e shrub	early spring	white flower	20cm (8in)	75cm (30in)
D. x burkwoodii 'Somerset'	s/e shrub	late spring	white/pink flower	1.4m (4ft 3in)	1.3m (4ft)
D. cneorum	e shrub	late spring	white/pink flower	10cm (4in)	50cm (19¹/₂in)
D. collina	e shrub	late spring	purple/pink flower	50cm (19¹/₂in)	50cm (19¹/₂in)
D. jasminea	e shrub	late spring-early summer-autumn	white/pink flower	8cm (3in)	30cm (12in)
D. petraea	e shrub	late spring	pink flower	15cm (6in)	25cm (10in)
Dicentra cucullaria	herbaceous perennial	spring	white flower	12cm (5in)	30cm (12in)
D. exima	herbaceous perennial	spring-early summer	white/pink flower	30cm (12in)	30cm (12in)
D. peregrina	tuft-forming perennial	spring-summer	pink flower	8cm (3in)	5cm (2in)
Dionysia aretioides	e cushion-forming perennial	early spring	yellow flower	5cm (2in)	25cm (10in)
D. tapetodes	e cushion-forming perennial	early spring	yellow flower	1cm (¹/₂in)	15cm (6in)
Dryas octopetala	e subshrub	late spring-early summer	white flower	5cm (2in)	45cm (18in)+
D. o. minor	e subshrub	late spring-early summer	white flower	3cm (1¹/₄in)	25cm (10in)+
Epimedium grandiflorum	carpeting perennial	all year	pink flower	30cm (12in)	30cm (12in)
Erinus alpinus	s/e perennial	late spring-early summer	pink/white flower	12cm (5in)	12cm (5in)
Eritrichium nanum	herbaceous perennial	spring-early summer	blue flower	2cm (1in)	3cm (1¹/₄in)
Erodium macradenum	herbaceous perennial	spring-autumn	pink flower	25cm (10in)	50cm (19¹/₂in)
Erythronium tuolumnense	tuber	all year	yellow flower	30cm (12in)	15cm (6in)
E. 'Pagoda'	tuber	spring	yellow flower	30cm (12in)	20cm (8in)
E. 'White Beauty'	tuber	spring	white flower	25cm (10in)	15cm (6in)
Fritillaria acmopetala	bulb	spring	green/blue flower	20cm (8in)	8cm (3in)
F. camtschatcensis	bulb	spring	black/purple flower	30cm (12in)	10cm (8in)
F. meleagris	bulb	spring	white mauve flower	25cm (10in)	8cm (3in)
F. pallidiflora	bulb	spring	green/yellow flower	15–60cm (6–24in)	10cm (4in)
F. pontica	bulb	spring	green flower	15–40cm (6–15in)	10cm (4in)
F. pyreniaca	bulb	spring	brown/blue/purple flower	15cm (6in)	8cm (3in)
F. uva-vulpis	bulb	spring	purple/yellow flower	15cm (6in)	8cm (3in)
Galax urceloata (syn. *G. aphylla*)	e perennial	late spring-early summer	white flower	15cm (6in)	30cm (12in)

plant	type	season	colour	height	spread
Gaultheria nummulariodes	e shrub	late spring	white/pink flower	10cm (4in)	20cm (8in)
Genista lydia	d shrub	late spring-early summer	yellow flower	50cm (19½in)	60cm (24in)
G. tinctoria 'Plena'	d shrub	spring-summer	yellow flower	50cm (19½in)	90cm (36in)
Gentiana excisa syn. *G. acaulis*	e perennial	spring-autumn	blue flower	2cm (1in)	10cm (4in)
Glaucidum palmatum	herbaceous perennial	all year	lilac flower	50cm (19½in)	50cm (19½in)
Globularia repens	e carpeting perennial	late spring-early summer	blue flower	2cm (1in)	8cm (3in)
G. trichosantha	e shrub	early spring	white flower	15cm (6in)	30cm (12in)
Haberlea ferdinandi-coburgii	e perennial	late spring-early summer	violet flower	10cm (4in)	30cm (12in)
H. rhodopensis	e perennial	late spring-early summer	violet flower	8cm (3in)	15cm (6in)
H. r. 'Virginalis'	e perennial	late spring-early summer	white flower	8cm (3in)	10cm (4in)
Hippocrepis comosa 'E R Janes'	herbaceous perennial	late spring-early summer	yellow flower	5cm (2in)	15cm (6in)
Hypericum aegypticum	e shrub	late spring-early summer	yellow flower	10cm (4in)	20cm (8in)
Iberis sempervirens	e subshrub	late spring-early summer	white flower	15cm (6in)	30cm (12in)
I. s. 'Schmeeflocke'	e subshrub	late spring-early summer	white flower	15cm (6in)	45cm (18in)
I. s. 'Weisswer Zwerg'	e subshrub	late spring-early summer	white flower	10cm (4in)	30cm (12in)
Iris bucharica	bulb	late spring	yellow/white flower	30cm (12in)	20cm (8in)
I. gracilipes	rhizome	late spring-early summer	lilac/white flower	15cm (6in)	45cm (18in)
I. innominata	herbaceous perennial	late spring-early summer	yellow/lilac flower	20cm (8in)	45cm (18in)
I. mellita	rhizome	mid-late spring	purple/brown flower	8cm (3in)	30cm (12in)
I. reticulata	bulb	early spring	violet flower	10cm (4in)	5cm (2in)
I. sibirica	rhizome	late spring-early summer	blue flower	50cm (19½in)	60cm (24in)+
I. winogradowii	bulb	early spring	yellow flower	8cm (3in)	6cm (2½in)
Jeffersonia dubia	herbaceous perennial	all year	lilac flower	12cm (5in)	20cm (8in)
Kalmiopsis leachiana	e shrub	early-late spring	purple/pink flower	30cm (12in)	30cm (12in)
Leiophyllum buxifolium	e shrub	late spring	pink/white flower	25cm (10in)	50cm (19½in)
Leontopodium alpinum	herbaceous perennial	spring-early summer	white flower	15cm (6in)	15cm (6in)
Leucojum nicaeense	bulb	early spring	white flower	10cm (4in)	6cm (2½in)
L. vernum	bulb	spring	white/green flower	12cm (5in)	10cm (4in)
Lewisia tweedyi	herbaceous perennial	spring	white/pink flower	15cm (6in)	12cm (5in)
Lilium nanum	bulb	late spring-early summer	pink flower	15cm (6in)	7cm (3in)
Lysichiton americanus	d perennial	all year	yellow flower	90cm (36in)	70cm (28in)
L. camtschatcensis	d perennial	all year	white flower	75cm (30in)	60cm (24in)
Mazus reptans	carpeting perennial	all year	purple/yellow flower	5cm (2in)	30cm (12in)
Minuartia stellata	cushion-forming perennial	late spring-early summer	white flower	2cm (1in)	10cm (4in)

plant	type	season	colour	height	spread
M. verna	cushion-forming perennial	late spring-early summer	white/purple flower	5cm (2in)	12cm (5in)
Moltkia petraea	s/e shrub	late spring-early summer	pink/purple flower	30cm (12in)	60cm (24in)
Muscari azureum	bulb	early spring	blue flower	10cm (4in)	5cm (2in)
M. botryoides	bulb	spring	blue flower	15cm (6in)	6cm (2^{1}/2in)
M. b. 'Album'	bulb	spring	white flower	12cm (6in)	5cm (2in)
Narcissus asturiensis	bulb	early spring	yellow flower	5cm (2^{1}/2in)	5cm (2in)
N. cyclamineus	bulb	early spring	yellow flower	7cm (3in)	5cm (2in)
N. rupicola	bulb	mid-spring	yellow flower	7cm (3in)	5cm (2in)
N. watieri	bulb	mid-spring	white flower	9cm (3^{1}/2in)	5cm (2in)
N. 'February Gold'	bulb	spring	yellow flower	25cm (10in)	10cm (4in)
N. 'Jenny'	bulb	spring	white/cream flower	25cm (10in)	10cm (4in)
N. 'Jumblie'	bulb	early spring	yellow flower	15cm (6in)	8cm (3in)
N. 'Sundial'	bulb	mid-spring	yellow flower	20cm (8in)	8cm (3in)
N. 'Tête à Tête'	bulb	early spring	yellow flower	15cm (6in)	8cm (3in)
N. 'Wee Bee'	bulb	early spring	yellow flower	10cm (4in)	7cm (3in)
Ornithogalum balansae	bulb	spring	white flower	10cm (4in)	5cm (2in)
O. nutans	bulb	spring	white/green flower	15cm (6in)	10cm (4in)
O. umbellatum	bulb	late spring	white flower	12cm (5in)	10cm (4in)
Orontium aquaticum	water plant	spring	yellow/white flower	1cm (^{1}/2in)	60cm (24in)
Paraquilegia anemonoides	tuft-forming perennial	mid-late spring	mauve/blue flower	12cm (5in)	18cm (7in)
Parnassia palustris	herbaceous perennial	late spring-early summer	white flower	20cm (8in)	8cm (3in)
Parochetus communis	e carpeting perennial	spring-autumn	blue flower	2cm (1in)	40cm (16in)+
Persicaria affinis	carpeting perennial	spring-autumn	pink/red flower	12cm (5in)	45cm (18in)+
P. a. 'Donald Lowndes'	carpeting perennial	spring-autumn	pink/red flower	15cm (6in)	60cm (24in)+
P. vacciniifolia	carpeting perennial	spring-autumn	pink flower	10cm (4in)	45cm (18in)+
Pleione formosana	orchid	spring	pink/yellow flower	8cm (3in)	20cm (8in)
Polygala calcarea	e perennial	late spring-early summer	blue flower	2cm (1in)	10cm (4in)
P. chamaebuxus	e subshrub	late spring-early summer	white/yellow flower	5cm (2in)	20cm (8in)
P. vayredae	e carpeting shrub	late spring-early summer	purple/yellow flower	7cm (3in)	30cm (12in)
Polygonum affine syn. *Persicaria affinis*	e perennial	all year	white, pink, mauve flower	8cm (3in)	15cm (6in)
Primula allionii 'Apple Blossom'	e perennial	spring	pink flower	8cm (3in)	15cm (6in)
P. a. 'Avalanche'	e perennial	spring	white flower	8cm (3in)	15cm (6in)
P. a. 'Marion'	e perennial	spring	pink/white flower	8cm (3in)	15cm (6in)
P. auricula	clump-forming perennial	spring	yellow flower	15cm (6in)	15cm (6in)
P. denticulata	herbaceous perennial	spring	lilac flower	45cm (18in)	45cm (18in)
P. edgeworthii	herbaceous perennial	spring	mauve flower	6cm (2^{1}/2in)	15cm (6in)
P. frondosa	herbaceous perennial	spring	pink flower	10cm (4in)	12cm (5in)
P. juliae 'Tawny Port'	herbaceous perennial	spring	red flower	12cm (5in)	25cm (10in)
P. j. 'Wanda'	herbaceous perennial	spring	red/purple flower	12cm (5in)	30cm (12in)
P. marginata	clump-forming perennial	spring	lilac flower	12cm (5in)	15cm (6in)
P. x *pubescens*	clump-forming perennial	spring	white, pink, lilac, purple flower	15cm (6in)	25cm (10in)
P. rosea	herbaceous perennial	early spring	pink flower	10cm (4in)	20cm (8in)
P. scapigera	clump-forming perennial	early spring	mauve flower	15cm (6in)	15cm (6in)

plant	type	season	colour	height	spread
Primula sonchifolia	herbaceous perennial	spring	blue/purple flower	25cm (10in)	25cm (10in)
P. veris	herbaceous perennial	spring	yellow flower	15cm (6in)	15cm (6in)
P. vialii	clump-forming perennial	late spring	mauve/red flower	40cm (16in)	25cm (10in)
Pulsatilla alpina	clump-forming shrub	spring	yellow flower	20cm (8in)	10cm (4in)
P. vernalis	tuft-forming perennial	spring	white flower	8cm (3in)	10cm (4in)
P. vulgaris	tuft-forming perennial	spring	purple, mauve, red, white flower	20cm (8in)	20cm (8in)
Puschkinia scilloides	bulb	early spring	blue flower	12cm (5in)	5cm (2in)
Ramonda myconi	e perennial	late spring-early summer	blue/mauve flower	8cm (3in)	10cm (4in)
R. m. 'Rosea'	e perennial	late spring-early summer	pink flower	8cm (3in)	10cm (4in)
R. nathaliae	e perennial	late spring-early summer	white, lilac flower	10cm (4in)	10cm (4in)
R. n. 'Alba'	e perennial	late spring-early summer	white flower	10cm (4in)	10cm (4in)
R. serbica	e perennial	late spring-early summer	lilac flower	10cm (4in)	10cm (4in)
Rhamnus pumila	d shrub	all year	green flower, blue/black fruit	10cm (4in)	30cm (12in)
Rhodohypoxis baurii	tuber	spring-early summer	pink flower	5cm (2in)	5cm (2in)
R. b. 'Albrighton'	tuber	spring-early summer	pink flower	8cm (3in)	8cm (3in)
R. b. 'Douglas'	tuber	spring-early summer	red flower	8cm (3in)	8cm (3in)
R. b. platypetala	tuber	spring-early summer	white/pink flower	8cm (3in)	8cm (3in)
Rhodothamnus chamaecistus	e shrub	late spring-early summer	pink flower	15cm (6in)	25cm (10in)
Romulea bulbocodium	corm	spring	lilac/white flower	8cm (3in)	5cm (2in)
R. ramiflora	corm	late spring	lilac/yellow flower	8cm (3in)	5cm (2in)
Salix apoda	d shrub	spring	yellow flower	15cm (6in)	45cm (18in)
S. hastata 'Wehrhahanii'	d shrub	early spring	silver/yellow flower	90cm (36in)	150cm (5ft)
S. lanata (male)	d shrub	late spring	yellow flower	60cm (24in)	90cm (36in)
S. reticulata	d shrub	spring	green foliage	5cm (2in)	40cm (16in)
Sanguinaria canadensis	rhizome	spring	white flower	15cm (6in)	45cm (18in)
S. c. 'Plena'	rhizome	spring	white flower	15cm (6in)	45cm (18in)
Saxifraga cortusifolia	e perennial	late spring-early summer	white flower	30cm (12in)	45cm (18in)
S. grisebachii 'Wisley'	e perennial	all year	red foliage	10cm (4in)	20cm (8in)
S. oppositifolia	e carpeting perennial	early spring	purple flower	2cm (1in)	15cm (6in)
S. o. 'Thoden'	e carpeting perennial	early spring	purple flower	3cm (1¼in)	20cm (18in)
S. umbrosa	e carpeting perennial	all year	white/pink flower	5cm (2in)	25cm (10in)
Scilla biflora	bulb	early spring	white, pink, blue flower	8cm (3in)	8cm (3in)
S. sibirica	bulb	early spring	blue flower	10cm (4in)	8cm (3in)
Shortia soldanelloides	e carpeting perennial	late spring	pink flower	8cm (3in)	15cm (6in)
S. uniflora	e carpeting perennial	all year	white/pink flower	8cm (3in)	25cm (10in)
Silene acaulis	e cushion-forming perennial	all year	pink flower	2cm (1in)	15cm (6in)
S. schafta	e carpeting perennial	late spring-late autumn	pink flower	10cm (4in)	10cm (4in)
Soldanella alpina	e clump-forming perennial	early spring	mauve flower	8cm (3in)	10cm (4in)
S. montana	e clump-forming perennial	early spring	blue flower	10cm (4in)	15cm (6in)

plant	type	season	colour	height	spread
Soldanella pusilla	e clump-forming perennial	early spring	violet flower	7cm (3in)	10cm (4in)
S. villosa	e clump-forming perennial	early spring	purple flower	10cm (4in)	15cm (6in)
Sternbergia candida	bulb	spring	white flower	15cm (6in)	10cm (4in)
Teucophilaea cyanocrocus	corm	spring	blue flower	8cm (3in)	6cm (2$\frac{1}{2}$in)
Tulipa aucheriana	bulb	early spring	pink/yellow flower	20cm (8in)	10cm (4in)
T. batalinii	bulb	spring	yellow flower	17cm (6$\frac{3}{4}$in)	12cm (5in)
T. clusiana	bulb	mid-spring	pink/white flower	30cm (12in)	12cm (5in)
T. humilis	bulb	early spring	pink, mauve flower	15cm (6in)	18cm (7in)
T. praestans	bulb	mid-spring	orange flower	20cm (8in)	15cm (6in)
T. pulchella	bulb	early spring	purple/yellow flower	15cm (6in)	18cm (7in)
T. saxatalis	bulb	mid-spring	lilac/yellow flower	20cm (8in)	20cm (8in)
T. sprengeri	bulb	late spring-early summer	orange/red flower	35cm (14in)	18cm (7in)
T. tarda	bulb	mid-late spring	white/yellow flower	12cm (5in)	25cm (10in)
T. urumiensis	bulb	mid-late spring	yellow flower	12cm (5in)	26cm (10$\frac{1}{2}$in)
Vaccinium angustifolium	e shrub	all year	white flower, blue fruit	70cm (28in)	80cm (32in)
V. corymbosum	d shrub	late spring	white/pink flower, blue/black fruit	1.5m (5ft)	1.5m (5ft)
V. oxycoccos	e shrub	late spring-early summer	pink flower, red fruit	25cm (10in)	40cm (16in)
Verbascum 'Letitia'	e shrub	late spring-mid-autumn	yellow flower	25cm (10in)	25cm (10in)
Veronica bombycina	cushion-forming perennial	all year	blue, lilac flower	5cm (2in)	8cm (2in)
Viburnum opulus 'Compactum'	d shrub	all year	white flower, red fruit	1.5m (5ft)	1.5m (5ft)
Vitaliana primuliflora	e carpeting perennial	all year	yellow flower	2cm (1in)	20cm (8in)
Weldenia candida	tuber	late spring-early summer	white flower	10cm (4in)	15cm (6in)

Summer

plant	type	season	colour	height	spread
Acaena affinis	e carpeting perennial	all year	pink flower	15cm (6in)	60cm (24in)
A. buchananii	e carpeting perennial	all year	green flower	2cm (1in)	75cm (30in)
A. microphylla	s/e carpeting perennial	all year	red flower	5cm (2in)	15cm (6in)
A. novae-zelandiae	carpeting perennial	all year	mauve flower	5cm (2in)	75cm (30in)
Acantholimon glumaceum	e perennial	all year	pink flower	10cm (4in)	20cm (8in)
Achillea ageratifolia	e perennial	mid-late summer	white flower	15cm (6in)	30cm (12in)
A. clavennae	e perennial	summer-autumn	white flower	15cm (6in)	25cm (10in)
Acorus gramineus 'Pusilllus'	s/e perennial	all year	green flower	10cm (4in)	10cm (4in)
Alchemilla alpina	herbaceous perennial	all year	green/yellow flower	15cm (6in)	60cm (24in)
Allium moly	bulb	summer	yellow flower	15cm (6in)	15cm (6in)
A. narcissiflorum	bulb	summer	white flower	15cm (6in)	10cm (4in)
A. orephyllum	bulb	summer	pink flower	8cm (3in)	10cm (4in)
A. sphaerocephalon	bulb	summer	mauve flower	60cm (24in)	10cm (4in)
Anacyclus pyrethrum depressus	carpeting perennial	all year	white flower	5cm (2in)	15cm (6in)
Androsace lanuginosa	e carpeting perennial	all year	pink flower	4cm (1$\frac{1}{2}$in)	20cm (8in)
Anemonopsis macrophylla	herbaceous perennial	summer	purple flower	45cm (18n)	60cm (24in)
Anthemis marschalliana syn. *A. biebersteinii*	e carpeting perennial	all year	yellow flower	20cm (8in)	40cm (16in)
A. punctata cupaniana	e perennial	all year	white flower	30cm (12n)	30cm (12in)
A. sancti-johannis	e perennial	all year	orange flower	60cm (24in)	60cm (24in)
Aquilegia flabellata nana	herbaceous perennial	summer	blue flower	15cm (6in)	15cm (6in)
A. jonesii	herbaceous perennial	summer	violet flower	1cm ($\frac{1}{2}$in)	5cm (2in)
A. scopulorum	herbaceous perennial	summer	blue flower	6cm (2$\frac{1}{2}$in)	10cm (4in)

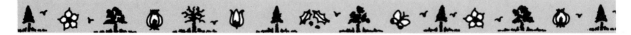

plant	type	season	colour	height	spread
Arctostaphylos uva-ursi	e shrub	all year	pink/white flower	10cm (4in)	50cm (19^1/$_2$in)
Arenaria montana	carpeting perennial	all year	white flower	5cm (2in)	15cm (6in)
Arisaema candidissimum	tuber	early summer	white/pink flower	12cm (5in)	40cm (16in)
A. consanguineum	tuber	summer	green/white/purple flower	75cm (30in)	40cm (16in)
A. triphyllum	tuber	summer	green flower	40cm (16in)	30cm (12in)
Artemisia glacialis	e perennial	all year	white flower	12cm (5in)	35cm (14in)
A. schmidtiana 'Nana'	carpeting perennial	all year	yellow flower	8cm (3in)	20cm (8in)
Arnica montana	rhizome	all year	yellow flower	30cm (12in)	15cm (6in)
Asperula gussonii	e perennial	early summer	pink flower	10cm (4in)	25cm (10in)
A. nitida	herbaceous perennial	early summer	pink flower	8cm (3in)	25cm (10in)
A. suberosa	herbaceous perennial	early summer	pink flower	8cm (3in)	15cm (6in)
Aster alpinus	herbaceous perennial	mid-late summer	purple flower	15cm (6in)	30cm (12in)
Azorella trifurcata	e perennial	all year	yellow flower	10cm (4in)	15cm (6in)
Calandrinia umbellata	carpeting perennial	all year	mauve flower	15cm (6in)	45cm (18in)
Calceolaria biflora	e perennial	all year	yellow flower	25cm (10in)	25cm (10in)
Calluna vulgaris	e shrub	mid-late summer	white, pink, purple flower	30cm (12in)	45cm (18in)
Campanula barbata	e perennial	all year	blue flower	20cm (8in)	15cm (6in)
C. cochleariifolia	carpeting perennial	all year	blue flower	8cm (3in)	45cm (18in)+
C. excisa	herbaceous perennial	mid-late summer	blue flower	5cm (2in)	10cm (4in)
C. piperi	herbaceous perennial	midsummer	blue flower	8cm (3in)	20cm (8in)
C. raineri	herbaceous perennial	summer	lilac flower	4cm (1^1/$_2$in)	8cm (3in)
C. rotundifolia	herbaceous perennial	summer	blue flower	15cm (6in)	20cm (8in)
C. zoysii	tuft-forming perennial	summer	lilac flower	5cm (2in)	20cm (8in)
Carlina acaulis	herbaceous perennial	all year	white flower	8cm (3in)	20cm (8in)
Celmisia argentea	tuft-forming perennial	all year	white flower	8cm (3in)	10cm (4in)
C. bellidioides	e carpeting perennial	early summer	white flower	2cm (1in)	15cm (6in)
C. spectabilis	e perennial	all year	white flower	30cm (12in)	45cm (18in)
Convolvulus sabatius	carpeting perennial	summer-early autumn	blue/purple flower	15cm (6in)	30cm (12in)
Coprosma petriei	e carpeting shrub	late summer	white/purple fruit	8cm (3in)	90cm (36in)
C. 'Indigo Lustre'	e carpeting shrub	late summer	violet fruit	8cm (3in)	40cm (16in)
Cornus alba 'Elegantissima'	d shrub	all year	white/green foliage	3m (9ft)	3m (9ft)
Crassula sarcocaulis	e subshrub	all year	red/pink flower	30cm (12in)	30cm (12in)
Crepis aurea	herbaceous perennial	summer	orange flower	20cm (8in)	15cm (6in)
C. incana	herbaceous perennial	summer	pink flower	20cm (8in)	10cm (4in)
Cyanthus microphyllus	carpeting perennial	late summer	blue flower	2cm (1in)	20cm (8in)
Cyclamen purpurascens	tuber	summer-autumn	red/purple flower	10cm (4in)	12cm (5in)
Cymbalaria aequitriloba	carpeting perennial	all year	purple flower	1cm (^{1}/$_2$in)	10cm (4in)
C. hepaticifolia	carpeting perennial	all year	lilac/purple flower	1cm (^{1}/$_2$in)	10cm (4in)
C. muralis 'Nana Alba'	carpeting perennial	all year	white flower	3cm (1^1/$_4$in)	10cm (4in)
Cytisus ardoinii	d shrub	early summer	yellow flower	8cm (3in)	35cm (14in)
Dianthus deltoides	e herbaceous perennial	all year	white, pink, red flower	10cm (4in)	30cm (12in)
D. microlepis	e herbaceous perennial	all year	pink flower	5cm (2in)	20cm (8in)
Diascia cordata	herbaceous perennial	all year	pink flower	15cm (6in)	20cm (8in)
D. rigescens	herbaceous perennial	summer-early autumn	pink flower	20cm (8in)	30cm (12in)
Dodecatheon meadia	herbaceous perennial	summer	pink flower	20cm (8in)	15cm (6in)
Dryas drummondii	e subshrub	early summer	cream flower	5cm (2in)	45cm (18in)+
D. x suendermannii	e subshrub	early summer	cream flower	5cm (2in)	45cm (18in)+
Epilobium canum	tuft-forming perennial	late summer-early autumn	red flower	45cm (18in)	45cm (18in)

plant	type	season	colour	height	spread
Eriogonum umbellatum	e herbaceous perennial	summer	yellow flower	10cm (4in)	30cm (12in)
Erysimum linifolium	s/e subshrub	early summer	lilac flower	30cm (12in)	20cm (8in)
Filipendula ulmaria 'Aurea'	herbaceous perennial	spring-autumn	white flower, yellow foliage	30cm (12in)	30cm (12in)
Frankenia laevis	e subshrub	midsummer	pink flower	10cm (4in)	30cm (12in)
F. thymifolia	e subshrub	midsummer	pink flower	15cm (6in)	30cm (12in)
Genista sagittalis	d shrub	early summer	yellow flower	8cm (3in)	30cm (12in)
G. s. delphinensis minor	d shrub	early summer	yellow flower	4cm (1½in)	15cm (6in)
Gentiana asclepiadea	herbaceous perennial	late summer-autumn	blue flower	70cm (28in)	60cm (24in)
G. a. alba	herbaceous perennial	late summer-autumn	white flower	65cm (26in)	55cm (21¾in)
G. clusii	e perennial	early summer	blue flower	5cm (2in)	20cm (8in)
G. gracilipes	s/e perennial	all year	purple/blue flower	15cm (6in)	20cm (8in)
G. × *macaulayi*	e perennial	late summer-autumn	blue flower	5cm (2in)	20cm (8in)
G. m. 'Kidbrooke Seedling'	e perennial	late summer-autumn	blue flower	5cm (2in)	20cm (8in)
G. m. 'Kingfisher'	e perennial	late summer-autumn	blue flower	5cm (2in)	20cm (8in)
G. m. 'Well's Variety'	e perennial	late summer-autumn	blue flower	5cm (2in)	20cm (8in)
G. saxosa	e perennial	early summer	white flower	5cm (2in)	15cm (6in)
Geranium farreri	herbaceous perennial	early summer	mauve/pink flower	10cm (4in)	15cm (6in)
G. sanguineum striatum	herbaceous perennial	all year	pink flower	10cm (4in)	13cm (5¼in)
Globularia cordifolia	e carpeting perennial	all year	blue flower	3cm (1¼in)	20cm (8in)
Gypsophila aretioides	cushion-forming perennial	midsummer	white flower	2cm (1in)	5cm (2in)
G. repens 'Dorothy Teacher'	s/e perennial	midsummer	pink flower	3cm (1¼in)	35cm (14in)
Haplopappus brandegeei	herbaceous perennial	summer	yellow flower	5cm (2in)	10cm (4in)
H. b. 'Canary Bird'	herbaceous perennial	summer	yellow flower	5cm (2n)	10cm (4in)
Hebe buchananii 'Minor'	e shrub	all year	white flower	8cm (3in)	6cm (2½in)
Helichrysum bellidioides	e shrub	all year	white flower	5cm (2in)	20cm (8in)
H. coralloides	e shrub	all year	yellow flower	18cm (7in)	15cm (6in)
H. frigidum	carpeting perennial	all year	white flower	8cm (3in)	20cm (8in)
H. milfordiae	e carpeting shrub	early summer	white flower, silver foliage	5cm (2in)	20cm (8in)
H. selago	e shrub	all year	cream flower	15cm (6in)	15cm (6in)
Hieraceum villosum	herbaceous perennial	all year	orange flower	15cm (6in)	30cm (12in)
Hosta sieboldiana	herbaceous perennial	early summer	lilac flower	90cm (36in)	1.2m (4ft)
Houttuynia cordata	herbaceous perennial	all year	white flower	20cm (8in)	1m (3ft)+
Hydrocharis morsus-ranae	water perennial	all year	white flower	1cm (½in)	30cm (12in)
Iris pseudacorus 'Variegata'	herbaceous perennial	all year	yellow flower, yellow and green foliage	2m (6ft)	2cm (6ft)
I. tenax	rhizome	early summer	lilac/blue flower	12cm (5in)	25cm (10in)+
Jasminum parkeri	e shrub	early summer	yellow flower	15cm (6in)	35cm (14in)
Leontopodium haplophylloides	herbaceous perennial	all year	white flower	30cm (12in)	30cm (12in)
Leucogenes grandiceps	e perennial	spring-early summer	yellow flower, white foliage	12cm (5in)	12cm (5in)
Lewisia cotyledon	e perennial	early summer	pink flower	30cm (12in)	20cm (8in)
Lilium mackliniae	bulb	early summer	pink flower	50cm (19½in)	15cm (6in)
L. formosanum pricei	bulb	summer	white flower	20cm (8in)	8cm (3in)
Linaria alpina	biennial	summer	violet/yellow flower	15cm (6in)	12cm (5in)
L. borealis americana	carpeting perennial	early-mid-	pink flower	8cm (3in)	20cm (8in)

plant	type	season	colour	height	spread
Linum perenne alpinum	herbaceous perennial	summer	blue flower	15cm (6in)+	15cm (6in)
Lithodora diffusa	carpeting perennial	all year	blue flower	12cm (5in)	30cm (12in)
Loiseleuria procumbens	carpeting shrub	early spring	pink flower	6cm (2¹/₂in)	15cm (6in)
Lotus corniculatus	herbaceous perennial	summer-autumn	yellow flower	6cm (2¹/₂in)	30cm (12in)
Lychnis alpina	tuft-forming perennial	all year	pink flower	8cm (3in)	12cm (5in)
L. flos-cuculi 'Nana'	e perennial	all year	pink flower	6cm (2¹/₂in)	20cm (8in)
L. flos-jovis	tuft-forming perennial	all year	pink flower	35cm (14in)	35cm (14in)
L. f-j. 'Nana'	tuft-forming perennial	all year	pink flower	10cm (4in)	15cm (6in)
Margyricarpus setosus	e shrub	early spring	white fruit	25cm (10in)	90cm (36in)
Mentha pulegium	carpeting perennial	all year	purple flower	5cm (2in)	45cm (18in)+
M. requienii	carpeting perennial	all year	purple flower	1cm (¹/₂in)	45cm (18in)+
Moltkia suffruticosa	d subshrub	all year	blue flower	30cm (12in)	30cm (12in)
M. x intermedia	e shrub	all year	blue flower	30cm (12in)	50cm (19¹/₂in)
Nomocharis aperta	bulb	early summer	pink flower	45cm (18in)	10cm (4in)
Nierembergia repens	carpeting perennial	all year	white/pink flower	5cm (2in)	20cm (8in)
Nuphar pumila	water lily	all year	yellow flower	1cm (¹/₂in)	75cm (30in)
Nymphaea 'Aurora'	water lily	all year	yellow flower	1cm (¹/₂in)	75cm (30in)
N. x helvola	water lily	all year	yellow flower	1cm (¹/₂in)	45cm (18in)
Oenothera acaulis	tuft-forming perennial	summer	white/pink flower	15cm (6in)	20cm (8in)
O. missouriensis	herbaceous perennial	summer	yellow flower	10cm (4in)	40cm (16in)
Ononis fruticosa	d subshrub	all year	pink flower	40cm (16in)	40cm (16in)
O. natrix	d subshrub	all year	yellow flower	30cm (12in)	30cm (12in)
O. rotundifolia	d s/e subshrub	all year	pink/red flower	25cm (10in)+	20cm (8in)
Origanum amanum	d s/shrub	all year	pink/white flower	15cm (6in)	15cm (6in)
O. laevigatum	d subshrub	all year	pink flower	25cm (10in)	20cm (8in)
Papaver alpinum	s/e perennial	all year	white, pink, yellow, orange flower	15cm (6in)	12cm (5in)
Paris polyphylla	rhizome	summer	green/yellow flower	60cm (24in)+	30cm (12in)
P. quadrifolia	rhizome	summer	yellow/green flower	25cm (10in)	30cm (12in)
Penstemon hirsutus	e subshrub	all year	purple, blue, white flower	60cm (24in)	40cm (16in)
P. h. 'Pygmaeus'	e subshrub	all year	white/purple/blue flower	8cm (3in)	8cm (3in)
Pernettya mucronata	e shrub	all year	pink foliage	1m (3ft)	1m (3ft)
P. prostrata	e shrub	all year	white fruit, blue/purple flower	20cm (8in)	30cm (12in)
P. pumila	e shrub	all year	white fruit white/pink flower	15cm (6in)	45cm (18in)+
P. tasmanica	e shrub	early summer	red fruit	10cm (4in)	45cm (18in)
Phlox adsurgens	carpeting perennial	all year	purple/pink/white flower	10cm (4in)	40cm (16in)
P. a. 'Wagon Wheels'	carpeting perennial	all year	pink flower	10cm (4in)	30cm (12in)
P. douglasii	e carpeting perennial	all year	white/pink/red flower	8cm (3in)	25cm (10in)
P. subulata	e carpeting perennial	early summer	white, pink, mauve, blue flower	10cm (4in)	20cm (8in)
P. s. brittonia 'Rosea'	e carpeting perennial	early summer	pink flower	10cm (4in)	20cm (8in)
P. s. 'G. F. Wilson'	e carpeting perennial	early summer	blue flower	10cm (4in)	20cm (8in)
P. s. 'Temmiskaming'	e carpeting perennial	early summer	mauve/purple flower	15cm (6in)	30cm (12in)
P. 'Kelly's Eye'	e perennial	early summer	white/pink flower	7cm (3in)	10cm (4in)
Physoplexis comosa	tuft-forming perennial	all year	violet flower	8cm (3in)	10cm (4in)
Potentilla aurea	tuft-forming perennial	late summer	yellow flower	10cm (4in)	20cm (8in)
P. nitida	carpeting perennial	early summer	pink flower	4cm (¹/₂in)	25cm (10in)
P. palustris	herbaceous perennial	early summer	purple/blue flower	30cm (12in)	40cm (16in)
Primula beesiana	herbaceous perennial	summer	pink flower	30cm (12in)	25cm (10in)
P. bulleyana	herbaceous perennial	early summer	orange flower	30cm (12in)	30cm (12in)
P. florindae	herbaceous perennial	summer	yellow flower	70cm (28in)	40cm (16in)
P. helodoxa	herbaceous perennial	summer	yellow flower	60cm (24in)	40cm (16in)
P. japonica	herbaceous perennial	early summer	red flower	45cm (18in)	40cm (16in)

plant	type	season	colour	height	spread
P. muscarioides	herbaceous perennial	early summer	purple flower	18cm (7in)	18cm (7in)
P. pulverulenta	herbaceous perennial	early summer	red flower	75cm (30in)	40cm (16in)
P. reidii	clump-forming perennial	early summer	white flower	8cm (3in)	12cm (5in)
P. r. williamsii	clump-forming perennial	early summer	blue flower	10cm (4in)	15cm (6in)
P. secundiflora	clump-forming perennial	summer	red/purple flower	40cm (16in)	30cm (12in)
P. sikkimensis	clump-forming perennial	summer	yellow flower	60cm (24n)	40cm (16in)
Ranunculus amplexicaulis	herbaceous perennial	early summer	white flower	25cm (10in)	10cm (4in)
R. crenatus	s/e perennial	all year	white flower	10cm (4in)	10cm (4in)
Saponaria 'Bressingham'	carpeting perennial	all year	pink flower	8cm (3in)	15cm (6in)
S. pumilio	cushion-forming perennial	early summer	pink flower	5cm (2in)	8cm (3in)
Saxifraga moschata 'Cloth of Gold'	e perennial	all year	white flower, yellow foliage	10cm (4in)	20cm (8in)
Scutellaria alpina	rhizome	summer	purple/white flower	15cm (6in)	40cm (16in)
Sorbus reducta	d shrub	early summer	white flower, pink/orange fruit	30cm (12in)	30cm (12in)
Tanacetum argenteum	e carpeting perennial	all year	white flower, silver foliage	15cm (6in)	15cm (6in)
T. densum amani	e carpeting perennial	all year	yellow flower, silver foliage	20cm (8in)	20cm (8in)
Teucrium aroanum	e carpeting subshrub	all year	purple flower	2cm (1in)	12cm (5in)
T. subspinosum	e carpeting subshrub	all year	pink flower	15cm (6in)	30cm (12in)
Thymus cilicicus	e shrub	early summer	lilac flower	8cm (3in)	10cm (4in)
T. membranaceus	e shrub	early summer-early autumn	white/pink flower	12cm (5in)	18cm (7in)
T. serpyllum	e carpeting perennial	early summer-early autumn	white, pink, mauve, red flower	1cm (^{1}/2in)	30cm (12in)
Vaccinium macrocarpon	e shrub	late summer	white/pink flower, blue fruit	35cm (14in)	50cm (19^1/2in)
V. myrtillus	d shrub	early summer	pink flower, blue/black fruit	15cm (6in)	30cm (12in)
V. praestans	d shrub	early summer	white/pink flower, red fruit	15cm (6in)	30cm (12in)
V. vitis-idaea	e shrub	early summer-autumn	pink flower, red fruit	5cm (2in)+	30cm (12in)+
Veronica fruticans	carpeting perennial	all year	blue flower	8cm (3in)	25cm (10in)
Wulfenia carinthiaca	e perennial	all year	violet flower	25cm (10in)	25cm (10in)
Zephyranthes candida	bulb	late summer-early autumn	white flower	17cm (6^3/4in)	20cm (8in)

Autumn

plant	type	season	colour	height	spread
Allium callimischon	bulb	autumn	white flower	20cm (8in)	15cm (6in)
Crocus banaticus	corm	autumn	violet flower	10cm (4in)	8cm (3in)
C. cancellatus	corm	autumn	lilac flower	8cm (3in)	8cm (3in)
C. goulimyi	corm	autumn	lilac flower	10cm (4in)	8cm (3in)
C. hadriaticus	corm	autumn	white flower	10cm (4in)	8cm (3in)
C. kotschyanus	corm	autumn	lilac flower	8cm (3in)	8cm (3in)
C. niveus	corm	late autumn	white flower	12cm (5in)	8cm (3in)
C. ochroleucus	corm	mid-late autumn	white flower	7cm (3in)	7cm (3in)
C. sativus	corm	mid-autumn	lilac flower	8cm (3in)	8cm (3in)
C. serotinus syn. C. astauricus	corm	autumn	violet flower	10cm (4in)	8cm (3in)
C. tournefortii	corm	autumn	lilac flower	10cm (4in)	8cm (3in)
Erica carnea 'Eileen Porter'	e shrub	late autumn-winter	red flower	20cm (8in)	45cm (18in)
Leucojum autumnale	bulb	early autumn	white flower	10cm (4in)	5cm (2in)
Saxifraga cortusifolia	s/e clump-forming perennial	early autumn	white flower	25cm (10in)	25cm (10in)
Sedum cauticola	carpeting perennial	early autumn	purple/white flower, blue/green foliage	5cm (2in)	20cm (8in)

plant	type	season	colour	height	spread
Sternbergia lutea	bulb	autumn	yellow flower	8cm (3in)	8cm (3in)
S. sicula	bulb	autumn	yellow flower	8cm (3in)	8cm (3in)
Zephyranthes citrina	bulb	early autumn	yellow flower	12cm (5in)	10cm (4in)

Winter

plant	type	season	colour	height	spread
Adonis amurensis	herbaceous perennial	late winter–early spring	yellow flower	25cm (10in)	30cm (12in)
Cornus alba (Dogwood)	d shrub	all year	red stem	3m (9ft)	3m (9ft)
C. a. 'Sibirica'	d shrub	all year	red stem	3m (9ft)	3m (9ft)
C. stolonifera 'Flaviramea'	d shrub	all year	yellow stem	3m (9ft)	3m (9ft)
Crocus chrysanthus	corm	late winter–early spring	white flower	8cm (3in)	8cm (3in)
C. laevigatus	corm	all year	lilac/purple stem	11cm (4½in)	8cm (3in)
C. tommasinianus	corm	late winter–early spring	lilac flower	8cm (3in)	8cm (3in)
Eranthis cilicica	tuber	late winter–early spring	yellow flower	8cm (3in)	10cm (4in)
E. hyemalis	tuber	late winter–early spring	yellow flower	8cm (3in)	10cm (4in)
Erica carnea 'Vivellii'	e shrub	late winter–early spring	purple/pink flower	10cm (4in)	35cm (14in)
Galanthus x *atkinsii*	bulb	late winter–early spring	white/green flower	15cm (6in)	10cm (4in)
G. ikariae	bulb	late winter–early spring	white/green flower	15cm (6in)	10cm (4in)
G. nivalis 'Viridapicis'	bulb	spring	white/green flower	20cm (8in)	10cm (4in)
G. plicatus	bulb	late winter–early spring	white/green flower	15cm (6in)	10cm (4in)
Iris danfordiae	bulb	late winter–early spring	yellow flower	8cm (3in)	5cm (2in)
I. histrioides	bulb	midwinter–early spring	blue flower	7cm (3in)	5cm (2in)
Narcissus cantabricus	bulb	all year	white flower	7cm (3in)	5cm (2in)
Ranunculus calandrinoides	herbaceous perennial	all year	white/pink stem	20cm (8in)	20cm (8in)
Scilla mischtschenkoana	bulb	late winter–early spring	blue flower	8cm (3in)	8cm (3in)
Tulipa biflora	bulb	late winter–early spring	white/yellow flower	8cm (3in)	8cm (3in)

USEFUL ADDRESSES

SPECIALIST ALPINE SOCIETIES

Great Britain

Alpine Garden Society
AGS Centre
Avon Bank
Pershore
Worcestershire
WR10 3JP
> Secretary: Michael Upward
> 61 Local groups in England, Wales and Ireland;
> 22 shows annually

Scottish Rock Garden Club
Groom's Cottage
Kirklands
Ancrum
Jedburgh
Roxburghshire
TD8 6UJ
> Secretary: Dr Jan E Boyd
> 15 Local groups in Scotland;
> 5 regional shows annually

Australia

Alpine Garden Society
Tasmania Group
Mrs S Collins
3 Lynton Avenue South
Hobart 7000

Victoria Group
Otto Fauser
7 Bella Vista Crescent
Olinda
Victoria 3788

Canada

The Alpine Club of British Columbia
c/o Frank Dorsey
4410 Ranger Avenue
North Vancouver
B.C.
Canada V7R 3L3

The Vancouver Island Rock and Alpine
Garden Society
PO Box 6507, Station C
Victoria, B.C.
Canada V8P 5M4

Denmark

The Alpine Garden Society
Per Husted
Helligsøvej 38
Helligso
7760 Hurup Thy
Denmark

France

Societé des Amateurs de Jardins Alpins
43 rue Buffon
77005 Paris
France

New Zealand

The New Zealand Alpine Garden Society
PO Box 2984
Christchurch
New Zealand

North America

The North American Rock Garden Society
Jacques Mommens
PO Box 67, Millwood
NY 10546
USA

OTHER GARDENING SOCIETIES OF INTEREST

The Hardy Plant Society
The Administrator
Bank Cottage
Great Comberton
Worcestershire
WR10 3DP

The National Council for the Conservation
of Plants and Gardens
The Pines, RHS Garden
Wisley
Ripley
Woking
Surrey
GU23 6QB

USEFUL ADDRESSES

The Royal Horticultural Society
80 Vincent Square
London
SW1P 2PE

The British Iris Society
C E C Bartlett
The Old Mill House
Shurton
Stogursey
Bridgwater
Somerset
TA5 1QA

There are also Iris Societies in the following countries: Australia, Belgium, Canada, Denmark, France, Germany, Italy, Japan, New Zealand, Russia, South Africa, Sweden, Switzerland.

Details are available from the British Iris Society.

The Cyclamen Society
Peter Moore
Tile Barn House
Standen Street
Iden Green
Benenden
Kent
TN17 4LB

The Saxifrage Society
Adrian N Young
19 Auriol Park Road
Worcester Park
Surrey
KR4 7DP

The American Primrose Society
9705 SW Spring Crest Drive
Portland
OR 97225
USA

FURTHER READING

  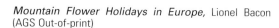

Mountain Flower Holidays in Europe, Lionel Bacon (AGS Out-of-print)

The Alpine Flowers of Britain and Europe, C. Grey-Wilson (Collins)

Collins Guide to Alpines and Rock Garden Plants, A. N. Griffith (Collins)

Flowers of Greece, A. Huxley/W. Taylor (Chatto & Windus)

Mountain Flowers of Europe, A. Huxley (Blandford)

Flowers of Greece and Balkans, O. Polunin (Oxford Univ. Press)

Flowers of the Mediterranean, O. Polunin/A. Huxley (Chatto & Windus)

Flowers of South West Europe, O. Polunin/B. E. Smythies (Oxford Univ. Press)

Flowers of the Himalaya, O. Polunin/A. Stainton, (Oxford Univ. Press)

INDEX

Numbers in **bold** indicate main entry

Aconite, winter, 10, **51**, 90, 118
Adonis, 36, 116, 118
    A. amuriensis, brevistyla, 23
    A. vernalis, 22–3, 129
Agapanthus, 115
Agrostis canina, tenuis, 40
Ajuga reptans, 40, 72
Allium, 9, 78, 81, 87, 94, 100, **124**
    A. beesianum, cyaneum, 78
    A. callimischon, 108
Allseed, 36
Alpine house, 8, 9, 10, 12, 48, 56, **84–7**, 101, 110, 116, 118; bulbs for, 87; heating, 87, 119; plants for, 84–5; shrubs for, 86; ventilation, 56, 110–11
Alyssum, 26, 33, 58, 100
Anacyclus depressus, 44, 53, 96
    A. pyrethrum depressus, 74
Andromeda, 63
    A. polifolia, 42, 55
Androsace, 69, 84, 125
    A. alpina, 114
Anemone, 33, 63, 80, 125
Anthemis, 40; 80, 106
    A. cinerea, montana, 74
Aphids, root, 13, 20, 28, **29**, 90
Aquilegia, 36, 80, 84
    A. alpina, 114
    A. jonesii, 84
Arabis, 17, 58, 80
Arisaema, **60**, 76
    A. candidissima, consanguineum, triphyllum, 60
Asplenium ceterach, 55, 58–9, 111, **120**
    A. trichomanes, 120
Aster alpinus, 48
Aubrieta, 17, 26, **30**, 33, 58
    A. deltoidea, 30
Autumn foliage, 111; flowering plants, 63, 110, **139–40**
Avens, Mountain, 92–3

Beds, peat, 62–3; plants for, 63; plunged, 96; raised, 8, 16–17; shrubs for, 62
Bloodroot, 30
Bog garden, 8, 9, 56, 66, **76–7**; plants for, 76–7; shrubs for, 77
Bog rosemary, 42
Box, false, 14; sweet, 14–15
Brachyglottis, 106
Broom, dwarf, 56, 60
Bugle, 40
Bulbs, 9, 10, 32, 33, 40, 41, 44, 55, 63, **81**, **94–5**, 110, **124–7**; frame, 91, 94–7; lifting, 69; planting, 40, 90, 91, 96; repotting, 81
Butcher's broom, 15
Calluna vulgaris, 62, 91, 110

Calochortus, 87, 95
Caltha palustris, 72, 76
Campanula, 28, 44, 48, 78, 80, 81, 84, 125
    C. barbata, cenisia, rupestris, 114
    C. cochleariifolia, 44
    C. zoysii, 115
Campion, dwarf, 82
Candytuft, 50
Cardamine hirsuta, 36
Carex, 55, 125
    C. buchananii, 98, 111, 120
    C. firma, 55, 120
    C. oshimensis, 98, 111
Cassiopes, 62, 63, 86, 125
Catalogues, 8, 110, 119
Catmint, 66
Celmisia, 118
Chamaecyparis, 90
    C. obtusa, 121
Chionodoxa, 69
Christmas rose, 111
Clematis, 42–3
    C. alpina, 43
    C. marmoraria, 42–3
Clump-forming plants, 28–9, 41
Colchicums, 88, 90, 91
Collecting, 110, 122–5
Composts, **12–13**, 25
Conifers, dwarf, 8, 9, 33, 55, 56, 69, 86, 90, 121, **128–9**
Containers, 8, 58–9, 106
Convolvulus, 84
    C. cneorum, 70
    C. sabatius, 52, **70**, 84
Coprosma, 37, **103**, 125
Corydalis, 39
    C. cheilanthifolia, flexuosa, transsilvanica, 39
Cotoneaster, 33
Cowslips, 41
Creeping plants, **40–1**, **44**, 46, 48, 78, 106
Crepis, 48
Crocus, 10, **15**, 36, 44, 55, 69, 80, 81, 87, 88, 90, 91, 94–6, **103**, 108, 110, 115, 116, 118, **124**, 125; autumn, 88, 90
    C. corsicus, 15
    C. goulimyi, 103, 110
    C. kotschyanus, 103
    C. minimus, 15, 95
    C. ochroleucus, tournefortii, 108, 110
    C. speciosus, 103, 110
Cuttings, 36, 48, 49, 68–9, 80, 101
    leaf, 58, **59**, plants for, 58
    root, **49**, 69, plants for, 48, 69
    stem, 49, **59**, 69, plants for, 48, 58, 68
Cyananthus, 84
Cyclamen, **22**, 84, 88, 110, 115, 118, **125**
    C. cilicium, purpurascens, 88
    C. coum, 22, 116, 118
    C. hederifolium, 22, 88, 90, 110, 111

    C. repandum, 22
Cypripedium acaule, 51
    C. calceolus, **50–1**, 63, 114
    C. reginae, 63

Daboecia, 48, 62, 110
Dactylorrhiza, 76
    D. incarnata, 64, 76
    D. majalis, 64
Daffodils *see* Narcissus
Daisy, Mount Atlas, 74
Daphne, 62, 125
    D. arbuscula, 55, 86, 91
    D. blagayana, 48, 91
Dead-heading, 58
Dianthus, 36, 37, 66, 80, 107, 125
Diascia, 66, **92**, 125
    D. cordata, rigescens, 92
Dionysia, 18, **23**, 84
    D. aretioides, tapetodes, 23
Dittany, 83
Dividing, **28–9**, 80–1; plants for, 81
Dog's tooth violet, 38
Dondia, 121
Draba, 44, 84, 125
Drainage, 9, 16, **17**, 40, 100, 110
Dryas drummondii, 93
    D. octopetala, 58, **92–3**, 127
Dryopteris dilatata, 72, 76

Epigaea asiatica, repens, 48
Epilobium canis, 110
Equipment, 9
Eranthis, 90
    E. cilica, hyemalis, tubergenii, 51
Erica, 62, 48, 91, 110, 111
    E. carnea, 98, 110, 111
Erigeron, 48, 80, 106
    E. karvinskianus, 9, 78
Erinus alpinus, 6, 44, 107
Eriogonum, 118
Eritrichium nanum, 84, 114
Erodium, 48
Erythronium, 63, 69, 81, 90, 91
    E. dens-canis, tuolumnense, 38
Expedition, planning, 114–15
Extension, 33, **68**

Ferns, 12, 21, 32, 33, 48, 55, 58, 63, **119**, **125**
    Royal, 72, 76, 77
    Rusty-back, 58–9, 120
Fertiliser, 18, **20–1**, 110
Fescues, 40
Festuca glacialis, 55
    F. ovina, rubra, tenuifolia, 40
Flaxes, 66, 106
Fleabane, 71
Flower of Job, 75
Foliage, dead, 9, **12**, 21, 90, 101, 111, 118
Foliage plants, 66, 111, **128–9**
Frame, 9, 10, 56, 69, 94–5
    bulb, 8, 91, **94–7**
Fritillaria, 36, 81, 87, 95, **125**

    F. meleagris, 41, 43, 91, **125**
    F. pyrenaica, **43**, 95
Fritillary, **43**, 96, **125**
    Snake's head, 41, **43**, 125

Galanthus, 69, 81, 87, 90, 91, 96, 110, **124**
    G. ikariae, nivalis, plicatus, 15
    G. reginae-olgae, 15, 87, 110
Gaultheria, 37, 62, 63, 91, 98, 111
    G. nummularioides, procumbens, 112
    G. trichophylla, 113
Genista, 55, 91
    G. lydia, 60
    G. sagittalis, **60**, 61, 86
Gentian, 125
    autumn, 63, **82–3**, 88
    spring, **38–9**, 44
    trumpet, 114
    willow-leaved, 92
Gentiana, 100, 125
    G. acaulis, 9, 39, 114
    G. asclepiadea, 92
    G. farreri, 83
    G. sino-ornata, 63, **82–3**
    G. verna, **38–9**, 44
Geranium, 33, 36, 48, 78, 125
    G. sanguineum striatum, 69
Geum reptans, 114
Gifts, 81, 119
Glaucidium palmatum, 36
Globularia, 40, 81, 85, 107
Grasses, 9, **40**, 55, 116
Gravelled areas, 8, 46, 104–7
Gunnera manicata, 77
Gypsophila paniculata, 78
    G. repens, 78, 85, 107

Haberleas, 59
Hairy bittercress, 36
Haplopappus brandegeei, 71
Haquetia epipactis, 121
Heathers, 33, 44, 63, 98, 101, 111
Hebes, 35, 81, 86, 91, 96, 125
Hedera helix, 111, 120–1
Helianthemum, 58, 66, 69, 80
Helichrysum, 85, 96, 115, 118
Hellebore, 11
    H. niger, orientalis, 111
Hepatica, 26, 116, 118, 125
Hygiene, **12**, 90, 101, 110, 118–19

Iberis, 33, 48, 58
    I. sempervirens, **50**, 128
Iris, 10, 18, 36, 56, 66, 69, 72, 76, 77, 81, 101, 125
    I. danfordiae, 87, 95, 118
    I. histrioides, 87, 95, 118, 127
    I. reticulata, 87, 91, 95, 116
    I. unguicularis, 111
Ivy, 111, 120–1

Jovibarba, 96, 124
Juniperus (Juniper), **56**, 90, 98, **121**
 J. communis, 55, 90, 98
 J. compressa, 98, 121

Kalmiopsis, 50
 K. leachiana, 50, 91
Knotweed, 40, 102

Lavender, 66
Lawn, alpine, 40–1; plants for 40–1, 126
 grassless alpine, 44–5; plants for, 44, 127
Leggy plants, 48
Leucojum, 18, 69, 81, 87
 L. autumnale, 55, 87, **88**
Lewisia, 37, **42**, 85
 L. cotyledon, tweedyi, 42
Lilies, 63, 80, 96, 100, 115
 water, 56, 66, 101
Lime-hating plants, 104–5
 -tolerant plants, 105
Linum arboreum, 6
Lobelia, 78, 100
Lychnis alpina, 75
 L. flos-cuculi, 56, 80
 L. flos-jovis, 75, 107
Lysichiton americanus, 76, 77
 L. camtschatcensis, 76

Maidenhair spleenwort, 120
Marsh marigold, 76
Meconopsis, 118
Mentha pulegium, requienii, 41
Mildew, 110
Milkwort, 14
Mimulus, 41, 72
Mints, 40–1
Mites, red spider, 20
Moles, 48, 97
Morisia, 31
 M. monanthos, 31
Muscari, 69, 81, 87, 116
 M. azureum, 81, 91
 M. botryoides, 81, 87
Musk, 41

Narcissus, 18, 55, 69, 80, 81, 87, 91, 95, 96, 110, **112**, 115, 125
 N. bulbocodium (Hoop-petticoat daffodil), 36, 41, 44, 91, 95, 108, 116
 N. cantabricus, 36, 87, 95, 108, **112**
 N. cyclamineus, 36, 41, 91, 95
 N. foliosus, 112
 N. Nylon, 113
 N. romieuxii, 87, 108, 112
Noah's-ark tree, 121

Oenothera, 37, 66, 81, **83**, 107
 O. acaulis, 83, 107
Orchid, **39**, 63, 66, 114, 126
 Lady's slipper, **50–1**, 63, 114, 115

Southern marsh, 64
Origanum, 125
 O. amanum, laevigatum, 83
Ornithogalum, 69, 81
Osmunda regalis, 72, 76, 77
Outcrop, 16, **24–5**, 46
Oxygenating plants, 73

Paraquilegia anemonoides, 36
Parochetus, 72, 124
 P. communis, 110, 111, 118
Pasque flower, 22
Paved areas, 8, 16, 104–7; plants for, 46, 106–7
Pearlwort, 36
Peat, 25, 62–3
Pennyroyal, 41
Penstemon, 74–5
 P. hirsutus, 74–5
Pernettya, 37, 62, 98
Persicaria affinis, **102**, 110
 P. vacciinifolia, 102
Pests, 13, 18, **20**, 28, 29, 48, 91, 96, 97, 101 *see also individual headings*
Petrocallis pyrenaica, 114
Pheasant's eye, 22–3
Phlox, 38, 48, 56, 65, 66, 81, 121
 P. adsurgens, 38
 P. borealis, 65
 P. Kelly's Eye, 65
 P. subulata, 38, 65
Phyllodoce, 62, 63
Pinks, 106
Planting, 28, 40, 90, 91, 96; out, 90
Pleione formosana, forrestii, 39
Pollination, 36, 37
Polygala calcarea, chamaebuxus, vayrediae, 14
Polygonum, 40, 107
 P. vacciinifolium, 78
Pool/pond, 8, 9, 56, 66, **72–3**, 101
Poppies, 106
Potentilla, 66
Potting up, 101
Pratia pedunculata, 78
Primroses, 41, 50
 Evening, 66, **83**
Primulas, 13, 17, 18, 22, **23**, 26, **31**, 36, 41, 48, **50**, **51**, 69, 72, 76, 77, 80, 81, 85, 100, 118, **123**
 P. allionii, 13, 22, 23, 36, 85, 114
 P. auricula, 13
 P. bellidifolia, muscarioides, vialii, 51
 P. denticulata, 80
 P. juliae 'Wanda', 30
 P. marginata, 13, 17, 34, 36, 37, 48, 85
 P. petiolares, 63
 P. pubescens, 13, 37
 P. reidii williamsii, 50
 P. rosea, 76

Propagation, 18, 56
Protection, 29, 100–1, 118
Pruning, 33, 58, 80, 101
Pulsatilla, 33, 58, 80, 85
 P. vernalis, 22, 85
 P. vulgaris, 22, 48
Puschkinia, 69
 P. scilloides, 81

Rabbits, 48–9, 97
Radiola linoides, 36
Ragged robin, 56, 80
Ramonda, 59, 85
 R. myconi, 59
Ranunculus, 36, 72, 81
 R. calandrinioides, 85, 116
 R. glacialis, 114
Raoulia, 81, 125
 R. australis, 44, 81, 111
 R. hookeri, 111
Red hot pokers, 115
Repotting, 13, 28, 81
Rhododendrons, 46, 62, 63, 86, 91, 125
Rhodohypoxis baurii, 60–1, 115
 R. platypetala, 61
Rock, stabilising, 28, 37, 118; type, 24, 25, 33
Romulea, 18, 87, 95
Rotting, 9, 12, 90

Sagina procumbens, 36
Salix, 86, 91
 S. boydii, 39, 55, 113
 S. lanata, 37, 72, 113
 S. reticulata, 37, 72, 86, **113**
Sanguinaria canadensis, 30
Sarcococca hookeriana humilis, 14–15
 S. ruscifolia, 15
Satin flower, 70–1
Saxifraga (Saxifrage), 18, 26, 33, 37, 44, 58, 69, 80, 81, 85, 107, 111, **123**
 Encrusted, 65
 Purple, 31
 S. frederici-augustii grisebachii, 64, 65
 S. oppositifolia, 31, 48
Scilla, 69, 81, 94, 95, 116
 S. scilloides, 88
 S. sibirica, 91, 95
Screes, 8, 9, 52–3; plants for, **53**, 65
Sedges, 9, 55, 98, 101
 Variegated, 120
Sedum, 28, 44, 59, 81, 110, 111, **123**
 S. acre, 59
 S. cauticola, 93, 110
 S. sieboldii, 93, 110
Seed, 110, **123–4**; sowing, **21**, 80, 101
Seedlings, 90–1
Sempervivums, 28, 33, 34, 81, 107, 111, **123**, 124
Shade, 48, 62, 69, 87
Shortia, 63
 S. soldanelloides, uniflora, 112

Shrubs, 8–10, 13, 32, 33, 46, 55, 62, **77**, 86, 91, 106, 122
Silene acaulis, 82, 85
 S. schafta, 82
Silver-leaved plants, 37, 106, 111
Sisyrinchium, 81
 S. graminoides, 71
 S. idahoense, 71; *album*, 70–1
Skimmia japonica, 37
Slugs, 13, 18, **20**
Snowdrop, 10, **15**, 63, 90, 116, 118
Societies, 8, 110, 119, **141–2**
Soil, 9, 12, 25, 33, 53, 62
Soldanella, 63, 114, 118
Spring-flowering plants, 129–35
Sternbergia, 69, 81, 90, **102**
 S. candida, 87
 S. lutea, sicula, 102
Stonecrop, 59, 63
Summer-flowering plants, 135–9

Thymus (thyme), 28, 40, **44**, 48, 66, 106, 125
 T. serpyllum, 40, **44**
Top-dressing, 18, 21, 28, 29, 37, 48, 53, 58, 63, 68, 91
Trees, 8–10, 13, 33, 46, **56**, 122 *see also conifers*
Trillium, 63, 81, 90, 91
Trough gardens, 8, 9, 36, **54–5**, 59, 106; plants for, 54–5, 65
Tulipa (tulip), 41, **43**, 44, 55, 69, 81, 87, 91, 95, 96, **125**
 T. biflora, 55
 T. greigii, kaufmanniana, 43
 T. sprengeri, 41
 T. tarda, 43, 91
 T. urumiensis, 43

Vaccinium, 37, 62, 80, 91, 98, 116
Veronica, 48, 81
Viola, 80, 81, 85, 100, 122–3, **123**
 V. cazorlensis, 115

Wall plants, 17
Water butts, 49, 68
Water plants, 66, 72–3
Waterfalls, 12, 72–3
Watering, **21**, 41, 56, **58**, **68**, 69, 80, 91, 97, **110**
Weeding, 18, **28**, 33, **36**, 41, 44, **58**, 68, 69, 104
Weedkiller, 28, **32–3**, 68
Weevils, vine, 13, 20, 28, **29**, 90
White fly, 20
Willow, reticulate, 37, **113**
Winter-flowering plants, 11, 95, 140

Zauschneria, 110
Zephyranthes, 81, 87, 94
 Z. candida, 88, 94